Mathematics
FOR EVERY YOUNG CHILD

Karen A. Schultz
Ron P. Colarusso
Virginia W. Strawderman

GEORGIA STATE UNIVERSITY

Merrill, an imprint of
Macmillan Publishing Company
New York

Collier Macmillan Canada, Inc.
Toronto

Maxwell Macmillan International Publishing Company
New York   Oxford   Singapore   Sydney

Macmillan Publishing Company
866 Third Avenue, New York, New York 10022

Macmillan Publishing Company is
part of the Maxwell Communication
Group of Companies.

Maxwell Macmillan Canada, Inc.
1200 Eglinton Avenue East
Suite 200
Don Mills, Ontario M3C 3N1

This book was set in Century Schoolbook.
Administrative Editor: Jeff Johnston
Developmental Editor: Amy Macionis
Production Coordinator: Linda Bayma
Art Coordinator: James H. Hubbard
Cover Designer: Cathy Watterson

Library of Congress Catalog Card Number: 88–61800
International Standard Book Number: 0-675-20425-9
Printed in the United States of America
 3 4 5 6 7 8 9—93

Preface

Mathematics for Every Young Child is written for teachers of 3- to 8-year-olds. Topics normally considered appropriate subject matter for beyond third grade, such as division of whole numbers or addition of decimals, are addressed from the perspective of the child's developmental readiness. The text supports the view of the National Council of Teachers of Mathematics's (1988) *Curriculum and Evaluation Standards for School Mathematics* that mathematical meanings are not passively obtained from the teacher, but rather constructed by the student. This book can be used as a text for early childhood and primary grade teacher education at the undergraduate level or as a reference manual for preschool and primary grade classrooms.

With more children in preschools and day care centers than ever before, opportunities to provide informal academic environments are increasing. One of our goals in writing this book was to provide mathematics background and guidance to preschool teachers in these environments.

Children bring to a learning environment experiences and understandings that contribute to pre-existing frameworks for classroom teaching. Throughout the book we suggest ways teachers can discover what mathematical understandings children already have so that classroom instruction can build upon them. We have taken the position that "learning problems" in mathematics are often a function of inappropriate teaching practices—practices that deny the natural learning behavior and stages of children.

Part 1 of the text discusses three different types of structures: the structures of learning, the structures of mathematics, and the structures of instructional planning. It provides the teacher with the basic background material necessary to successfully study and implement the teaching ideas that follow. Part 2 facilitates the instructional planning needed for the mathematics content. Chapters 4 to 7 discuss arithmetic; specifically, numbers and operations on those numbers. Chapter 8 is about geometry and Chapter 9 is about measurement. Because language development is so important in young children's learning, all of the chapters in Part 2 start with vocabulary for teachers and vocabulary for children. Each chapter walks through content, both from a mathematical perspective and a developmental learning perspective, with a final consideration for how to plan for instruction. An Instructional Planner in each chapter is followed by many activities to get teachers started. Problem solving, estimation, and technology are considered for each major content area. Finally, reflective thinking as well as children's participation in constructing their own mathematical knowledge is emphasized throughout the book.

Acknowledgments

Writing this book has been a learning experience for each of us. We contributed and learned from our collective experiences in cognitive development, special education, and developmental studies in mathematics education. Many teachers and children facilitated the refinement of our thinking—they taught us the realities of the mathematics teaching/learning process. We especially wish to acknowledge the preschool teachers, children, and parents of The Heiskell School of Atlanta and the primary grade teachers, children, and parents of West Side Elementary School in Marietta, Georgia who graciously allowed us to take photographs to use for this book. We appreciate our reviewers who contributed substantially to the quality of our work: Grace M. Burton, University of North Carolina at Wilmington; Douglas Cruikshank, Linfield College; Ann Harsh, The University of Southern Mississippi; Hiram Johnston, Georgia State University; Jane Ann McLaughlin, Trenton State College; Linda Jensen Sheffield, Northern Kentucky University; and Elaine Surbeck, Arizona State University. In addition, we wish to thank Jeff Johnston and Amy Macionis, our editors at Merrill, for their expertise, guidance, encouragement, and endless patience. The contributions of Annamaria Farlizio, free-lance copyeditor; Linda Bayma, production coordinator; and Jim Hubbard, art coordinator, deserve notice. Lannda Oden and Barbara Wilson, who assisted with the clerical preparation of this manuscript, also deserve to be recognized. Closer to home, we wish to acknowledge our families for their thoughtful and loving support.

K. A. S.
R. P. C.
V. W. S.

Contents

6
Multiplication and Division   145

7
Rational Numbers   207

PART 1

Foundations for Learning and Teaching Mathematics

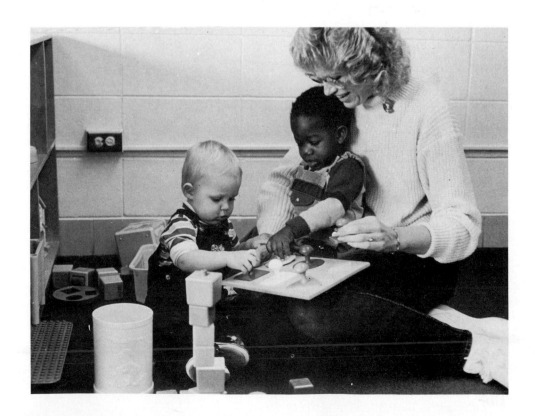

implications for the classroom. Piaget established that children pass through four stages of cognitive growth. The approximate ages for each stage are presented as follows, but variation between children should be expected.

1. sensorimotor (birth to 2 years)
2. preoperational (2 to 7 years)
3. concrete operational (7 to 11 years)
4. formal operational (11 and older)

The early learning of mathematics addressed in this text occurs during the **preoperational** and **concrete operational** stages. Therefore, this discussion will focus on these two stages. However, the importance of the **sensorimotor** stage must not be overlooked. During his or her first 2 years of life, the child explores the world by making comparisons in space and discriminating between three-dimensional objects. These abilities are prerequisite to classifying and grouping objects and events. Without these abilities, a true understanding of many mathematical concepts would be very difficult, if not impossible.

The basis for understanding mathematics continues to develop during the **preoperational** stage. The child attends to *specific* attributes of a situation at a time, cannot process multiple comparisons, and does not have the ability to conserve quantity. However, the child does make global comparisons and thus learns how to classify. *Classification* is the ability to group objects that are similar or have common characteristics. At this level, the child can discriminate visually among shapes, sizes, and colors. At the start, the child merely uses these characteristics to group objects. Later, the child can compare representations of objects (such as pictures of blocks or sticks) to represent numbers. The child can also address questions like, "Which does not belong?" *One-to-one correspondence* is also developed at this stage, making it possible for the child to learn how to count, add, and subtract. The basic skill required is matching, beginning with similar objects and then advancing to the matching of different objects and sets of objects. *Seriation* is a prerequisite to understanding the meaning and order of numbers. Seriation skills may begin with simple ordering of objects by size, texture, taste, or color. This task can be accomplished in either ascending or descending order. Near the end of this stage, the child can order according to quantity. Throughout this stage, the child is functioning at a perceptual or intuitive level and is developing many necessary skills that lead to the performance of higher level mathematics.

During the **concrete operational** stage, children begin to question perceptions and to learn logical reasoning. They begin to manipulate their environment, mainly through mental pictures. There is still a great need for manipulatives at this developmental stage. At this time children achieve flexibility and reversibility of thought as well as an understanding of conservation. *Flexibility* involves the ability to understand that an object belongs to more than one category. The child understands that $2 + 3 = 5$, and that $1 + 4 = 5$, too. Thus, the child can think about something from more than one point of view. *Reversibility,* on the other hand, is prerequisite to understanding the relationship between addition and subtraction. For example, $2 + 3 = 5$ and $5 - 2 = 3$. This ability is best learned through manipulatives such as counters or Cuisenaire rods. *Conservation* is critical to the understanding of number. The child must understand that a set is not changed quantitatively by changing the arrangement or shape of a set (that is, not adding to or taking away units).

Learning behaviors develop as the child progresses through the stages of cognitive development. During this development, the young learner interacts with the environment by employing perceptual skills. Therefore, mathematics instruction for the young learner should focus on concrete learning experiences. These learning experiences should provide opportunity for experimentation, discovery, flexibility of thinking, peer interaction, and problem solving. The teacher should focus on the child's perspective of a situation in order to be better able to facilitate the child's construction of mathematical ideas. This method is referred to as a constructivist approach, where the mathematics is to be constructed by the learner (Schoenfeld, 1987; Silver, 1987).

Ways of Knowing

Jerome Bruner (1960, 1966), in his study of thinking processes, focuses on levels of knowing and translates these levels into a hierarchy of learning processes. These processes give direction to the types of instruction necessary for learning to occur. He believes that there are three forms or levels of knowing related to instruction: enactive, iconic, and symbolic.

Enactive knowledge involves the physical manipulation of concrete objects and one's own physical movement. This concrete level of knowledge is demonstrated in mathematics by the ability to sort objects such as blocks and chips. Number can be understood and represented through the manipulation of concrete objects.

Iconic knowledge involves the mental manipulation of concrete objects that are representations of objects. This task is accomplished through images of the object in picture or diagram form. Therefore, the emphasis is visual, perceptual information. At this level, the child deals with number by mentally manipulating pictures and other representations of objects. The child can solve a problem by drawing pictures or symbols for the number of objects specified.

Symbolic knowledge involves the ability to use abstract symbols to represent objects, relations, or operations in the problem-solving process. The child uses numerals rather than the objects (or their pictorial representations) to experience mathematical ideas or to solve problems. The goal in teaching mathematics is to reach this highest level of knowledge because it frees the individual from the limitations of perceptions, allowing for more complex abstract learning.

Bruner developed the spiral curriculum model based on these three levels of knowing. This curriculum philosophy stresses beginning with concrete interactions that allow the child to manipulate the objects involved. When knowledge at the enactive level is achieved, concepts are advanced to more abstract forms requiring mental images and symbols. Finally, the child can demonstrate the knowledge of concepts through the use of abstract symbols such as numerals.

While it is possible to avoid enactive learning activities by training students to manipulate symbols (symbolic level), there is a real danger that understanding of the concept has not been achieved. This fault is demonstrated in many instances when a child can use an algorithm in a drill situation without error but is not capable of applying the skills in a problem-solving situation or cannot explain the meaning of the process. Bruner's model addresses the levels of knowing and provides a sequence of teaching activities ranging from the concrete to the abstract.

Gagné looks at the learning process from a behavioral viewpoint and focuses on the hierarchy of learning concepts and skills. The focus is the developmental hierarchy of tasks involved in the mastery of a concept and the concurrent skills required to master the concept. The developmental sequence for learning mathematics is most important because new learnings build upon earlier concepts and skills. The hierarchy of mathematical content is well established (with some minor variations among authorities). This sequence will be discussed throughout the remainder of the text.

Information Processing

Language is integral to the cognitive process. While the relationship between language and thinking is not completely understood, we know that language plays an important part in the thinking process. Language is required for learning to develop to a level of abstract thinking and problem solving. The hierarchy of language skills develops in the following order: (a) listening, (b) speaking, (c) reading, and (d) writing.

The learning process requires the ability to receive and send information. **Receptive** abilities used by young children to learn are listening and seeing. The early stages of these abilities are concrete. For example, a child listens to the sounds of an object while looking at the actual object or representation of the object instead of reading about it. **Expressive** abilities include manipulating, sorting, saying, drawing, and, later, writing.

Teaching mathematics to young children requires more careful attention than teaching students on higher cognitive levels. The need for more concrete communication is required. Table 1–1 presents the hierarchy of receptive and expressive skills used in the early learning of mathematics. This hierarchy ranges from the lowest level of touching and sorting to the highest of reading and writing.

TABLE 1–1
Communication Hierarchy in Early Mathematics Learning

Level	Receptive (input)	Expressive (output)
high	reading	writing
	listening	saying
	seeing	drawing
low	touching	sorting

MATHEMATICS LEARNING MODEL

When planning lessons in mathematics, three areas must be considered in order for successful learning to occur. First, the hierarchy of mathematical objectives ensures that learning proceeds in a sequence believed to be best for the overall development of mathematical abilities. Second, the cognitive level of functioning and related levels of knowing must be considered. This area addresses learning at the early concrete level, matching the concrete with the abstract at a transitional level, and using abstract symbols at the abstract level. Third, the teaching plan should consider the child's information processing skills when presenting information to the child and when requiring the child to respond. Table 1–2 presents a teaching model that considers both the child's level of cognitive functioning and his or her communication behaviors when planning lessons to meet the selected mathematical objective. The model

TABLE 1–2
Hierarchy of Mathematical Learning Behaviors

Type of Cognitive Interaction	Learning Interaction	Mode of Information Processing	
		Receptive	Expressive
Type 1: Concrete	*Concrete manipulations and/or pictorial representations* Emphasis is on manipulation of actual objects to problem solve.	Seeing Listening Touching	Sorting Speaking Drawing
Type 2: Transitional	*Manipulation of concrete objects and/or their pictorial representations* Emphasis is on matching the abstract symbols (numerals) with the objects in the problem-solving process.	Reading Seeing Listening Touching	Writing Sorting Speaking Drawing
Type 3: Abstract	*Problem solving using abstract symbols (numerals)*	Reading Listening	Writing Speaking

specifies the level of cognitive interactions from the concrete to the abstract. Corresponding to each level are the learning interactions and the modes of information processing (communication channels).

Concrete Level

The young child is capable of solving mathematical problems but is limited to those that are concrete, meaningful, and in the here and now. Information is processed at this early learning level mainly by touching and manipulating the actual objects. For the child to be able to match information with what he or she sees is essential. The child may not be able to remember information, therefore, the concrete objects allow for checking visually. While visual information is essential, listening skills are also important since they allow the child to focus on following simple directions and answering questions directly related to the visual information presented.

The child expresses solutions to problems mainly through manipulation of the concrete objects of the drawing or marking of simple images. The child at this level will know simple number/object correspondence and is capable of responding verbally.

Transitional Level

For the transitional level of learning mathematics, the major focus is the transition to abstract symbols from concrete objects or, preferably, their representations in picture form. The intent is for the child to learn that numerical symbols represent mathematical ideas as do objects or pictures.

Information processing at this level requires the child's understanding of quantitative relations through concrete objects and their corresponding numerals. At this time the transfer from concrete to abstract occurs. While mathematical information is also presented verbally, the majority of information is presented visually. The limited memory capacity for auditory information usually requires the child to translate auditory information to visual information by writing the number symbol, drawing marks, or drawing representations of the figure.

At this level, the child should express solutions to problems by writing the mathematical symbols. Manipulating objects and drawing pictures may still be necessary for some; however, this strategy is employed more as a technique for solving problems than in expressing results.

Abstract Level

The abstract level is the most efficient level of learning and problem solving in mathematics because it does not rely on concrete representations of objects. The child is capable of thinking mathematically and solving problems symbolically. Due to the requirements of dealing with many numerals at the same time, the written symbol is necessary and useful for processing information. The solutions to problems are usually written as numerals or graphs. However, from the start emphasis should be placed on activities that foster mental computation. Every time a new mathematical concept or procedure is being developed, the teaching plan should account for the movement from the concrete to the abstract. Piaget refers to this movement as horizontal decalage.

LEARNING PROBLEMS AND DISABILITIES IN MATHEMATICS

Understanding normal development and the hierarchies of the learning process is the first step toward good teaching. Many children, who otherwise might experience problems in learning mathematics, will find it an enjoyable experience when appropriate materials are presented through teaching strategies that consider the child's level of functioning. However, there are other factors that must be considered when children are having learning problems in mathematics.

Teaching

One factor leading to learning problems has to do with teaching methodology. Teaching has become so technical and behavioral that we never look at the general goal. Much of our teaching has been focused upon the specific steps (task analysis) necessary to perform a task, without including application activities that ensure understanding and the ability to apply the learned skill appropriately. Take multiplication, for example. Many children can execute complicated multiplication problems without understanding the underlying concept and/or without being able to apply it appropriately to a real-life situation. Also, as teachers we tend to focus on *repeated* practice rather than *varied* practice. A problem similar to this one is overlearning; we give children a large number of computation problems to perform but never allow for generalization or application of the computational skills in varied and real situations.

Information Processing

In analyzing learning problems one must look at the child's ability to process information. To perform mathematics at a useful level the child must be able to process abstract (symbolic) information and concepts. Prerequisite to abstract reasoning is reasoning at the concrete level, which requires classification and discriminating abilities.

Throughout most learning activities, the child processes information visually and aurally. While there are other means by which information is received, such as by touch, these are the two main sources. At the concrete level the child deals with real objects. The child asks: Which set has more blocks? Which is more: four apples or two apples? At the abstract or symbolic level, the number becomes larger and the comparisons become more abstract so they don't lend themselves to concrete representation and must be dealt with symbolically. Therefore, we must determine if a child can receive information both visually and aurally at his or her level of functioning (concrete or abstract). We must also realize that the more extensive and complicated mathematics becomes, the greater the need to visually process abstract symbols (numerals) because of the limited ability to store (remember) verbal information.

Some children may receive information with no difficulty but have problems expressing it. Expression in mathematics is usually spoken or written. While we require children to express themselves verbally at times, most responses in mathematics are pictorial responses such as drawing figures (concrete level) or producing numerals (abstract level). Young children may experience difficulty in completing mathematics assignments that require motor responses beyond their capacity. Therefore, teachers should be certain to plan learning tasks within the child's verbal and motoric abilities.

To determine if a child has a learning problem that is receptive or expressive, each area should be tested *separately*. For example, to assess receptive abilities, allow the child to give a yes-no response or to select from a multiple choice. If testing for an expressive problem, use an activity that you are sure the child understands and vary the type of response required.

Prerequisite skills to the higher level of processing in mathematics are the ability to discriminate, identify, and name quantities or geometric forms as well as produce them. Often, a teacher encounters a child with a motor problem who can't produce numerals or who makes reversal errors. The teacher comes to the conclusion that the child doesn't know the numerals. In most cases, however, a child who makes errors of this nature can usually discriminate correctly. The errors occur when the child is required to produce the form or symbol. Therefore, it is necessary to determine if the problem is receptive, or expressive, and at what level. The three levels are discrimination, identification, and naming. Developmentally, discrimination requires only that the child determine whether numerals are the same or different. The next level requires that the child identify numerals by pointing to the correct numeral when it is named. The last level is naming that requires the child to say the correct name when a numeral is presented. For example, when presented with 6 and 9, can the child respond correctly to the following?

Discrimination: Are they the same or different?

Identification: Show me the nine.

Naming: (pointing to one of the numerals) What do we call this number?

Most receptive errors are at the identification and naming levels (which are memory skills), rather than the discrimination level (which is more perceptual). The child who can do all three but makes errors when writing them is having expressive problems. This trouble may indicate a coordination or motor planning problem. However, remember that reversals at early ages (even up to 7 years) are not uncommon. Boys do not develop fine motor skills as early as girls and placing too much pressure on motor performance too soon is not good for any child.

Attending

Attending ability is an important factor. Hewett (1968) presented a hierarchy of learning abilities and identified attending as the first step in the learning process. Keogh and Morgolis (1976) analyzed the components of attending in the learning process and identified three areas: (a) coming to attention, (b) decision making, and (c) maintaining attention. These three attending abilities are applicable to mathematical abilities and should be assessed. Coming to attention and maintaining attention are figure-ground abilities. The child must be able to focus on the relevant information and maintain this focus until the task is completed. Decision making involves the plan of action for problem solving. Young children with learning problems are impulsive problem solvers. They don't attend to all the stimulus information before taking action and many times select an inappropriate approach in solving a problem. These are the children who complete a page of addition and/or subtraction problems without an error. However, when given problems that require following directions or problem solving, they lack the ability to determine the appropriate methods and use the wrong algorithm.

Attending behavior for mathematics should be assessed in two different ways. To determine if a child can come to attention and maintain attention requires the selection of problems the child has already mastered. When teachers assign mathematics problems that children are capable of performing, the focus is placed on the ability to attend to the work. If the child doesn't know the assigned algorithm, we cannot be sure that there is an attending problem. In assessing the decision-making ability in attending, the child should be presented with situations that require a decision as to the correct algorithm needed to complete a problem. An impulsive child will make errors in selecting the appropriate algorithm rather than computing incorrectly. Attending behaviors may also be affected by the child's ability to perform a task over time, especially when fine motor skills are weak or still developing. Some children who appear to have attending problems may actually have problems in fine motor coordination and struggle with mathematics solutions that involve lots of writing. When asked to perform with few or no written responses, such children can complete the required task with little difficulty or frustration.

Reading

While the mathematics level where a child functions should not be determined by reading level, mathematics problems should be written on the child's independent reading level. A child who is performing computations at a fourth grade level but reading at a second grade level will stumble if the problems read at the fourth grade level. Therefore, the teacher must ask: Is the level of reading in mathematics beyond the child's ability? Is the real mathematics learning problem the inability to understand what is required rather than the mathematical concept?

We know that we must understand a lot more than mathematics in order to teach mathematics. We must constantly explore how children learn and how best to facilitate their discovery of mathematical concepts and procedures.

SUMMARY

This chapter reviewed the stages of cognitive development, the ways of knowing, and how information is processed. It reviewed common learning problems and disabilities of young mathematics learners and concluded with a model that explains how the learner processes mathematics—whether the learner is a preschooler or a third grader.

STUDY QUESTIONS AND ACTIVITIES

1. Observe a child's ways of solving mathematical problems. If at all possible, videotape the child in different types of mathematical activities or lessons. Study the tape for evidence of the following:
   a. stages of cognitive development
   b. ways of knowing
   c. receptive and expressive processes
   d. mathematical learning behaviors (see Table 1–2)
2. Skim through the student activities at the ends of the chapters in Part 2 of this book. Respond to the following:
   a. Which ways of knowing are addressed?
   b. Which kinds of receptive and expressive processes would be employed in the activities?

REFERENCES AND RESOURCES

Bruner, J. S. (1960). *The process of education*. New York: Vintage Books.

Bruner, J. S. (1966). *Toward a theory of instruction*. New York: Norton.

Copeland, R. W. (1984). *How children learn mathematics: Teaching implications of Piaget's research*. New York: Macmillan.

Dienes, Z. P. (1963). *An experimental study of mathematics learning*. London: Hutchinson.

Dienes, Z. P. (1971). *Building up mathematics*. London: Hutchinson Educational.

Flavell, J. H. (1963). *The developmental psychology of Jean Piaget*. New York: Van Nostrand Reinhold.

Gagné, R. M. (1965). *The conditions of learning*. New York: Holt, Reinhart & Winston.

Gagné, R. M. (1974). *Essentials of learning instruction*. Hinsdale, IL: Dryden Press.

Ginsburg, H. P. (Ed.). (1983). *The development of mathematical thinking*. New York: Academic Press.

Hewett, F. M. (1968). *The emotionally disturbed child in the classroom*. Boston: Allyn & Bacon.

Keogh, B. K., & Margolis, J. (1976). Learn to labor and wait: Attentional problems of children with learning disorders. *Journal of Learning Disabilities, 9*, 276–286.

Labinowicz, E. (1985). *Learning from children*. Menlo Park, CA: Addison-Wesley.

Schoenfeld, A. H. (1987). Cognitive science and mathematics education overview. In A. H. Schoenfeld (Ed.), *Cognitive science and mathematics education* (pp. 1–31). Hillsdale, NJ: Lawrence Erlbaum Associates.

Silver, E. A. (1987). Foundations of cognitive theory and research for mathematics problem-solving instruction. In A. H. Schoenfeld (Ed.), *Cognitive science and mathematics education*. (pp. 33–60). Hillsdale, NJ: Lawrence Erlbaum Associates.

Thornton, C. A., Tucker, B. F., Dossey, J. A., & Bazik, E. F. (1983). *Teaching mathematics to children with special needs*. Menlo Park, CA: Addison-Wesley.

Wadsworth, B. (1971). *Piaget's theory of cognitive development*. New York: David McKay.

2

Mathematical Structures

THIS CHAPTER PRESENTS the mathematics teachers should cover in an early childhood curriculum. Prior to the 1960s, the term used was *arithmetic* and children focused on acquiring computation skills and applying them in limited, concrete situations. Since the inclusion of geometry and measurement, the term commonly used is *modern mathematics* (National Council of Teachers of Mathematics [NCTM], 1970). By *mathematics*, then, we mean "arithmetic, measurement, and geometry." Figure 2–1 indicates the relationship among these three areas. While we will address these areas separately, the interrelationship becomes evident when geometric concepts are used to teach the understanding of numeration.

Discussion of each of these areas will focus on the child's understanding of concepts during the early childhood years. For the purpose of clarity, some discussion of the topics will go beyond what are usually considered "the early childhood years." In determining how far students usually progress, it is necessary to establish general guidelines concerning the skills that typical

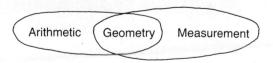

FIGURE 2–1
The Three Components of Mathematics

young children acquire through age 8. Figure 2–2 is a reminder that progress is enhanced when mathematics is related to the real world.

In the area of arithmetic, 8-year-old children can generally multiply two- and three-digit numbers by one-digit numbers and are able to learn the division facts. Though they are not yet operating with fractions, they are recognizing, naming, and comparing fractional parts.

By age 8, children should be able to recognize, name, and construct various three-dimensional shapes (prisms, pyramids, and polyhedra associated with the circle), two-dimensional shapes (polygons), and one-dimensional shapes (lines, line segments, and rays). Constructions can be done with clay, paper folding, ripping, or cutting; pipe cleaners and straws; paper and pencil; geoboards, plastic or wooden boards with nails or pegs in an array on which rubber bands can be stretched; or other media common to young children. Children at this age would have an intuitive understanding of symmetry, congruence, and similarity. They would have mastered the topological notions of proximity, order, enclosure, and separation as well as attained an understanding of shape and size relative to Euclidean geometry.

The basic concepts of measurement are understood, but the fact that both customary and metric systems are to be learned is confusing. Estimation, problem solving, and the use of calculators are essential in all areas of mathematics and should be an integral part of the early childhood curriculum beginning in kindergarten. Students should be able to use estimation skills as well as other strategies useful in applied and nonapplied problem solving. By

FIGURE 2–2
This bulletin board relates mathematics to the real world.

second grade, children should already be comfortable with the calculator as a tool used to learn arithmetic concepts, properties, facts, procedures, and algorithms. They should also be comfortable with the calculator as a tool in nonroutine problem solving.

ARITHMETIC

Arithmetic includes numbers and numeration, operations on these numbers, properties associated with the operations, and number theory. Arithmetic enables us, for example, to tell how many and how much. The following topics are further developed in Chapters 4–7.

Numbers

The ten digits 0, 1, 2, 3, 4, 5, 6, 7, 8, 9, what they mean, and how to use them constitute the topic of numbers and numeration. Depending on how these digits are used, they can express the set of whole numbers, counting (natural) numbers, integers (positive and negative whole numbers), and rational numbers (expressed as fractions, decimals, or percents).

Whole numbers	0, 1, 2, 3, 4, . . .
Counting numbers	1, 2, 3, 4, 5, . . .
Integers	. . . , -3, -2, -1, 0, $+1$, $+2$, $+3$, . . .
Rational numbers	
Fractions	Numbers in the form of a/b; where a and b are integers, and a does not equal 0
Decimals	Both terminating (e.g., 0.5) and repeating (e.g., 0.333 . . .)
Percents	A ratio between some number and 100

The Hindu-Arabic Numeration System

How to use the numbers previously described is determined by the following information (Kennedy, 1984):

1. There is a base number of 10.
2. There are as many digits as the base.
3. The symbol 0 is used as a placeholder in a numeral like 104, where the 0 indicates that there are no tens.

4. A place-value system is used with the ones place on the right, a base position to the left of the ones place, a base times a base position next, and so on.

5. It is possible to carry out computations using this system.

Operations

As you know, there are four operations: addition, subtraction, multiplication, and division. Addition, a more efficient way of counting, is the operation that assigns a sum to two addends. For every addition statement with different addends, there are two related subtraction statements. Therefore, it helps students to define subtraction in terms of addition. Subtraction is the operation that assigns to a sum and an addend, the other addend (often called the difference).

$$\underline{\text{addend} + \text{addend} = \text{sum}} \qquad 2 + 3 = 5$$
$$\underline{\text{sum} - \text{addend} = \text{addend}} \qquad 5 - 2 = 3$$
$$5 - 3 = 2$$

Multiplication assigns a product to two factors. For every multiplication statement with different factors, there are two related division statements. So again, it helps to define division to children in terms of multiplication. Division assigns to a product and a factor, the other factor.

$$\underline{\text{factor} \times \text{factor} = \text{product}} \qquad 3 \times 2 = 6$$
$$\underline{\text{product} \div \text{factor} = \text{factor}} \qquad 6 \div 3 = 2$$
$$6 \div 2 = 3$$

The examples shown previously use whole numbers. These operations can also be applied to other number systems, such as integers and rationals.

Properties

After some experience with the operations applied to the various number systems (wholes, integers, rationals), you can see that certain patterns occur. These patterns are properties, rules, or principles that reveal the structure of each system under the respective operations.

The **commutative property** applies to the operations of addition and multiplication for every number system but does not apply to subtraction or division. When a number system is commutative under addition or multiplication, the order of the elements to be added or multiplied can be changed without affecting the solution.

If $a = 5$ and $b = 4$

then $a + b = c$ or $5 + 4 = 9$

$b + a = c$ or $4 + 5 = 9$

or $a + b = b + a$ or $5 + 4 = 4 + 5$

and $a \times b = c$ or $5 \times 4 = 20$

$b \times a = c$ or $4 \times 5 = 20$

or $a \times b = b \times a$ or $5 \times 4 = 4 \times 5$

The **associative property** applies only to addition and multiplication for every number system. When a number system is said to be associative under addition or multiplication, the grouping of elements undergoing the same operation can be changed without affecting the solution.

If $a = 5$, $b = 4$, and $c = 3$

then $(a + b) + c = a + (b + c)$ or

$(5 + 4) + 3 = 5 + (4 + 3)$

$9 + 3 = 5 + 7$

$12 = 12$

and $(a \times b) \times c = a \times (b \times c)$ or

$(5 \times 4) \times 3 = 5 \times (4 \times 3)$

$20 \times 3 = 5 \times 12$

$60 = 60$

The **distributive property** applies to multiplication over addition or subtraction, and to division over addition or subtraction, for any number system. The most commonly used applications are multiplication or division over addition. These more common applications are illustrated as follows.

If $a = 5$, $b = 4$, and $c = 3$

then $a \times (b + c) = (a \times b) + (a \times c)$

or

$5 \times (4 + 3) = (5 \times 4) + (5 \times 3)$

$5 \times 7 = 20 + 15$

$35 = 35$

and if $a = 20$, $b = 4$, and $c = 2$

then $(a + b) \div c = (a \div c) + (b \div c)$

or

$(20 + 4) \div 2 = (20 \div 2) + (4 \div 2)$

$24 \div 2 = 10 + 2$

$12 = 12$

There are two **identity elements** that occur in every number system. In addition problems, when 0 is added to any number, the result is that number; likewise, when 1 is multiplied by any number, the result is that number.

$$\text{If} \qquad a = 8$$
$$\text{then} \qquad 0 + a = a + 0 = a \quad \text{or}$$
$$0 + 8 = 8 + 0 = 8$$

$$\text{and} \qquad 1 \times a = a \times 1 = a \quad \text{or}$$
$$1 \times 8 = 8 \times 1 = 8$$

MEASUREMENT

Attributes

Discrete things are *counted*; continuous things are *measured*. Measurement occurs when we use numbers to describe various continuous attributes of geometric figures (such as length, area, volume, or capacity), or other attributes such as temperature, change (time), and value (money). Two major considerations for this section are what (attribute) is measured and the systems available with which to measure. Chapters 3 and 9 present a description of the learning stages children go through when learning to measure, and Chapter 9 develops measurement in further detail. The attributes and what they represent are as follows:

Attribute	Representation
Length	Distance along one dimension
Area	Surface of a two-dimensional shape
Volume	Interior of a three-dimensional shape
Capacity	Amount of liquid an object can hold
Mass	Amount of matter an object has
Temperature	Heat
Change (time)	Continuous measure of change
Value (money)	How much something is worth

Systems of Measurement

The two systems available for measurement are the customary system (inches, pounds, etc.) and the metric system (meters, grams, etc.). The former is sometimes referred to as the English system and the latter is part of a larger, highly technical International System of Units (SI). Children study only the parts of the SI that concern length (including square and cubic measure), mass, capacity, and temperature as well as certain non-SI metric units dealing with time, angles in a plane, and money.

The customary system has irregular relationships among and within units; but familiarity has made it possible to develop efficiency with the system. The metric system, on the other hand, has regular and consistent relationships among and within units; but lack of familiarity and consistent use has made it difficult for us to feel comfortable with it.

Three characteristics of the metric system that characterize it as a "system" are the following:

1. Length, area, volume, capacity, and mass are all based on the meter. That is, a decimeter (1/10 of a meter) determines a square decimeter, which is used to determine a cubic decimeter. A cubic decimeter of liquid, then, is said to be a liter (liquid capacity). If this liquid is water, held constant at 4°C, it is said to have the mass of 1 kilogram (kg).

2. The metric units are based on the decimal system. Specifically, this fact means that each measure has an interrelationship of units determined by multiplying or dividing by 10. For example, 1 decimeter (dm) is 1/10 of a meter.

3. Further, to facilitate the use of this system, each basic standard unit uses a uniform set of prefixes.

Memorizing these prefixes becomes simple if you know their translation from the Latin. For example, *deci* means "one tenth."

Regardless of the system being used, there are certain important aspects of measurement.

1. Measurement is a comparison between an object's attribute and a unit, which results in a number used to describe the attribute of the object.

2. These comparisons are direct when one can physically compare the object being measured with the instrument or material used for the unit of measure. Examples of direct comparisons are placing liquid in a container to measure capacity or placing sugar cubes in a container to measure volume. Comparisons are indirect when the attribute being measured is compared mathematically with an instrument. Examples are a calibrated scale used to measure mass, a computation used to find area, or a chemical used such as in a thermometer to measure temperature.

3. Choice of unit is arbitrary, although eventually it is more efficient to use standard units.

4. All measurement is approximate.

5. The precision of the measurement depends on the choice of unit. An inch, for example, is more precise than a foot, and a gram is more precise than a kilogram.

GEOMETRY

There are similarities between geometry and arithmetic. In arithmetic, there are numbers, operations on those numbers, and properties. In geometry, there are shapes of varied dimensions, transformations of those shapes, and properties. Geometry as taught in early childhood education refers mostly to nonmetric geometry rather than metric geometry. Nonmetric geometry has been realized as important since geometric models are used to learn and understand arithmetic ideas. This section will discuss the three major components of a sound early childhood geometry curriculum: dimensions, transformations, and properties. The following is a brief discussion of each of these components. These ideas are further developed in Chapter 8.

Dimensions

There are three-, two-, one-, and zero-dimensional shapes. Other names for **three-dimensional** shapes are *solids* and *space figures*. We will refer to a sugar cube, a child's wooden building block, and a baseball as examples of solids; and a room, a shoe box, and an empty ice cream cone as examples of space figures. The term used for a **two-dimensional** shape is a *plane figure*; examples of plane figures are the surface of a valentine heart, a throw rug, or a piece of paper. A **one-dimensional** shape is a line or a path, such as the path a person walks on a sidewalk, the edge of a page of a book, and the path of a zipper. A **zero-dimensional** shape is a point. Examples are the corner of a room, where two walls and a floor meet; the place where three edges meet on a toy building block; and the place where two lines cross, such as where two strings cross on a wrapped package.

These shapes represent ideas that can only be embodied by objects around us or by pictures. However, it's like the number/numeral issue of the 1960s. To the child, a hula hoop *is* a circle. It is impossible and unnecessary to convince any child that the hula hoop is merely a model of a circle.

Transformations

There are two hierarchical levels of three types of geometric understanding that children acquire. These levels concern invariance (conservation)—an idea that is basic to geometry—number, and measurement. In these, geometric invariance of certain properties of objects is studied when the objects undergo specific transformations. Since geometry is the study of space and shapes in space, transformation geometry is the study of transformations on these shapes. The two geometry levels are (a) topological and (b) projective and Euclidean. Since children acquire projective and Euclidean concepts simultaneously, the two are considered to develop on the same level.

Topological transformations create changes in both shape and size. These changes are sometimes referred to as *stretching* and *shrinking* changes. They occur when the distance between an object and an observer decreases and increases. An embodiment of this phenomenon is found when inflating and deflating a balloon with a picture on it, or stretching or shrinking a sheet of rubber with a picture on it. These stretchings and shrinkings can either be uniform or not uniform. Projective transformations create changes in shape and/or size and occur when one's visual perspective is altered to include the possibility of larger or smaller images. An embodiment of this phenomenon appears in shadows of shapes from different angles to the light source and/or different distances from the light source. Activities of this kind are usually referred to as *shadow geometry*. Euclidean transformations create changes in location while still conserving shape and size. Children study three kinds of Euclidean transformations: (a) translations (slides), (b) reflections (flips), and (c) rotations (turns). Other kinds of Euclidean transformations are rigid motions or rigid transformations. (See Chapter 8 for more detailed development of these transformations.)

Properties

Children first acquire understanding of the topological properties. These include proximity, order, enclosure, and separation. Projective and Euclidean properties acquired simultaneously include those that are topological, as well as those of shape and size. In the case of projective geometry, there are properties such as straightness that appear unchanged while a change in point of view occurs. In the case of Euclidean geometry, there are properties such as angularity, parallelism, and distance that remain invariant while a change in location occurs as a result of translations, reflections, or rotations.

Constructions

While the early years should focus on informal play with geometric figures, a significant aspect of informal and formal geometry learning should be through constructions. Use whatever materials and procedures are available and appropriate. Some examples of materials/activities are clay, straws, pipe cleaners, paper folding, paper cutting, paper ripping, use of the Mira (See Figure 8–11.) and geoboard, as well as the early play activities associated with learning about shape.

SEQUENCE OF LEARNING

The expected order of children's learning is **concepts, properties, facts, procedures,** and **skills** (Sowder, 1980; Suydam & Dessart, 1980). In mathematics (as well as other content areas) this order may vary and overlap. There are no specific points where one learning skill stops and another begins. In many cases, more than one skill is being learned at the same time. Efforts should be made to facilitate these learnings in a problem-solving environment, where the teacher strives to understand the learner's perspective. This strategy makes it possible to assist the learner in an individual understanding of mathematics. The following discussion is presented according to types of learning as they relate to arithmetic, geometry, and measurement. Table 2–1 shows the order of learning for each area in comparison to the usual sequence of learning skills.

Arithmetic learning can be expanded to concepts, properties, facts, procedures, algorithms, and skill with problem solving. To illustrate, children should learn the *concept* of multiplication before the commutative and identity properties of multiplication. When the teacher thinks that the concept of the operation is understood, the *properties* can be presented intuitively. It is at this time that children get the idea of *facts*—that a certain combination of factors will always yield the same product. While children are memorizing the facts, they can accomplish early work on the *algorithm* of the multiplication operation. This learning requires understanding a series of *procedures* that make up the algorithm, such as aligning factors so the ones and tens are properly arranged, applying the distributive property, recording partial products, and finally adding the partial products. These procedures are generally learned over the course of time with factors that increase in the numbers of digits. Computational *skill development* is better tempered by estimation and calculator skill. It is not necessary to wait until algorithms are mastered before nonroutine problem solving is presented to children. There are many problems with varying degrees of sophistication, that relate to real-life situations requiring division. Furthermore, calculators can be used in problems where the problem solver knows that division is the required operation, but is unable to carry out the operation. Or the problem solver can use the calculator to explore with repeated subtraction. Problem solving and calculators can serve to encourage children to explore in the world of mathematics and to make discoveries.

The sequence of geometry learning can be described as concepts, properties, facts, and transformations acompanied by problem solving. For example, children need to know the *concept* of dimensions—that a shoe box is three-dimensional and has edges, corners, and sides. Then they should know that it

TABLE 2–1
The Learning Sequence of Arithmetic, Geometry, and Measurement

Arithmetic	Geometry	Measurement
concepts	concepts	concepts
properties	properties	
facts	facts	facts
procedures	transformations	procedures
algorithms		algorithms

has certain characteristics or *properties*, such as shape and size. *Facts* include the number of sides, edges, and corners (vertices). *Transformations* are the "operations" on a shape, such as topological, projective, and Euclidean transformations.

Measurement learning builds on some of the skills learned in arithmetic and geometry such as properties, transformations, and algorithms. Types of measurement learning are concepts, facts, procedures, and algorithms accompanied by problem solving. *Concepts* refer to attribute recognition, where a child must understand the attribute (e.g., mass) of an object before being expected to measure that attribute. *Facts* refer to the knowledge of number and the standard units needed to measure. Facts also include knowledge of the relationships among units. *Procedures* refer to the direct or indirect application of iteration when measuring. Or, in the case of area or volume, we mean the procedures for measuring needed dimensions in order to apply the appropriate *algorithm*. (For example, finding the length, width, and depth of an object in order to compute the volume.)

In closing, there needs to be a shift from teaching for skill development to teaching for thinking skills. It is more important that children know how to think, estimate, and use the calculator or computer in order to solve problems than to be efficient and proficient with computation. This strategy is in keeping with the mathematical demands of the 20th century.

SUMMARY

This chapter reviewed arithmetic, geometry, and the area of mathematics that integrates arithmetic and geometry—measurement. The origin of the numeration system, along with operations and properties associated with those operations, were discussed. Attributes and systems of measurement were detailed. Dimensions, transformations, properties, and constructions as aspects of geometry were also discussed. Finally, a sequence of learning was recommended.

STUDY QUESTIONS AND ACTIVITIES

1. Skim through Chapters 4 through 7 on arithmetic to identify instances where intuitive understandings of geometry are important. For example, the addition table is arranged in a vertical/horizontal orientation, and models such as blocks (cubes) or Cuisenaire rods are shown to support the development of operating with whole numbers.

2. Skim through Chapter 9 on measurement to identify instances where numbers (Chapters 4 through 7) are applied to objects in the environment (Chapter 8).

REFERENCES AND RESOURCES

Callahan, L. G. (1985). One point of view: Pressing problems in primary mathematics programs. *Arithmetic Teacher, 33*(2), 2.

Flavell, J. (1963). *The developmental psychology of Jean Piaget.* New York: Van Nostrand Reinhold.

Hendrickson, A. D. (1983). A psychologically sound primary school mathematics curriculum. *Arithmetic Teacher, 30*(5), 42–47.

Hollis, L. Y. (1981). Mathematical concepts for very young children. *Arithmetic Teacher, 29*(2), 24–27.

Kennedy, L. M. (1984). *Guiding children's learning of mathematics.* Belmont, CA: Wadsworth.

Labinowicz, E. (1985). *Learning from children.* Menlo Park, CA: Addison-Wesley.

Mueller, D. W. (1985). Building a scope and sequence for early childhood mathematics. *Arithmetic Teacher, 33*(2), 8–11.

National Council of Teachers of Mathematics. (1970). *A history of mathematics education in the United States and Canada.* Washington, DC: Author.

Nelson, D., & Reys, R. E. (Eds.). (1976). *Measurement in school mathematics.* Reston, VA: National Council of Teachers of Mathematics.

Reisman, F. (1981) *Teaching mathematics: Methods and content* (2nd ed.). Boston: Houghton Mifflin.

Schultz, K. A. (1986). Representational models from the learners' perspective. *Arithmetic Teacher, 33*(6), 52–55.

Sowder, L. K. (1980). Concept and principle learning. In R. J. Shumway (Ed.), *Research in mathematics education* (pp. 244–285). Reston, VA: National Council of Teachers of Mathematics.

Spencer, P. J., & Lester, F. K. (1981). Second graders can be problem solvers! *Arithmetic Teacher, 29*(1), 15–17.

Suydam, M. N., & Dessart, D. J. (1980). Skill learning. In R. J. Shumway (Ed.), *Research in mathematics education* (pp. 207–243). Reston, VA: National Council of Teachers of Mathematics.

3

Planning for Instruction

A PRIMARY CONCERN for all teachers is that children will be prepared for the real world. It is particularly critical in mathematics education for children to be ready for the kind of problem solving they will face in the age of information and technology. Like the child in Figure 3–1, children should have exposure to the computer at an early age. Various professional groups have tried to help curriculum developers and teachers to identify the structure of mathematics education today. Unfortunately, change is slow. Recommendations made as long ago as 1977 are still not followed in some school programs. Results of international studies indicate that we must follow these recommendations if we want the children of today to be the competent problem solvers of tomorrow.

THE MATHEMATICS CURRICULUM: DIRECTIONS FOR CHANGE

Before specific mathematics objectives can be established for a classroom, general curriculum goals must be established. Three documents have provided general curriculum goals that reflect the changing times and needs. In 1977, the National Council of Supervisors of Mathematics published the following list of basic skill areas:

1. Problem solving
2. Applying mathematics to everyday situations

FIGURE 3–1
Familiarity with the computer at an early age is important.

3. Alertness to the reasonableness of results
4. Estimation and approximation
5. Appropriate computational skills
6. Geometry
7. Measurement
8. Reading, interpreting, and constructing tables, charts, and graphs
9. Using mathematics to predict
10. Computer literacy (p. 20)

In 1980, the National Council of Teachers of Mathematics (NCTM) published *An Agenda for Action,* recommendations for school mathematics of the 1980s. The NCTM recommended the following:

1. problem solving be the focus of school mathematics in the 1980s;
2. basic skills in mathematics be defined to encompass more than computational facility;

3. mathematics programs take full advantage of the power of calculators and computers at all grade levels;

4. stringent standards of both effectiveness and efficiency be applied to the teaching of mathematics;

5. the success of mathematics programs and student learning be evaluated by a wider range of measures than conventional testing;

6. more mathematics study be required for all students and a flexible curriculum with a greater range of options be designed to accommodate the diverse needs of the student population;

7. mathematics teachers demand of themselves and their colleagues a high level of professionalism;

8. public support for mathematics instruction be raised to a level commensurate with the importance of mathematical understanding to individuals and society. (p. 1)

In 1985, NCTM published "The Impact of Computing Technology on School Mathematics" (Corbitt) with recommendations for curriculum, instruction, and teacher education. The report emphasized that the major influence of technology on mathematics education is its potential to shift emphasis from computational skills to concepts, relationships, structures, and problem solving:

> Much of the instructional time currently devoted to acquiring proficiency with paper-and-pencil algorithms should be reallocated to support a range of new or previously neglected topics that have a valid place in the K–12 mathematics curriculum . . . . To do arithmetic today, mental operations are best for obtaining quick approximations; calculators are the tools of choice for one-time computations; and computers are most appropriate for repetitive calculations. (pp. 14–15)

This report also included the following list of recommendations for the K–4 mathematics education curriculum:

1. Calculators should routinely be available to students in all activities associated with mathematics learning, including testing. Students should be taught to distinguish situations in which calculators are appropriate aids to computation from situations in which mental operations or paper-and-pencil computations are more appropriate.

2. Emphasis should continue to be placed on students' knowledge of basic facts required for proficient mental arithmetic and estimation. However, significant portions of elementary curricula devoted to algorithms for multiple-digit calculations can be eliminated.

3. Instruction must shift to emphasize the meaning of arithmetic operations. Such understanding is essential for problem solving.

4. Experience with physical manipulatives and other concrete representations of concepts must continue to be an important phase of learning mathematical ideas. Because of the increased instructional emphasis on meaning and under-

standing, this activity must not be overlooked as the curriculum evolves to take advantage of computers and calculators for instruction.

5. Because computers and calculators can be used effectively in teaching mathematical concepts, no a priori assumptions should be made about the appropriateness of any given mathematical topic for elementary students. For instance, decimals, negative numbers, and scientific notation appear naturally when using calculators and can be taught as they arise. Computers facilitate an early introduction to geometric concepts such as transformations, congruence, and vectors; statistical concepts such as randomness; and algebraic concepts such as variable and function.

6. Preprogramming activities and simple computer programming in Logo or BASIC can be done by students as early as the kindergarten level to convey both mathematical and computer concepts. Computer literacy should come as a natural by-product of such experiences rather than as a special addition to the elementary school curriculum. (p. 15)

Because of the strength of the problem-solving movement, Schoenfeld (1983) cautions us to take care to instill respect for and develop strength in basic understandings and basic facts; otherwise, we could find ourselves in a back-to-back-to-basics movement!

All the previous points are important and must be considered when determining which mathematical objectives should be integral to the curriculum. We are in a problem-solving movement. At the same time, we are attempting to determine the place of the computer in the teaching of mathematics. Thus, we should not lose sight of the importance of problem solving (as a thread throughout the curriculum), new technology, and basic skills when considering the needs and abilities of the individual learner.

TYPES OF STRUCTURE: LEARNING, MATHEMATICAL, AND INSTRUCTIONAL

Good planning for instruction implies a knowledge of who is being instructed and what is being instructed. Effective planning for instruction is done by teachers who have a sensitivity to the makeup of the child—psychological, cognitive, physiological, social—and how the child is constantly undergoing change. Furthermore, effective instructional planning requires a knowledge of the mathematical structures and how these structures correspond with learning in mathematics. Instructional structures provide a framework or a system by which a teacher can determine what will be learned, in what order it will be learned, and how it will be learned.

There are three major categories of mathematical structures in the elementary school curriculum: arithmetic, geometry, and measurement. The following are instructional planners recommended for each area.

THE INSTRUCTIONAL PLANNER

For Arithmetic

The Instructional Planner for Arithmetic is presented in Table 3–1 (Schultz & Strawderman, 1980) It lists the types of learning and provides space for the inclusion of mathematical objectives. It also provides space for descriptions of activities, sorted according to the types of behavior and experiences sought during learning. The end of each arithmetic chapter (chapters 4–7) includes a hierarchy of mathematical objectives and their corresponding types of learning. These mathematical objectives are not presented in the traditional behavioral form, which is often seen and labeled "behavioral objectives." The types of behavior and experiences to consider for each objective are specified across the upper right of the planner and are labeled Type 1 (concrete and pictorial), Type 2 (transitional), and Type 3 (abstract) according to how concrete or abstract the lesson might be for each objective. Types of behavior and experiences also include the specific receptive and expressive modes listed in Table 1–2. (These are not included on the Instructional Planner for Arithmetic in order to conserve space, but the teacher needs to keep them in mind while planning for instruction.) Recall from Table 1–2 that the Type 1 behavior and experiences in Table 3–1 are touching, listening, and seeing (receptive); and drawing, speaking, and sorting (expressive). Type 2 behavior and experiences are touching, listening, seeing,

TABLE 3–1
Instructional Planner for Arithmetic

			Types of Behavior and Experiences			
Age	Types of Learning	Mathematical Objectives	Type 1 Concrete	Type 1 Pictorial	Type 2 Transitional	Type 3 Abstract
	concepts					
	facts					
	properties					
	procedures					
	algorithms					
	skills					

Sources: Adapted from Figure 1 in "Representational Models from the Learner's Perspective" by K. A. Schultz, 1986, *Arithmetic Teacher, 33*(6), p. 52. Copyright 1986 by NCTM. Adapted by permission; Figure 3 in "Diagnostic-Prescriptive Mathematics Teaching and the Teaching Cycle Model" by K. A. Schultz and V. W. Strawderman, 1980, *Focus on Learning Problems in Mathematics, 2*(4), p. 32. Copyright 1980 by CTLM. Adapted by permission.

and reading (receptive); and drawing, speaking, sorting, and writing (expressive). Finally, Type 3 behavior and experiences are listening and reading (receptive), and speaking and writing (expressive). These types of behaviors and experiences are in hierarchical form just as the mathematical objectives are.

Lessons can be planned according to the intersection of the hierarchy of mathematical objectives and the hierarchy of behavior and experiences. In some cases, it would not be appropriate to have a lesson for every behavior listed. For example, a Type 3 lesson would not be taught for the concept of addition, since concept learning at this level requires much discussion and hands-on experience and would warrant Type 1 experiences.

For Geometry

The Instructional Planner for Geometry is different than the one for arithmetic due to the content of geometry and the natural development of geometric ideas in young children. Table 3–2 presents the format for planning for geometry. On the left of the planner is the list of dimensions describing the shapes to be studied. Keep in mind that children generally experience or construct three-dimensional shapes first and later focus attention on shapes with fewer dimensions. By Grade 4, children should have formal instruction with models of each dimension, including the formal terminology. For example, *corners* should be understood as *vertices*. A good geometry curriculum should focus not only on the facts about the different shapes, but also on transformations (operations) on these shapes. Attention should be given to the properties of shapes that change or remain the same. Topological transformations change the properties of shape and size without changing the properties of proximity, order, enclosure, or separation. Thus, these four invariant properties are called *topological*. Projective transformations change shape and/or size, also keeping the topological properties invariant. Euclidean transformations do not change shape, size, or the topological properties. Shape and size, therefore, are named *Euclidean properties*.

TABLE 3–2
Instructional Planner for Geometry

Dimensions	Transformations			Properties			Constructions
	Topological	Projective	Euclidean	Topological	Projective	Euclidean	
three							
two							
one							
zero							

Generally, geometry should be approached through hands-on activities. Nonroutine problem solving should include the development of geometric concepts, facts, constructions, transformations, and properties. The Instructional Planner for Geometry will help teachers consider a total geometry curriculum when planning lessons. Teachers should be aware of the importance of geometry experiences in preschool as well as in the early grades.

For Measurement

The Instructional Planner for Measurement presented in Table 3–3 shows how lesson or activity planning can be guided by an intersection of two sets of ideas. For each attribute we measure, the list of developmental stages that young children go through while learning to measure is considered. Notice that volume and capacity are combined because during early childhood, they have basically the same meaning. The stages are (a) attribute recognition, (b) conservation, (c) comparison of the same attribute between objects, (d) application of nonstandard units, (e) application of standard units, and (f) conversion within each system. Again, problem solving is a thread throughout all stages. Although the list of developmental stages is presented in hierarchical order, the attributes are not necessarily in the order they are naturally learned. For example, though temperature is near the bottom of the list, we know that a toddler learns the concept of hot and cold before the concepts of length, area, or volume. Keep in mind that children in the United States are

TABLE 3–3
Instructional Planner for Measurement

Attributes	Attribute Recognition	Conservation	Comparison	Application of Nonstandard Unit	Application of Standard Unit	Conversion
			Stages			
length						
area						
volume/capacity						
mass						
temperature						
time (change)						
money (value)						

learning two systems of measurement. Therefore, we must teach both the customary and metric systems of measurement with informal conversions between systems.

The instructional planners presented previously are discussed in further detail in their respective chapters in Part 2 of this book. Most instruction with 2- through 5-year-olds will be in the first four stages. By Grade 3, children will be able to do some work with standard units, conversion within the systems, and problem solving.

TYPES AND USES OF REPRESENTATIONAL MODELS

When models are made available to middle school students for voluntary use during problem solving, some students prefer certain types of models over others (Schultz, 1984). Some models seem to increase problem-solving ability more than others. The factors that contribute to increased problem-solving ability are concreteness of models, meaningfulness of models, and use of models, as shown in Table 3–4 (Schultz, 1986).

Concreteness

Classifying types of representational models into **concrete, pictorial,** and **symbolic** has long been a useful reference to teachers and researchers (Bruner, 1960, 1966; Dienes, 1963; Flavell, 1963). Examples of concrete models are blocks, sticks, chips, Cuisenaire rods, and Dienes blocks. Examples of pictorial models are pictures of blocks, sticks, chips, Cuisenaire rods, and Dienes blocks. These pictures can be on worksheets, textbook pages, bulletin

TABLE 3–4
Types and Uses of Representational Models

	Concrete	*Pictorial*	*Symbolic*
meaningful			
indirectly meaningful			
nonmeaningful			

Note: Materials in each frame above can be *actively manipulated, passively manipulated* (by watching another actively manipulate materials), or *not manipulated* at all.

Source: Adapted from Figure 2 in "Representational Models from the Learner's Perspective" by K. A. Schultz, 1986, *Arithmetic Teacher, 33*(6), p. 54. Copyright 1986 by NCTM. Adapted by permission.

boards, paper cutouts, felt cutouts, or picture cards. Symbolic models are numerals on worksheets, textbook pages, chalkboards, bulletin boards, number cards, or number tiles.

Meaningfulness

Directly meaningful, indirectly meaningful, and **nonmeaningful** classifications are then applied across the concrete, pictorial, and symbolic types of models. That is, a concrete model could be directly meaningful, indirectly meaningful, or nonmeaningful. Examples of directly meaningful models are pennies for problems about pennies; Cuisenaire rods for problems about Cuisenaire rods; pictures of baseball players for problems about pictures of baseball players; and sticks for problems about sticks, where they could be bundled to represent groups of ten. That is, directly meaningful models are the actual items that relate to a problem. Indirectly meaningful models are representations of real objects, such as pictures of rabbits for problems about rabbits, toy cars for problems about cars, or pictures of baseball players for problems about baseball players. Nonmeaningful models are bottle caps used to represent people and blocks used to represent books. In other words, children wouldn't know what a nonmeaningful model represented unless they were told.

Another way to describe models is according to their uses. We have not referred to "manipulative" materials in this section, but, instead, we have referred to "representational models" for reasons that will be outlined in the next section.

Manipulation

Each intersection of the two classifications of representational models classified by meaningfulness and concreteness can be further classified according to use, that is according to **active manipulation, passive manipulation,** and **nonmanipulation** of models. Active manipulation of a concrete model is Bruner's (1966) "enactive" learning, which involves a rich and meaningful direct hands-on experience—the key to readiness. Students' active manipulation can include more than just concrete models; it can also include cutout pictures or number tiles. Flexibility of thinking is enhanced by this action approach to learning in problem-solving situations.

When students observe the teacher manipulating models to demonstrate a concept or procedure, these models are passive manipulatives for the students. There are critical moments in learning when active manipulation is essential. However, at times, being one step removed from the action encourages students to develop their abilities with abstract concepts. Likewise, when models are present, but not manipulated at all, they become nonmanipulatives. Examples of nonmanipulatives include a display of Dienes blocks, models on a bulletin board, and, the most common, pictures on worksheets and textbook pages. These nonmanipulatives require spatial visualization skills. Children refer to models on display and imagine some action on them.

Many of the educational microcomputer software packages in homes and schools offer opportunities to "directly manipulate" pictures or numerals by moving, removing, drawing, or otherwise transforming them on the monitor (Champagne & Rogalska-Saz, 1984). "Passive manipulation" images are programmed to appear, disappear, or transform in some way on the monitor, outside the user's control. Likewise, "nonmanipulative" experiences occur when images remain static until a response is given and/or the return key is pressed.

ASSESSMENT AND EVALUATION

It makes sense that the purpose of testing be established before testing materials are selected and testing procedures are established. Assessment is the process of determining the child's specific abilities and functioning level and is used for the purpose of selecting appropriate teaching strategies. Evaluation is the process of determining the effectiveness of the teaching strategy employed.

Most school systems employ standardized tests to assess children's abilities in mathematics. These standardized achievement tests are useful in identifying the grade level where a child is functioning and in making preliminary decisions, such as grouping by instructional level. However, criterion-referenced tests are much more useful for the purpose of identifying specific teaching objectives for individual children and pinpointing specific deficiencies in the hierarchy of mathematics skills. Therefore, the practice of using one standardized test to make several decisions is questionable. Different testing techniques and materials should be employed depending on the purpose for testing.

Assessment

The assessment process involves two steps: (a) screening to determine grade level and preliminary grouping, and (b) analyzing specific skills to determine specific teaching strategies and specific instructional points. While the most efficient method for screening is the group-administered achievement test with norm references, a criterion-referenced test is recommended for determining the specific instructional strategies and teaching objectives. Many instructional series include criterion-referenced tests as a part of their curriculum. Some of the more recent achievement tests such as the KeyMath Diagnostic Arithmetic Test (Connolly, Nachtman, & Pritchett, 1971, 1976) and the Stanford Diagnostic Mathematics Test: 3rd Edition (SDMT) (Beatty, Madden, Gardner, & Karlsen, 1983, 1984) have made attempts to combine both features. For example, the SDMT provides comprehensive norms as well as a specific diagnostic analysis of the child's strengths and weaknesses.

Evaluation

The evaluation process determines if the teaching/learning process is working effectively. Evaluation allows the teacher to determine if the child has mastered the objectives of the lessons taught so that the decision to reteach or move forward can be made. Short-term evaluation is usually done at the end of a specific unit using a criterion-referenced test. Long-term evaluation is accomplished using standardized achievement tests at the end of the school year. It is best to use the same test at the beginning and end of the year to evaluate progress.

The Testing Procedure

Teachers should question test results because results reflect only a specific situation and may be inaccurate and misleading. Several points should be considered. A test may be assessing a child's ability to take that test rather than testing the child's knowledge. Test items should match the objectives of the school mathematics curriculum. In addition to tests, teachers should use a variety of means to assess learning. Some of these means are seat work, homework, observation, interview, information from parent conferences, and performance in real situations. Test scores should be used by teachers and administrators who are fully aware of what they imply; today too much interpretation of student ability or achievement is made solely by scores.

Testing should be done in the same mode that was used in the teaching/learning process. For example, if children were learning a concept through a Type 1 *concrete* experience, they should be tested in a Type 1 *concrete* situation (not in a Type 1 *pictorial* format). If they were taught through a Type 2 experience, they should be tested in Type 2 format (not Type 3). A short period of instruction may indicate that the test results were not a true indicator of the child's level of functioning. Therefore, after a short period of actual instruction, you will probably need to adjust the grouping of students.

In closing, the teacher of mathematics must consider many models and structures when planning lessons or activities. The structure of the mathematics itself cannot be superimposed upon the learning process. The structure must be built up within children's minds. The teacher should carefully consider the instructional readiness of the child and the structures and processes to be used when planning an instructional sequence and selecting types of models. Finally, the child must be evaluated in an appropriate manner for the teacher to know how complete and correct (or how incomplete and erroneous) the child's mathematical understanding is at particular points in time.

SUMMARY

This chapter combined information about the instructional readiness of the learner in chapter 1 and the structures of mathematics in chapter 2. The results are the instructional planners for arithmetic, geometry, and measurement. We covered some very important facts about assessment and evaluation. We concluded that the key to successful instruction and testing is attending to the hierarchy of learning behaviors. Also, since the role of hands-on materials is emphasized so much, we included a thorough survey of what *concreteness* means, what *meaningfulness* means, and what *manipulation* means in relation to choosing instructional materials that assist the teaching and learning process. We are now ready to move into Part 2 of this text to begin our study of mathematics content and how to teach it.

STUDY QUESTIONS AND ACTIVITIES

1. Effective mathematics instruction involves the teacher's understanding of the child's interpretation of a mathematical idea or procedure. Interview several children ages 2 to 9. Choose from among the following items according to the age of the child. Ask the children to respond to the items, but do not instruct. Report accounts of their responses.
   a. Show a picture of a circle. Say something equivalent to "Tell me all you can about this picture."
   b. Show the fraction $\frac{1}{2}$. Say something equivalent to "Tell me all you can about this number."
   c. Show the expression $2 + 1 = 3$. Say something equivalent to "Tell me all you can about this."
   d. Show the expression $10 \div ? = 5$. Say something equivalent to "What does this mean to you?"
2. Look at the materials used in the student activities at the end of chapter 4. Identify each set of materials according to the following: (a) concreteness, (b) meaningfulness, and (c) manipulation.

REFERENCES AND RESOURCES

Beatty, L. D., Madden, R., Gardner, E. F., & Karlsen, B. (1983, 1984). *Stanford Diagnostic Mathematics Test*: 3rd Edition. Cleveland: Psychological Corporation.

Bruner, J. S. (1960). *The process of education*. New York: Vintage Books.

Bruner, J. S. (1966). *Toward a theory of instruction*. New York: Norton.

Champagne, A. B., & Rogalska-Saz, J. (1984). Computer-based numeration instruction. In V. P. Hansen & M. J. Zweng (Eds.), *Computers in mathematics education* (pp. 43–53). Reston, VA: NCTM.

Connolly, A. J., Nachtman, W., & Pritchett, E. M. (1971, 1976). *KeyMath diagnostic arithmetic test* Circle Pines, MN: American Guidance Service.

Corbitt, M. K. (Ed.). (1985). The impact of computing technology on school mathematics: Report of an NCTM conference. *Arithmetic Teacher, 32*(8), 14–18.

Dienes, Z. P. (1963). *An experimental study of mathematics learning.* London: Hutchinson.

Flavell, J. H. (1963). *The developmental psychology of Jean Piaget.* New York: Van Nostrand Reinhold.

Hoffer, A. (1983). Van Hiele-based research. In R. Lesh & M. Landau (Eds.), *Acquisition of mathematics concepts and processes* (pp. 205–227). New York: Academic Press.

Labinowicz, E. (1985). *Learning from children.* Menlo Park, CA: Addison-Wesley.

Lindquist, M. M. (1987). *Learning and teaching geometry, K–12: 1987 Yearbook.* Reston, VA: NCTM.

National Council of Supervisors of Mathematics. (1977). Position paper on basic skills. *Arithmetic Teacher, 25*(1), 19–22.

National Council of Teachers of Mathematics. (1980). *An agenda for action: Recommendations for school mathematics of the 1980s.* Reston, VA: Author.

Schoenfeld, A. H. (1983). The wild, wild, wild, wild, wild world of problem solving: A review of sorts. *For the Learning of Mathematics, 3,* 40–47.

Schultz, K. A. (1984). Self-directed use of different types of representational models in middle school problem solving. In J. M. Moser (Ed.), *Proceedings of the Fifth Annual Meeting of the North American Chapter of the International Group for the Psychology of Mathematics Education* (pp. 153–158). Madison, WI: University of Wisconsin.

Schultz, K. A. (1986). Representational models from the learner's perspective. *Arithmetic Teacher, 33,* 52–55.

Schultz, K. A., & Strawderman, V. W. (1980). Diagnostic-prescriptive mathematics teaching and the teaching cycle model. *Focus on Learning Problems in Mathematics, 2*(4), 27–36.

PART 2

Planning for Instruction

4

Numbers and Numeration

TIIIS CHAPTER will set the pace for Part 2 of the book, where content is studied in detail. Each chapter in Part 2 will start with vocabulary for teachers and students since language development is such a significant part of both teaching and learning mathematics. Following the vocabulary, there is a discussion on readiness—a very important topic for number and numeration. All preschool learning is readiness for early understanding of number and numeration. Number answers: "How much?" or "How many?" Numeration is the system used to name numbers.

VOCABULARY FOR TEACHERS

Teaching early number and numeration concepts might appear to be fairly straightforward and simple. In reality, however, the language and concepts are quite specific and deserve careful attention. To appreciate the detail involved, let's examine the vocabulary for teachers.

Fifteen years ago, teachers discriminated between **number, the idea,** and **numeral, the symbol for the idea.** Children, especially at very early ages, were unable to understand the difference between the terms. Today, teachers should know the difference themselves, but their students are not expected to make the distinction. For all practical purposes, the term *number* is now used in the classroom; learning is not dependent upon students' understanding of the differences in the terms.

Numeration is the term applied to the system of naming and using numbers. Our system is the Hindu-Arabic numeration system. Teachers need to be intimately familiar with all the aspects of this system in order to teach it, although children need not know the term *numeration*.

Classification is the identification of objects according to a particular attribute. For example, very young children learn to classify objects according to size, color, shape, or use. As children get older they eventually classify according to number. **Cardinality** is the property of defining the number of objects in a group or set. For example, a group of 10 objects has cardinality 10, a group of 6 objects has cardinality 6, and so on. Teachers should be interested in the child's ability to count the members of a set as well as to understand the concept of "one more than." The children will use **one-to-one correspondence** by matching objects from one group with objects from another group in order to determine if each group has an equal number of objects. At first, children manually match each object from one set to an object in the other set. Older children progress to visually matching objects. Finally, children's early work in patterns and **seriating** objects (ordering objects according to increasing or decreasing degrees of different attributes—rough to smooth or small to large) prepares them to order numbers according to the patterns of "one more than" and "one less than." These four terms are not expected to be used by children.

VOCABULARY FOR STUDENTS

The following is a sampling of the terminology that should be used in the classroom and understood by children.

Sorting is usually the term children will use when they are engaged in classification activities. The children may need to be formally introduced to the term if it is not yet a part of their everyday language. **Matching** is a term that is probably familiar to most children in preschool and will be important when learning one-to-one correspondence. Matching naturally leads to the ideas of *greater than* and *less than*. Teachers should be aware that children don't think of numbers as being greater or less than other numbers, but rather bigger or smaller. In response to the child's "Five is bigger than four," say "Yes, five is greater than four." This gentle correcting will assist the children in making the transition to the correct terms.

Readiness for numeration includes the concepts of *groups* and *grouping*. Children may not know these terms at the late preschool or kindergarten levels when they will be asked to group objects into a given number. Groups may be explained in terms of sets if children are familiar with that term. If the children don't know *set,* they probably know the word *bunch*.

At first, the use of the term *place value* causes considerable confusion! One reason is the lack of understanding of the concept of group. In addition, children's understanding of the words *place* and *value* is not strong, nor is their ability to have an intuitive feel for the concept of place value. This term needs to be carefully developed for students. A similar problem will arise with the term *placeholder*.

Finally, some discussion concerning *renaming, trading,* and *regrouping* is important here. The term **renaming** should be used when working with numbers. **Regrouping**, however, should be used when working with the objects that are actually regrouped. An example of renaming occurs in the problem 21 − 3, where one thinks of or rewrites the number 21 to be "1 ten and 11 ones" in order to subtract 3 from it. An example of regrouping is when a rubber band is placed on or removed from a bundle of sticks. **Trading** should be used when it actually occurs, such as when a bundle of sticks is traded for 10 single sticks. Ample opportunity exists for confusion and contradiction in the children's use of all these terms, and teachers must take great care in the development of these concepts.

READINESS

Now that we have a foundation in some of the vocabulary involved in the teaching of number and numeration, our next consideration is children's readiness to learn these mathematical ideas. Young children naturally invent and use counting strategies (Carpenter & Moser, 1979). In fact, research has shown that children already have a great deal of knowledge and ability when they enter the first grade (Carpenter, Hiebert, & Moser, 1984; Carpenter & Moser, 1979; Fuson, 1986). When planning instruction, teachers should take advantage of these natural abilities. Children learn best when ideas are meaningful and related to previous knowledge and skills. Every effort should be made to determine the children's understanding and functioning levels so they can be involved in the construction of their own mathematical ideas (Schoenfeld, 1987).

Prenumber concepts and skills are critical in early mathematics learning. The prenumber components of classification and seriation, discussed briefly earlier, lay the groundwork for early number concepts and facilitate perceptual discrimination skills, language development, and motor skills. A more detailed discussion of each component follows.

1. Classification is based on many characteristics (also referred to as attributes or properties) that children perceive such as length, mass, color, taste, sound, and shape. At the same time, children are learning that quantity is also a characteristic to be classified. For example, children will identify or create groups of one, two, three, or more based on familiar objects; children can see there are two legs on a body, two books on the shelf, and two wheels on a bicycle.

According to Piaget (Flavell, 1963), children develop the ability to classify in three stages. Stage one, which begins around 2 years of age, is called the stage of figural collections. At this stage, children are unable to sort objects when told to look for a particular characteristic like shape or color. Also, children tend to randomly change their criteria for sorting objects and sometimes arrange objects into the shape of a familiar object like a smiley face or house. In this process, the child may sort objects so the eyes on the smiley face are each blue buttons, or the wheels on the train are each bottle caps, but the end product is not the result of sorting objects according to a given characteristic.

Stage two is characterized by the making of nonfigural collections by a 5-year-old, as shown in Figure 4–1. At this stage, the child can classify according to a given characteristic, but is unable to see a subclass as a part of a class of objects. For example, the child can sort red attribute pieces, but is unable to see that the red squares are a subclass of the red shapes. Stage three has been reached when the child can both sort according to a given characteristic and identify subgroups within a group. It could be as late as age 6 before some children have successfully shown characteristics of stage three, though many will do so by ages 4 or 5.

2. Concurrently with learning to classify objects, children learn seriation—ordering of objects according to a particular characteristic or attribute. These are attributes that can be found in varying degrees, such as length, mass, sweetness, temperature, shades of a color, and loudness. Ultimately, children will recognize that quantity can be ordered. The "one more than" notion leads them to see that one more than one is two; one more than two is three; one

FIGURE 4–1
A 5-year-old shows her nonfigural collections of objects.

more than three is four; and so on. Eventually, the children will comprehend that the listing of numbers "one, two, three, four, . . ." is in that order for a reason.

Experience with finding, completing, and creating patterns is important at an early age and will strengthen the child's understanding of the pattern of increasing degrees of an attribute. Several factors must be taken into consideration when anticipating the level of a child's performance. These factors are the attribute to be seriated, the method assigned to seriate, and the degree of difference in the objects or conditions presented. When teaching this concept to less mature children or those with learning problems, it is critical to provide many simple concrete experiences. It is also important not to move to a higher ability level until the student has demonstrated a generalized understanding of the concept. Understanding has been accomplished when the child can perform the same skill in different settings using different materials.

Piaget (Copeland, 1984) identified three stages through which children progress in their ability to seriate sticks according to length. Stage one, around age 4 or 5, called the uncoordinated series stage, is when the child starts out incapable of ordering any sticks and progresses to ordering clusters of 2 or 3 sticks at a time where there are sticks missing in between. Figure 4–2 illustrates the uncoordinated series stage.

During stage two, at 5 to 6 years of age, called the trial and error stage, the child is able to seriate 10 sticks, but only after a laborious series of trial and error activities between successive pairs of sticks. It is only in stage three, around 6 years of age, the stage of operational seriation, that the child is able to use relational thinking when ordering the sticks. For example, during stage two rod 2 might be compared with rod 4. Then, rod 3 would be compared to both rods 2 and 4 before determining that 2–3–4 is the correct order (4–3–2 would also be acceptable if the direction was not specified). Then, rod 1 would be

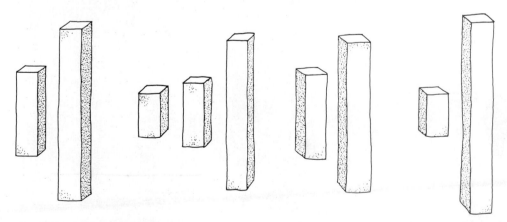

FIGURE 4–2
Uncoordinated Series

compared to all of the others individually before the child determines that 1–2–3–4 is correct. During stage three, rod 2 might be compared with rod 4. Then, rod 3 would be compared to rod 2 and 4 to get 2–3–4. Then, rod 1 would be compared only to rod 2 to get 1–2–3–4. See Figure 4–3 for a 6-year-old who has advanced to ordering all 10 rods. Therefore, the child would understand that if rod 1 is shorter than rod 2, it will also be shorter than rods 3 and 4. This more efficient strategy enables the child to bypass the numerous comparisons of two sticks at a time. Instead, the child makes use of the knowledge that if the first stick is shorter than the second stick, it is also shorter than the sticks longer than the second stick, and so on. The process is systematic and completely operational.

The previous section on readiness discussed the importance of experience and success with classifying and seriating as readiness for learning number. Preschool environments rich with opportunities to classify and seriate will facilitate the successful development of number in children.

NUMBER

This section begins with the five principles upon which counting with understanding is built (Kulm, 1985). Following these principles is a discussion of special considerations when teaching number. We describe why a child's lack of understanding of conservation can hamper the child's understanding of number. Zero is given special consideration because of the confusion surrounding its use. Sight groups are mentioned as a possible aid in identifying how many objects are in a group. We also consider ordinality, a common aspect of

FIGURE 4–3
Ten rods have been successfully ordered by this 6-year-old.

number experienced by children long before they start kindergarten. Then, we build up to counting and understanding—the focal points of this section. We then discuss how children learn to write numerals and how they learn to make and use the number line.

We know from research that arithmetic instruction can successfully build on counting strategies that children have developed by themselves during preschool. Some of these counting skills are not expected until second grade or later! The following paragraphs name and describe five principles that children must understand in order to use counting effectively. These principles should be incorporated into instruction, from as early as age 4, to ensure that the most effective use of counting will occur.

1. The **stable ordering principle** refers to counting in a fixed sequence, that is, "one, two, three," and so on. Research has indicated that children who count "one, two, three, five, seven" show an understanding of the stable ordering principle with some numbers simply missing (Thornton, Tucker, Dossey, & Bazik, 1983). The following suggested activities help develop stable ordering: rhymes, fingerplays, and songs; simple board games in which the child counts while moving a game piece; and oral counting.

2. The **one-to-one matching principle** is applied between objects and numbers. The child matches each object with a number. However, at the same time that this principle is being learned, the child is also engaged in matching objects, such as straws with paper cups, napkins with crackers, and children with chairs. Eventually, the child will be able to match a variety of more abstract objects, such as pictures of rabbits with pictures of carrots and blocks with chips. Outgrowths of matching are the concepts of "greater than" and "less than" (or in the child's terms, "bigger than" and "smaller than"). Also, the concept of "one more than" should merge with the principle of one-to-one matching, as shown in Figure 4–4. One-to-one matching is taught by having children physically move or touch objects as they count, by having them count while watching objects being moved or touched one at a time by someone else, and by having them count while looking at objects or while listening to particular sounds, such as bells.

3. The **total number principle** refers to the child's ability to understand that the number matched with the last object counted in a given group tells how many objects there are in the group. By correctly identifying the number of objects in a set, the child has demonstrated an understanding of cardinality. To teach this principle, have children count to find out how many objects there are or how many sounds are heard. Then, repeat the last number to emphasize "how many."

4. The **different objects principle** refers to the child's ability to understand that the objects in a group do not all have to be of the same type in order to count them. Teachers can help children to develop this ability by having them compare the number of related objects within a group, such as socks within a group of shoes and socks, or compare the number of similar objects with a same number of mixed objects, such as a group of six pencils with a group of three rulers and three erasers.

Teacher: "Are there more cups or more straws?"

Student: "There are more straws."

FIGURE 4–4
Comparison of Sets Using One-to-One Matching

5. **Different order** is the principle that a set of objects can be counted in a variety of ways. That is, no matter which object is counted first the result is always the same number of objects in all. To help children develop this ability, the teacher can have children count objects in a group, each time with a different starting point. Children should compare the total each time.

Conservation

Related to the previous principles is conservation of number. **Conservation** is the ability to not fix on the physical characteristics of objects like size or arrangement when determining if two sets are equal in number. An example of conservation is when children compare the number of chairs stacked up on one another with the same number of chairs placed around a table.

Zero

Mathematically, zero precedes all nonzero whole numbers. However, children's understanding of zero does not precede understanding of nonzero whole numbers. Children's personal experiences offer an early intuitive understanding of "nothing" or "all gone." Therefore, the first formal work with the concept of and notation for zero should be done with care in order to build on these early personal experiences.

Zero should not be introduced formally until several nonzero numbers have been successfully introduced and used. Remember that it is more difficult for children to understand the concept of a number when symbolic representations are used than when concrete representations are used, especially for zero. Children have difficulty understanding zero because, visually, there are no objects, but there *is* a symbol to use. Children tend to think "no objects, no number." Thus, great care should be exercised by the teacher to not equate "none" or "nothing" with zero. When four objects are taken away from four objects, the result is zero objects. Children tend to confuse the whole number zero with the concept of "nothing left."

Sight Groups

Learning to recognize how many are in a group without counting is a useful skill for children to develop. Practice should be provided to enable children to glance at an arrangement of objects, or at flashcards showing an arrangement of pictures of objects, and have them state how many objects they saw without providing enough time to count. When counting objects in larger groups, such as a group of nine beans where four are clustered, the child can be taught to say "four" and then to count from four to determine how many in all.

Ordinality

Ordinality refers to the relative position of an object or event in relation to other objects or events. For example, we say "first" in line, "second" in line, and so on. Since young children are egocentric, they will have some difficulty in determining position relative to other persons or objects instead of relative to themselves. Therefore, activities that include the child as one of the members of a set are good for early understanding of this concept. An example might be to assign the child to different positions in the group during different activities, such as lining up to go to lunch. Figure 4–5 illustrates a dialogue a teacher might have with students to reinforce the concept of ordinality.

Sally   Tyrone   Cleo   Marshall

Teacher: "Who is first in line?"   (Marshall)
          "Who is second?"   (Cleo)
          "What is Tyrone's position?"   (Third)
          "Which place is Sally in?"   (Fourth)

FIGURE 4–5
Ordinality

Up to this point, we have discussed many concepts related to children's early knowledge of numbers and counting. To encourage the fullest teaching and learning processes in the preschool or primary classroom, the teacher should carefully and deliberately determine the quality of thinking already in effect in the child's attempts at counting. Activities assigned should be used to diagnose, correct, practice, or extend the child's counting ability with the ultimate goal being *to count with understanding*. Once this understanding is reached, children can master writing numerals and the number line more easily (Kulm, 1985).

Counting with Understanding

Children who count with understanding do more than just recite the auditory pattern of "one, two, three." These children know that there is a class of single-object sets, a class of two-object sets, a class of three-object sets, and so on. They know that one more than one is two, one more than two is three, and one more than three is four. They know that there is a fixed order of number names. Also, they understand that when matching these number names to objects, the last number named tells how many objects are in the set. They know that objects can be different, rearranged, large or small, and counted in different orders without changing the number of objects in a set.

Children as young as 4 years can count past 10, often to 20 or more. However, this doesn't imply that they understand place value! They have merely memorized the number names since they have heard them so often at home, in day care, from siblings, and on television. By the first grade, formal instruction in place value will begin.

Writing Numerals

There are four general rules to follow when teaching children how to write numerals. First, it is best if children start to write numerals after they can associate the meaning of the number represented. However, they can practice writing numerals while they are still in the process of stabilizing their understanding. In this case, the writing should be done with representational models available, either in pictorial or concrete form, to reinforce the meaning of the number.

It is important for teachers to avoid situations and materials that encourage frustration, even for children who have no learning or behavior problems. Therefore, the second general rule is that writing should progress from using gross motor to fine motor movements. If the child does not have the fine motor skills required to write numerals, provide activities such as writing in the air or using materials like Play Doh, blocks, or sticks to make the shapes of the numerals. Figure 4–6 shows a sandbox and chalkboard as two more examples.

The third general rule is to avoid tracing dotted or dashed lines. The dots or dashes indicate to the child how a perfect numeral looks. The young child, however, is incapable of tracing well enough to feel satisfied. Even adults have

FIGURE 4–6
Writing Numerals

difficulty staying on the line—try it yourself! An alternative approach is to have the child practice writing a numeral next to the numeral already written. The sample nearby might reduce the possibility of the child getting frustrated because of not staying on the lines.

The fourth general rule is to use media that reduce the opportunity to remember an error. If a child makes a reversal error while writing with his or her finger in a sand or salt box, the child can quickly shift the sand or salt around to "erase" the mistake. A penciled numeral on a piece of paper is much more difficult to erase—becoming in itself a frustration. Air writing is the least frustrating since the focus is on process, not product. Other easily correctable media are Play Doh, sticks, plastic chains, strings, finger paints, and pudding "paints." No matter what medium is used, verbal prompting is very important, and children should be encouraged to verbalize the process themselves. For example, note the verbalization for writing the numeral 2 in Figure 4–7.

Number Lines

The use of number lines is particularly common among primary grade instructional materials. Mathematically, the number line is a logical model for number. However, cognitively, young children have trouble using the model successfully (Bright & Behr, 1984). This is because geometric, measurement, and numerical systems are superimposed on this one model. Children are expected to use this picture of a horizontal line with segments of equal measure labeled in order with each numeral to strengthen their understand-

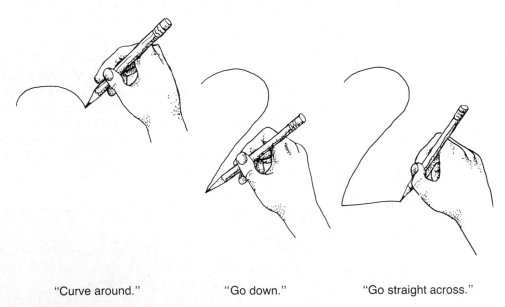

"Curve around."   "Go down."   "Go straight across."

FIGURE 4–7
Verbalizing Writing Numerals

ing of number. Unfortunately, this understanding is challenged by the inherent difficulties of superimposing the three mathematical systems onto the one model!

Therefore, the teacher should be sure to carefully develop each system—one at a time—to prepare children to use the model for number. The first exposure to the model should be a numberless line where children are actively engaged in determining equal segments. Children should completely understand this step before numerals are designated for the segments. Since this model has nothing to do with everyday life, we suggest some meaning be put into it. For example, the children could pretend a certain frog jumps in straight lines, and each jump is the same distance (see Figure 4–8). Have children

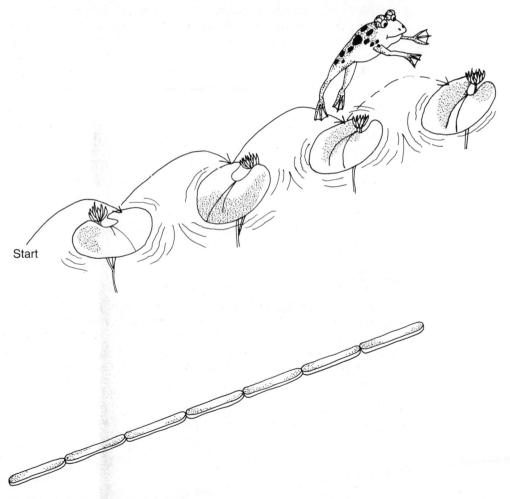

FIGURE 4–8
Modeling Number Line Concept

construct their own interpretations by having them draw pictures, use string, or use sticks. At the very least, the first number line children use should be the one they make themselves!

Arrows on number lines signify infinity, a concept children are unable to understand at the time the number line is first introduced. It is advisable to avoid these arrows. Because arrows have a multitude of meanings in early mathematics, they should not be used unless completely understood by the children. Figure 4–9 shows three uses. There are many more!

This section covered the most significant aspects of learning the concept of number as well as what counting is all about. Formation of these concepts is essential before children formally study numeration—the system of naming numbers. Preschool teachers should pay particular attention to the five principles upon which counting with understanding is based. The activities suggested to facilitate the understanding of these principles can be woven into the preschool curriculum starting with ages 3 and 4.

NUMERATION

We begin this section on numeration by first addressing the concept of grouping as preparation for counting groups as well as counting groups of groups. Then, the importance of children's understanding of place value is explained. Readiness for place value can occur in preschool with grouping activities. Formal instruction occurs at the end of first grade. Second grade is the critical year for laying a firm foundation. At the end of this section, naming, writing, and counting numbers are covered. Special attention is given to ordering, zero, and number lines.

Grouping

The first step toward an understanding of the Hindu-Arabic numeration system is the concept of grouping. Our system is based on groups of 10, but that should not limit children from experiencing other numbers in groups while learning the concept of grouping. As an activity, children can be provided with containers like $2\frac{1}{2}$-ounce paper drinking cups or soufflé cups into which they

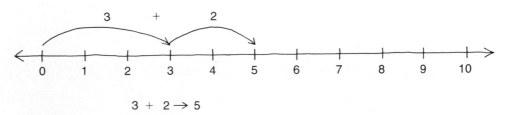

FIGURE 4–9
Number Line with Three Different Uses of Arrows

will count out announced numbers of beans, chips, or other small, discrete objects.

This activity is similar to many of the early number activities children have completed. The difference is that the activity will go beyond just counting a given number of objects and making groups. Special attention will be given to naming the grouping number, perhaps calling it the "magic number" or "special number." The number should have a name that makes it special and different from other groups of objects. When children are grouping in tens, let them know that this is the most important "magic number" or "special number" and that they will be grouping in tens for a long, long time to come. Ten is our friend! This lays the groundwork for calling ten the base.

While children are grouping according to various group numbers, get them involved in a discussion of how many groups of a particular number they have. For example, as in Figure 4–10, if the group number is five, and they have arranged three cups of five chips each, ask "How many do you have in one group?" and "How many groups of five do you have?"

Children are at a critical point in their understanding of many-to-one and one-to-many correspondences when confronted with these questions. They now have three groups of five. Often this is a difficult concept to grasp. They have worked so hard to understand what five of anything means, and now they are asked to call the five marbles a "one," that is, "one group of five." It certainly appears to be a contradiction in terms! Therefore, teachers' sensitivity to the potential confusion with the concept and the language involved can help offset trouble for children in the future. Teachers should go slowly and easily with these ideas; taking time now will save time later!

The teacher should provide some clear notion of what constitutes a group or where a group is to be placed. For example, in Figure 4–10, the counted marbles in the cups define the group. Other possibilities are buttons in egg cartons, Unifix Cubes in connected sections, Cheerios on paper plates, and crayons in cans.

Teachers should have several different models prepared for classroom use to assist in developing the grouping concept. As always with young children, the more meaningful and the more concrete the models, the more easily children will be able to learn the mathematical concepts. Because children

FIGURE 4–10
Group Number and Number of Groups

already have a language for familiar objects, they can more easily understand and articulate what they or someone else is doing with those objects. Also, the more personal the involvement children have with manipulations (as opposed to observing someone else do the manipulating), the stronger their conceptual knowledge will be. They are constructors and "owners" of the mathematics.

Place Value

Generally, by the middle of first grade, children should be directed to handle models that lend themselves to a place-value chart and to bundling or connecting. Even though other groups are possible, most of the work at this time should be focused on groups of 10, which will be the most usable group from this point on. Bundled popsicle or coffee stir sticks are ideal models. Drinking straws are inconvenient, since they roll. If the children are unable to manage rubber bands, they can still count out the groups of 10 sticks that the teacher can bundle. If the teacher prepared "trade" boxes filled with bundled and loose sticks like those shown in Figure 4–11, then the children could simply take out 10 ones for 1 group of 10 or 1 group of 10 for 10 ones. The children can physically see and feel that these are fair trades.

Allowing children to do the bundling and unbundling encourages the development of eye-hand coordination. This process is more time-consuming and there is a greater chance of error in counting sticks, but the advantage of the children's increased learning is worth it. A teacher should always be aware of the disadvantages in every situation and plan lessons that will foster the greatest learning for the students.

FIGURE 4–11
These children are using "trade" boxes filled with bundled and single sticks.

Other popular grouping models are Dienes blocks; a paper version of Dienes blocks, usually called *grid paper* or *squared paper*; and bean sticks, made of lima beans glued onto tongue depressors. Notice that these models do not need to be on a place-value chart for the user to know the value of each part. However, it would be appropriate to use these models on a place-value chart. For example, children can see that a single bean represents 1. One stick with 10 beans glued onto it represents a group of 10, and a flat of 10 bean sticks represents a group of 100.

Figure 4–12 shows a nongrouping model, representing 647, in which a group of 10 is represented by a single stick in a pocket chart instead of a group of 10 sticks. Other examples of nongrouping models are chips on a place-value chart and an abacus. These models require a large cognitive leap. They require the young mind to accept the fact that even though there is only 1 chip in the tens place, it represents a group of 10. This is very abstract and requires conceptual knowledge on the part of the child. This conceptual leap can only be possible with a solid grounding in and understanding of grouping models.

Naming and Writing Numerals

Only after children can state a two-digit number orally when given a model representation and can give a model representation when given the oral cue for a number, can they be expected to make the connection with the written symbol. Special care should be given to the naming irregularities of the numbers 11 through 19. These irregularities should be considered formally after students work with the 20s and 30s. Beginning with a less formal

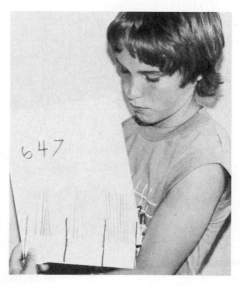

FIGURE 4–12
Nongrouping model of a pocket chart and sticks shows the number 647.

approach will give children a chance to appreciate patterns in the numbers and begin to get a sense of what place value means. These important levels of understanding come gradually and should never be underestimated.

Explain to the children that it might have made more sense to name the numbers 11 through 19 "tenty-one," "tenty-two," "tenty-three," and so on. Instead, children have to say "eleven" for one 10 and one 1, and "twelve" for one 10 and 2 ones. This inconsistency isn't even consistent! "Thirteen" through "nineteen" name the ones first, departing again from the patterns present in naming numbers greater than 20. It's understandable why a child might write 91 for 19! Languages other than English also have irregularities in the names of the counting numbers.

While children refine their understanding of two-digit numbers and number names as represented by models, children can begin to make symbolic connections. Teachers' expectations should be low at first, since children's understandings are being challenged. According to Piaget, children are trying to establish equilibrium with their understandings of number and numeration without the presence of symbols. When written symbols are matched with the words and models, children's minds tend to go into disequilibrium. Understanding is slow. Children need consistency in the way symbols are presented and in the terminology they hear. All other concepts should remain static while a new component is introduced to their communication systems. In some cases, teaching the same lesson several times may be appropriate, especially for transitional lessons that slowly remove the models and symbols. These lessons should be kept short the first time and then repeated. Consider loose number cards like those shown in Figure 4–13 or a number flip chart on a place-value chart. Children shouldn't always be required to write their responses. If they know the number but are not good at writing it yet, they will get frustrated. The cards provide a quick manner of symbolically representing numbers. Number tiles work, too, and may be easier for some children to handle.

When writing is first assigned, models on a place-value chart should be close and accessible. Gradually, make the models less accessible; perhaps place them on a nearby table. Movement from transitional to abstract types of learning is critical and should never be hurried. Extra time spent with models to ensure understanding will undoubtedly be offset by the time that will be saved by not having to remediate later!

Counting

Lessons, activities, and games could include counting up by ones and down by ones, first by using grouping, then nongrouping models. This is a valuable experience for learning the concept of base place value; it also serves as readiness for adding and subtracting where renaming is necessary. Later, counting up and down by twos, fives, and tens can be done. This type of counting serves as readiness for multiplication and division.

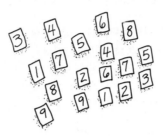

FIGURE 4–13
Using Numerals with a Place-Value Chart

Ordering Numbers

Ordering numbers, finding numbers missing in a sequence, and identifying the next in a sequence of numbers strengthen understanding. Typically, rote counting to 100 is as far as children go in the first grade, but after first grade these activities should expand to three-, four-, and five-digit numbers.

Zero

Consider the use of zero as a special case. As mentioned earlier, zero should not be introduced as a placeholder until children have a fairly firm conceptual knowledge of place value. Also, remember to use the term *placeholder* with caution. The term tends to be used as if children know what it means without much explanation. The use of number cards on a place-value chart is particularly useful when introducing zero (see Figure 4–14). Zero tells us that there are no objects in that place. Care should be exercised not to interchange the words "zero" and "nothing."

Number Lines

Sometimes it is useful to show counting by fives, tens, hundreds, and so on using a number line. This type of counting might be done in the first, second, or third grades. Make sure that the children are properly prepared to see increments of multiples of numbers, such as multiples of fives, tens, or hundreds. For example, they might not understand what happened to the numbers between 40 and 50. It would be important to show the progression of

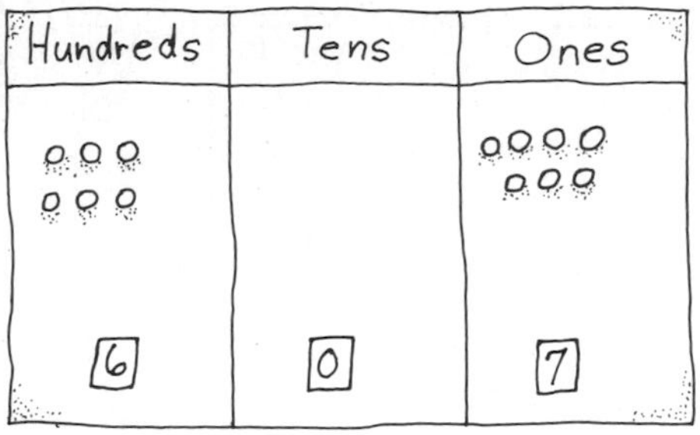

FIGURE 4–14
Using Zero as a Placeholder

number lines with consecutive numbers to number lines whose numbers are increments of two or more, such as those shown in Figure 4–15.

The study of numeration is exciting, because for the first time children can use number names to talk about and explore large quantities or measures. First and second graders are particularly fascinated with queries such as, "How many leaves are there on a tree?" and "How many days have I lived so far?" The study of numeration should include ideas of estimation (see the Problem Solving and Estimation section), since no one really knows exactly how many leaves are on a given tree!

PUTTING IT ALL TOGETHER

By third grade, children will be taught how to read and interpret six-digit numbers, such as 100,000. There is nothing particularly easy about learning the names for larger numbers. Although there are some predictable patterns, there are also some surprises. One surprise, already discussed, is the names for the numbers 11 through 19. Another surprise occurs when naming thousands. Even though it is acceptable for 1,200 to be read as either "one thousand, two hundred" or "twelve hundred," the number 1,200,000 can only be read "one million, two hundred thousand." It is not acceptable to read it "twelve hundred thousand." Most curricula address millions in the fourth grade.

A place-value chart with removable number cards is very useful for acquainting children with names for larger numbers. However, children should not depend too much on the chart. They should be told that they will eventually be expected to think about the new mathematical ideas without the models. On the other hand, children should not be expected to perform without representational models and other aids until they are ready. Teachers need to develop a keen sensitivity to these critical moments of learning.

Through their many experiences with number and numeration, children will come to know that our Hindu-Arabic numeration system has the following characteristics:

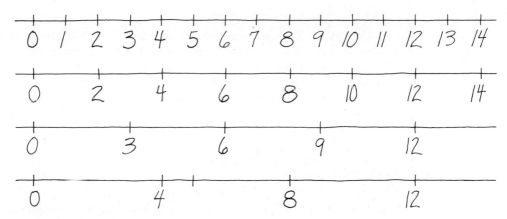

FIGURE 4–15
Consecutive Number Lines

1. The system is determined by base number, and that base number is 10.
2. The system has a symbol for zero.
3. There are ten symbols that can be used to name any number.
4. Intuitively, at least, children will know that our system is multiplicative (that is, 30 means three tens or 3 × 10) and additive (that is, 32 means 30 + 2).

Children's understanding of these characteristics creates the foundation for further learning in mathematics.

USING THE CALCULATOR TO LEARN ABOUT NUMBERS AND NUMERATION

Calculators should be incorporated into number and numeration learning. The type of calculator most appropriate for young children is the most basic kind. All calculators have the digits from 0 through 9 and the four operations +, −, ×, and ÷. If the calculator is not solar powered, there will be an on/off switch. All calculators have a clear button for clearing unwanted entries. Memory, percent, or square root are not necessary, but calculators with these extras can still be used. The teacher should ignore those buttons unless a child asks about them. In that case, the teacher might give a response that is suitable for the age level, such as "Oh, that helps us read numbers smaller than one." Some calculators make a slight beep sound when an entry is made. This is actually delightful to children and reassures them that contact has been made. The following is a list of suggestions and steps to follow when incorporating the calculator in the classroom.

Make the distinction between (a) the calculator as the object of instruction so children will become calculator literate, and (b) the calculator as a tool for learning and problem solving. The former must be addressed in the classroom before the latter. Suggestions listed for preschool are essentially addressing the calculator as an object of instruction; children learn what the calculator is and how it works. The kindergarten children in Figure 4–16 are learning what the calculator is through free play. The suggestions listed for kindergarten and beyond address the calculator as a tool for learning mathematics.

Preschool/Age 4

1. Introduce the calculator as something that helps us with numbers.

2. Teach the children how solar-powered and battery or rechargeable calculators are turned on and off. Emphasize the importance of turning the latter types off when they are finished using them.

3. Use correct terminology. Numbers are "entered," and keys or buttons are "pressed" or "pushed." We do not "punch" or "hit." Refer to the "display" when looking for results of an action on the calculator. And "clear" the display when you want to start over.

4. Provide free play with the calculator and have children verbalize what they can do with it. Coach their language development. In the beginning they will not have the language to describe what they are doing and seeing.

FIGURE 4–16
These kindergarten students are engaged in free play with a calculator.

5. Have children tell you what they see after they press various keys. For example, after entering 2, they will see 2 on the display, whereas after entering the + sign, they will see the previous number that was entered and not the + sign. Ask them what they see right after they turn the calculator on or after it is cleared. Ask them if they see a point (dot) in the display and if they can make it move to different places.

Kindergarten
1. Display 1 through 9; be sure the display between each entry is cleared.
2. Show 1 through 9 by adding 1 to each previous number.
3. Show 9 through 0 by subtracting 1 from each previous number.
4. Enter two-digit numbers.

First Grade
1. Show 1 through 30 or higher; clear the display between entries.
2. Show three-digit numbers on the calculator.
3. Show 1 through 30 or higher by adding 1 to each previous number, then by adding 2, 5, or 10 to each previous number.
4. Show 30 through 0 by subtracting 1 from each previous number, then by subtracting 2, 5, or 10 from each previous number.

Second Grade
1. Show four-digit numbers on the calculator.
2. Show two-, three-, and four-digit numbers as sums of their expanded parts. For example: Show that 1,234 is the same as $1000 + 200 + 30 + 4$.

Third Grade
1. Show five-digit numbers on the calculator.
2. Show five-digit numbers as the sums of their expanded parts.

USING THE COMPUTER TO LEARN ABOUT NUMBERS AND NUMERATION

In recent years, great strides have been made in developing software for young children. Color, sound, and animation techniques have been combined with effective teaching principles to create quality programs. Children as young as age 3 or 4 can become fascinated by the computer and find it fun. There are commercial programs available that deal with counting, number recognition, and numeration. Teachers have a responsibility to select good software that enhances the development of mathematical concepts for children. Teachers should ask for demonstrations and have clear objectives in mind when they select software. Because developing software is so time-consuming, many teachers will want to rely upon commercial programs. Quality programs are sound in their teaching strategies, mathematically correct, and help to build the child's confidence rather than undermine it.

PROBLEM SOLVING AND ESTIMATION

One excellent resource for incorporating problem solving into the primary grades is Nelson and Worth's *How to Choose and Create Good Problems for Primary Children* (NCTM, 1983). Nelson and Worth point out that the purpose of mathematics instruction is to show order and meaning in everyday situations, and the purpose of problem solving is to recognize relationships between an event or situation and its mathematical model.

For the preschool and primary grade levels, Nelson and Worth offer the following suggestions for incorporating problem solving into mathematics instruction:

1. The problem should be of significance mathematically.
2. The situation in which the problem occurs should involve real objects or obvious simulations of real objects.
3. The problem situation should capture the interest of the child.
4. The problem should require the child to move, transform, or modify the materials.
5. The problem should offer opportunities for different levels of solution.
6. The problem situation should have many physical embodiments.
7. Children should be convinced that they can solve the problem, and they should know when they have a solution for it. (p. 3)

Nelson and Worth offer the following as a sample problem:

The ferry must be used to get these cars across the river. If the ferry can carry only three cars at a time, how many trips must the ferry make to get all the cars across?

Three- and four-year-olds will not have a strategy, other than trial and error, for solving this problem, whereas older children, with some assistance, will eventually see that cars can share a ferry with other cars (see Figure 4–17).

Since most of our real world problem solving is done through estimation, it makes sense to start early in teaching children estimation as a major problem-solving strategy. For example, as early as age 3, teachers can have children guess how many blocks will fit into a container. In this case, "how many" shouldn't be described in terms of numbers, but by referring to a pile of blocks. By age 4 and up, children should routinely be prompted to guess a number of objects present before counting them. The previous problem can also be approached from a "guess then test" perspective.

Along with the early use of calculators, children should be developing a responsibility to consider the "reasonableness of results" of a calculator action.

FIGURE 4–17

For example, if a child attempts to enter 12 + 1 on the calculator and gets 23 as the result, he or she should have a sense that there is something wrong with the solution. In this case, the child accidentally entered 12 + 11. Children should be directed to always view the display after their entries to see if what they expect and what they get match.

In closing, number and numeration concepts are the foundation of mathematics for young children. Our place-value system is a very powerful system. Although children may not be able to appreciate its simplicity and beauty, they should learn how and why it functions. Helping a child build a clear conceptual understanding of the place-value system will ensure greater facility with operations on numbers for that child.

SUMMARY

In this chapter, number concepts and how they are acquired were discussed. We developed the concept of number starting with conservation of number, then the concept of zero, and then to sight groups and ordinality. Counting and numeral writing processes were also developed from the perspective of the young learner. The hazards of number lines were explained. The discussion of numeration centered on grouping and place-value concepts, naming and writing numerals, and counting and ordering numbers. Also included was the important role zero plays in numeration. Guidelines for organizing instruction were given along with hints on how to incorporate the use of calculators, computers, problem solving, and estimation in teaching numbers and numeration.

PLANNING FOR INSTRUCTION

As teachers construct their lessons on numbers having more than one and two digits, heavy emphasis on concrete representations should be consistently made. These concrete references should be easily interchangeable with the oral and written representations.

The following Instructional Planner shows the sequence of objectives according to grade and age and according to type of learning. The numbers correspond to the activities that follow in the Activities Section. Recall from chapter 3 that these objectives are not presented in the traditional behavioral form which is often seen and labeled "behavioral objectives." The behaviors for each topic are specified across the upper right of the planner and labeled Type 1, Type 2, or Type 3 according to how concrete or abstract the lesson might be for each objective. These types of behaviors are in hierarchical form just as the structure of mathematics is.

INSTRUCTIONAL PLANNER
Number and Numeration

			Types of Behavior and Experiences			
Age	*Types of Learning*	*Mathematical Objectives*	*Type 1 Concrete*	*Type 1 Pictorial*	*Type 2 Transitional*	*Type 3 Abstract*
2	Skill	Rote count to 2				1
	Concept	All		2		
	Concept	All gone		2		
3	Skill	Rote count to 5				1
	Concept/Skill	Count to 3 with understanding	3	3		
	Concept	Concept of zero	4			
	Concept	More or less	5	5		
4	Skill	Rote count to 10				1

INSTRUCTIONAL PLANNER (continued)
Number and Numeration

Age	Types of Learning	Mathematical Objectives	Type 1 Concrete	Type 1 Pictorial	Type 2 Transitional	Type 3 Abstract
			Types of Behavior and Experiences			
	Concept/Skill	Count to 10 with understanding	3	3		
	Skill	Numerals 1–10				6
	Concept	First, last, middle	7	7		
5	Concept/Skill	Sort and classify according to nonnumerical and numerical properties	8			
	Concept	One-to-one correspondence	9		9	
	Concept	Equivalent sets	10	10	10	
	Concept	More than and less than	11			
	Skill	Numerals 0–10 in order				12
	Concept/Skill	First, second, middle, last	13			
6	Concept	Set and subset	14	14		
	Concept	Count from 1–20 with understanding	3	3		
	Concept	Ordering of numbers 1–100				15
	Concept/Skill	Multiples of 10 less than 100			16	
	Concept	Place value up to 3 digits	17		17	
	Concept	Ordinal numbers 1st through 5th	18		18	
7	Concept/Skill	Ordering of numbers 1–1000				15
	Concept	Place value up to 4 digits	17		17	
	Concept	Odd and even numbers	19			
	Concept	Ordinal numbers 1st through 10th	18		18	
	Concept/Skill	Round off to nearest 10s and 100s	20			
8	Concept	Place value up to 5 digits	17		17	
	Concept	Round off to nearest 10s, 100s, 1000s	20			
	Concept/Skill	Estimation		21		
	Skill	Ordinal numbers 1st through 12th	18		18	

ACTIVITY 1

Type 3: Abstract

Age:	2—4
Objective:	Counting by rote
Materials:	(none needed)

Instructions: For children age 2, repeat the words "one, two" while clapping your hands twice or while holding up one finger then two fingers. For children age 3, do the same sort of patterning for counting up to 5; the children should repeat the pattern with you. Four-year-olds should repeat the numbers from 1 to 10 while they clap their hands or sing-song the words with rhythm. The idea is to get the auditory pattern well established so that it can be applied with understanding at a later time. The children must have the words readily available in order to apply them in the counting-with-meaning situation.

ACTIVITY 2

Type 1: Concrete

Age:	2—3
Objective:	Concepts of all and all gone
Materials:	Small objects such as milk cartons, raisins, crackers, etc.

Instructions: Use opportunities that occur during a routine day to introduce these concepts. For example, form small groups of three to five children for snack time and give each group a number of cartons of milk or juice, not necessarily corresponding to the number of children in the group. Distribute the milk for a group and ask the children if *all* of the children have milk now. Ask them how they know and let them respond. You can also ask what could be changed so that *all* of the children have milk, or alternately, what could be changed so that *all* of the milk is given out. Accept creative answers to these questions, as well as practical ones, to stimulate the discussion. When crackers or raisins are distributed on plates or napkins to the children and they have eaten some of them, ask the children whose crackers are *all gone.* If no one has eaten all of his or her crackers, ask the group how they could make the snacks *all gone.* At clean-up time, you can ask that the children make sure the toys are *all gone* from the table or floor, or that *all* the toys have been put away. There are many such opportunities to talk about *all* and *all gone.* Look for these opportunities and ask questions that give children options for responding in a variety of ways.

ACTIVITY 3

Type 1: Concrete

Age: 3—6

Objective: Counting with understanding

Materials: Small ordinary objects such as buttons, crayons, shells, cups, etc.

Instructions: Put a set of objects and a small container on the table in front of each child. Make sure they all have the same number of objects. Three-year-olds can have as many as 3 objects; four-year-olds can have as many as 10 objects; and six-year-olds can have as many as 20 objects. Show the children how to put an object in the container as the group counts "one," "two," "three," and so forth—as appropriate for the ages of the children. Children can also take objects out one at a time while the group counts. Smaller children may need to use gross muscle movements to accentuate the touching of the objects as the words are said. After several experiences with counting in which you do the leading, ask the children to count out loud while you watch. Have them hand you the objects as they are counting; then count out loud as you hand the objects back to them. Giving children many and varied experiences with counting is important. Take opportunities when going to lunch or out to the playground to count objects such as toys, pictures on the walls, etc.

Type 1: Pictorial After the children have had experiences counting objects that can be moved and handled, encourage them to begin to count pictures of objects. Most mathematics books have many pictures of objects that children can use to practice counting.

ACTIVITY 4

Type 1: Concrete

Age: 3—6

Objective: Concept of zero

Materials: Small snacks such as crackers or raisins and paper plates or napkins

Instructions: Put the children in small groups for snack time. Give each child a paper plate or napkin and a small number of snacks. Ask them to put their crackers on their plates and tell you how many there are on the plate. Let them eat some of the snacks and ask again how many are on the plate. Their answers will vary. When a child has an empty plate, point to it and ask the group to tell you about the crackers. Ask, "Are there any crackers on the plate?" or "How many crackers are on the plate now?" Young children will probably not use the term *zero*. Accept answers that are related to the concept of zero. However, it is important to keep in mind that the answer to the question of "how many" is a real number. Zero is the name of a number, whereas "nothing" is not the name of a number.

ACTIVITY 5

Type 1: Concrete

Age: 2—5

Objective: More or less

Materials: Small objects such as crackers, straws, crayons, beans, etc.

Instructions: Put two piles of beans on a table, one pile with many more beans than the other. Ask the children to point to the pile with more beans. Ask them to point to the pile with "less" beans. Ask them how they can tell which pile has more. You may not get well-thought-out answers, but your purpose is to get the children to begin to think about these concepts and for you to understand their thinking. Do this same sort of activity in many different settings. Use it as a developmental activity for the concepts of length, mass, volume, etc., by taking opportunities during the day to ask who has more crayons, which cup has less milk, and similar questions.

Type 1: Pictorial Use pictures of objects instead of real objects to help the children focus on more and less. Magazines and mathematics books are useful sources of pictures that may be simple enough, yet interesting to the children.

Note: The concepts just addressed are leading toward an understanding of greater than and less than, the terms applied to number. However, if children learn these concepts from concrete objects, they will use "more" and "less" first, instead of "more" and "fewer"—the more grammatically correct terms. Eventually, "greater" and "less" will be used when referring to numbers.

ACTIVITY 6

Type 3: Abstract

Age: 4—6

Objective: Numerals 1—10

Materials: Modeling clay, sand tray, chalkboard

Instructions: Show the children how to write numbers in the air. Get their larger muscles involved by "air" writing very large numbers that have been written on the chalkboard. Gradually ask the children to "air" write smaller numbers. Let the children have a card with a number on it and ask them to make another one like it out of modeling clay or draw one like it in a sand tray or on the board.

ACTIVITY 7

Type 1: Concrete

Age: 4—5

Objective: First, last, middle

Materials: (none needed)

Instructions: Let a group of three children line up at the door of the room. Point to each of the children and tell the class who is first, who is in the middle, and who is last. Have the children change their positions and let the others tell who is first, in the middle, and last. Do the position change again and again; ask who has which position. Let other groups of children participate as those who line up at the door.

Type 1: Pictorial Use pictures of people in lines or lines of objects to ask the children which one is first, last, and which ones are in the middle. This activity can be extended to groups of more than three because every person or object that is not first or last will, of necessity, be in the middle.

ACTIVITY 8

Type 1: Concrete

Age: 5—7

Objective: Sort and classify according to nonnumerical and numerical properties

Materials: Small objects (such as buttons) that have different characteristics (size, shape, color, number of holes, number of bumps, etc.)

Instructions: Give the children collections of objects and ask them to put the objects into two different groups. Ask the children why they put their objects into those groups. Listen carefully to what they say, since they may be using a classification scheme you have not thought of. At the younger ages, do not "correct" a child's sorting of objects, rather let the child discover from listening to classmates how to make clearer distinctions. After the children have had several opportunities to make their own classifications of groups, give them specific instructions, such as putting the objects in groups according to color. Next, let them sort according to shape or size. Finally, ask them to sort their objects according to the number of holes or number of bumps or some other numerical feature.

ACTIVITY 9

Type 1: Concrete

Age: 4—6

Objective: One-to-one correspondence

Materials: Small objects such as Styrofoam packing "peanuts," chips, cubes, cups, straws, etc.

Instructions: Introduce the concept of one-to-one correspondence in a natural way by asking the children to get "just enough" straws for their group (Kamii & DeVries, 1976). The children will find out whether they succeed without being told they got it right or didn't. Young children will probably take a trial-and-error approach to these types of tasks.

Show the children a set of small objects and ask them to make a set of objects that "match" your set. They can check their own sets by matching their objects with yours. Show the children how to line up the objects of your set and the objects of their sets, or pair them up. Very young children may have some difficulty for awhile because they will not understand the importance of lining them up to match exactly.

Offer many experiences with this concept and let children discover the importance of careful matching. Older children can be coached to count the objects for each set, if they are having trouble. Don't expect this activity to make sense to everyone until there have been many varied experiences. Putting straws in drinking cups, planting one seed in each pot, giving one crayon to each child, and providing just enough paper plates for the children at their table are some of the wide variety of experiences from which children can form the concept of one-to-one correspondence.

Type 2: Transitional   After many experiences with matching sets of objects, children can be asked to begin matching pictures of objects with sets of real objects. Ask the children to put a chip on each flower in the picture or put a pencil on each crayon in the picture. Eventually, it will be possible for the children to match pictures with other pictures.

ACTIVITY 10

Type 1: Concrete

Age: 4—6

Objective: Equivalent sets

Materials: Sets of small objects such as pencils, crayons, chips, beans, and paper plates or other small containers

Instructions: Give each of the children a set of objects on a paper plate and place a collection of objects on the tables. Ask the children to make another set with just as many objects in it as they have on their plates. Ask them how they can find out if the two sets have the same number of objects. Encourage them to match the sets and make corrections as needed. Snack time lends itself to this type of activity. The children can be asked to pass out the raisins or crackers at their table so that everyone has the same amount on his napkin. There will be lots of supervisors for this task who will make sure the number of snacks will be the same!

Type 1: Pictorial   After many experiences with making equivalent sets with real objects, the children can be asked to create sets of objects that are equivalent to ("have the same number as the") sets of objects that are pictured.

Type 2: Transitional   To create a Type 2 experience with equivalent sets give children numbers on cards and ask them to create or find sets that have the same number of objects as the number on the card. Pairing the number with sets that have the same number of objects can lead to creative set combinations.

ACTIVITY 11

Type 1: Concrete

Age:	5– 7
Objective:	More than and less than
Materials:	Groups of snacks such as popped popcorn, raisins, crackers, and paper plates or napkins

Instructions: Let the children pass out a napkin to each child in their small groups. Give each child a few pieces of the snack food, but not the same amount to everyone. Give a napkin to yourself and place some of the snack food on it. Ask each child to tell you how many snacks he or she has in comparison with yours. Ask the child how he or she could find out which of you has the most. Guide the children to match the sets if they don't make this suggestion. Then ask the children to find someone in the group who has more snacks than they do. Have them find someone who has less snacks than they do. Ask them how they could tell who had more and who had less. Then ask the children what would be needed for all the children to have the same number of snacks to eat. Let them equalize the sets before they eat them, so they all have the same number. Help them with this last part of the activity if they need it. Some children will be able to count to find if more snacks are needed for a child, while others may not be able to count.

ACTIVITY 12

Type 3: Abstract

Age: 5—6

Objective: Numerals 0—10 in order

Materials: Cards with the numbers 0 through 10 printed on them, crayons and newsprint, and a chalkboard with chalk

Instructions: Give a set of number cards to a small group of children and ask them to put the cards in order from the smallest number to the largest. After they have the cards arranged, let the children copy the numbers in a sand tray or in modeling clay. Gradually, let the children practice writing the numbers with crayons on newsprint or at the chalkboard. At first, use the medium that is least permanent, so mistakes are not as noticeable. You can have the whole class practice "air writing" the numbers as they name them in order from 0 to 10.

ACTIVITY 13

Type 1: Concrete

Age: 5—6

Objective: First, second, middle, last

Materials: Games that the children play in groups of three or more

Instructions: The concepts of first, second, and last can be taught in a natural way when children are playing board games. When a group of children are playing such a game, ask who finished first, then ask who finished second, and who finished last. You can ask the person who finished first (who may or may not have "won" by being the first to finish) to come and stand by you, with the second person next to the first person and the others next to them followed by the person who finished last. One part of the objective of this activity is to help the children recognize that the conventional method of ordering objects is to start from the left and proceed to the right.

The next stage of this activity is to use opportunities that occur naturally, such as putting away toys or eating snacks. Ask the children to place the toy that will be put away first at a particular spot on the table. To the left of it, have them place the toy that will be put away second. The toy that will be put away last should be placed to the left of all the other toys. The concept of middle will, for children of these ages, be comprised of all objects or events anywhere between first and last. Lining up snacks on a napkin and eating them in a specific order can be another experience in ordinal numbers.

ACTIVITY 14

Type 1: Concrete

Age: 6—8

Objective: Set and subsets

Materials: Collections of objects such as pattern blocks, attribute pieces, or shells that have different attributes, and a large index card or paper plate

Instructions: Give the children a set of objects and ask them to describe their collections. Try to help them focus on an inclusive term such as triangles, seashells, fasteners, or toys. Offer the children other objects. Ask them whether these new objects belong with their set and why or why not. At this age, it is wise to accept whatever reason the child gives for inclusion in or exclusion from the set. However, it is appropriate to help the children think through their choices by asking them questions for clarification. After they have had several experiences with sets as whole collections, it would be appropriate to focus on the concept of subset in an informal way. Give each of the children a set of objects and an index card. Ask them to put all of the blue objects on the card. Then, have them put the original set back together, and ask them to put the red ones on the card. Let them explore by making subsets of their own. Listen to their explanations about how they chose the ones they placed on the card. After children have had some experience with the concept of subset, you can use this as a readiness activity for addition and subtraction. Ask the children to count how many objects are in the "big" set before they put any objects on the card. Later, ask them to count the objects on the card (and not on the card) after the "little" set has been taken out of the whole collection. At this time, you do not need to ask the children to do more than count the two subsets and the original set. Many of them will be able to form their own conclusions about the relationships.

Type 1: Pictorial This type of activity can be naturally extended to pictures. Sometimes textbooks will have pictures of things that belong together—pictorial representations of sets. There are many other opportunities to work with pictures of sets and subsets. Be alert to them and use them.

ACTIVITY 15

Type 3: Abstract

Age: 6—7

Objective: Ordering numbers

Materials: Hundred charts, index cards, adding machine tape, crayons, and small game markers

Instructions: Ordering numbers includes putting numbers in sequence, finding missing numbers in a sequence, and finding numbers that occur next in a sequence. Let the children write numbers on the index cards and paste them in order from 1 to 100 (older children can write the numbers to 1,000) on the adding machine tape. Put it up on a wall or bulletin board so they can see it. Give six or seven children index cards with numbers written on them. Ask these children to stand in the front of the room. Then, ask them to go to the number tape and stand in front of their number and hold their cards up. Ask the other children in the class to write down the numbers in order from smallest to largest on their papers. Finding missing numbers in a sequence can be done in the same way; leave out a number in the sequence and ask the children where it should go. The pattern for finding numbers that occur next in a sequence can be done in a similar fashion by encouraging the whole class to work together. For individual work, a hundred chart will serve. Older children may want to have ten of the hundred charts so they can "see" the numbers from 1 to 1,000 laid out before them. Small game markers are used to mark the number patterns when exploring sequences or ordering numbers.

ACTIVITY 16

Type 2: Transitional

Age: 6—7

Objective: Multiples of 10 less than 100

Materials: Small objects for counting such as chips or blocks, index cards, and markers

Instructions: Let the children help make a 10-by-10 array of chips or blocks on a table or the floor. Gather the children, in small groups, around the table. Ask them how they could count all of the chips. Let them respond. If no one in the group can count that high, you can count them out, pointing as you go. Then, tell the children that there might be an easier way. Encourage the children to take turns counting the rows. As a child gets to the end of a row, mark a card with the symbol for 10, 20, 30, etc., and place it at the end of that row. Ask the children what they think these symbols mean. Ask them how many chips were in each row, and remind them of the pattern for counting they heard. If needed, count the chips again for them and continue to ask what they think these symbols mean. After doing this activity, the children could put the chips and the cards on a number strip.

ACTIVITY 17

Type 1: Concrete

Age: 6—8

Objective: Place value for three-, four-, or five-digit numbers

Materials: A place value chart, popsicle sticks, twist ties, number cards, dice, marked appropriately, or an appropriately marked spinner

Instructions: Give each of the children a place-value chart, a group of sticks, and twist ties. With younger children, start by playing a special number game. Tell them that the special number is 3 or 4. (Use dice or spinners marked with number dots or numbers that are at least one less than the special number.) Show them how to roll a die or spin the spinner to get a number. Take that number of sticks and put them in the right column of the place-value chart. Roll or spin again and put that number of sticks with the others in the right column. Count how many you have now. Continue until you have more than the special number of sticks. When you are counting your sticks and you reach the special number, make sure the children notice. Remind them about the special number, if necessary. Take those sticks and put a twist tie around them and move them into the next column. You may have to demonstrate this activity more than once for the children to understand clearly how to play the game.

As the children play, watch their progress. When a child has the special number in the second column, bring this to the attention of the group. Show the children that someone has the special number in the next column. Show them how to make a big bundle from the little bundles and put it in the next column. Let the children play this game with small special numbers at first (waiting to get 7 or 10 per column makes young children frustrated with the game). After children play the game with small special numbers, they can graduate to the all-important 10, which is used as a special number. Multibase blocks can be used as a variation on this activity. Only after the children have a well-developed concept of moving bundles of popsicle sticks should bottle caps or chips replace the sticks. In the case of chips, when the special number is reached, that number of chips is "traded" for one chip that goes into the next column. Be sure to emphasize that this chip represents a group of ten because it is in the tens place.

Another game that can be played is a pay-back game where children roll the dice or spin in order to find out how much they should pay back to the "bank." Let them start with two or three bundles or chips in each column.

Type 2: Transitional   When the children have had considerable experience with the sticks and/or chips in the special number game, they can use number cards on the place-value chart with the sticks to keep track of their materials. This pairing of the number symbols and the bundles in the columns of the place-value chart is an important step. At some point, give the children two or more number cards and ask them to show with the chips or sticks the largest number they can make with those cards. Next, ask them to show the smallest number they can make with those same cards. The physical bundles will reinforce that in the number 236 the digit 2 means something different than it does in the number 632. Older children can be expected to work with numbers greater than 1,000 and even 10,000. Of course, when working with these numbers, they will need to use chips or bottle caps because too many popsicle sticks would be required.

ACTIVITY 18

Type 1: Concrete

Age: 6—8

Objective: Ordinal numbers

Materials: Objects in the classroom such as books, cups, toys, or games

Instructions: As discussed in Activity 13, ordinary situations such as choosing sides in playground games, playing board games, and going out to play offer opportunities to talk about who finished first, which team made the third pick, what is the number of the seventh bus or the color of the tenth car in the parking lot. Books and toys can be arranged in lines, and their relative positions can be discussed. When talking about an arrangement of books, get the children to discuss how the relocation in the arrangement affects the position of the book. For instance, ask them where *Little Women* would have to be placed for it to be changed from sixth place to fourth place. Then ask what happens to the order of the rest of the books in the arrangement. There are a multitude of situations for discussing ordinal numbers. Look for these situations and use them as they develop.

Type 2: Transitional Pictures of objects that have some linear or vertical arrangement can also be sources for discussions about ordering. The children can be asked to color only the third and fifth balloon, to draw a hat on the sixth person shown, and so forth.

ACTIVITY 19

Type 1: Concrete

Age: 7—8

Objective: Odd and even numbers

Materials: Small snacks, such as raisins, and napkins

Instructions: Give each child two napkins and a small number of raisins. Ask the children to "deal out" the raisins onto the napkins, one at a time, first one napkin, then the other. Then ask them if the number of raisins on the napkins is the same. Ask them how many raisins they have altogether. During another snack time, when the children have raisins, ask them to find out how many they have. Then have them line the raisins up two-by-two. Ask them if they have any that are "left over." Encourage the children to explore the two-by-two lineup with different numbers of raisins.

ACTIVITY 20

Type 1: Concrete

Age: 7—8

Objective: Round off to the nearest ten, hundred, and thousand

Materials: Place-value charts, chips or popsicle sticks, number cards

Instructions: Give each of the children a place-value chart and chips as well as cards with two-digit numbers on them. Ask the children to show their number using the chips on the chart. Ask the children to add chips to the ones column until they have enough to trade for a ten. Ask them to group the chips that were added in a stack. Then, have them show their original number on the chart, and ask them to take away chips from the ones column until it is empty. Have them put these chips in another stack. Ask them which needed more chips, adding on or taking away. Ask them which tens number was closer to their original number. You can explain that usually a five is rounded up to the next highest number. A similar activity can be done with three- and four-digit numbers and a place-value chart.

ACTIVITY 21

Type 1: Concrete

Age: 7—8

Objective: Estimation

Materials: Collections of small objects such as chips, blocks, or straws

Instructions: When a rather large collection of objects is available in the classroom, perhaps before the distribution of snacks or chips for an activity, ask the children to estimate how many objects are in the collection. Let them count the objects or use another technique for getting either an exact number or verifying the estimate more closely. For example, the number of raisins in a box could be estimated with some accuracy if the children find out how many raisins fill a bottle cap and then find out how many bottle capfuls of raisins are in the box. Have children estimate how many cars are in the parking lot at the school or how many seats are in the auditorium. There are many quantities that children can estimate if you will point these situations out and help children to devise schemes for checking on the accuracy of their estimates.

STUDY QUESTIONS AND ACTIVITIES

1. Describe a Type 1, Type 2, and Type 3 activity where the objective is to construct a bar graph for the numbers and kinds of pets children have at

home. Explain how the following can relate to this activity.
  a. classification
  b. one-to-one matching
  c. ordering
  d. conservation
  e. zero

2. Reflect on what you think children in preschool or first grade might think when they hear the following.
  a. Seven is a bigger number than two.
  b. How many groups in ten ones? (Assume children are working in base 10.)
  c. Show me the numeral for the number three.
  d. Eighteen is one ten and eight ones.

3. Observe and interact with a preschool child who is engaged in counting activities of different kinds. Observe and make note of the child's status with respect to the five principles which are the foundation for counting with understanding. Videotape, if possible, for group review. The principles are listed below.
  a. stable order principle
  b. one-to-one matching principle
  c. total number principle
  d. different objects principle
  e. different order principle

4. What questions could you ask to help you determine a child's understanding of each of the following:
  a. what 0 means in a number like 203 (second grade)
  b. the difference between 23 and 32 (first and second grade)
  c. why 10 pennies stacked up are the same amount of money as 10 pennies spread out (kindergarten)

5. Count 25 chips (or other counters) using 3, 5, and then 10 as the base (we've also called this the "magic" or "special" grouping number). Show your results on a place-value chart and record your numbers.

6. Write at least five tasks that challenge the children's reversibility of thought. One example for place value is: "Give me a number that has 8 in the 10s place. Give me another. Another. How many are there?"

REFERENCES AND RESOURCES

Baratta-Lorton, M. (1976). *Mathematics their way*. Menlo Park, CA: Addison-Wesley.

Beattie, I. D. (1986). The number namer: An aid to understanding place value. *Arithmetic Teacher, 33*(5), 24–29.

Bright, G., & Behr, M. (1984 April). *Identifying fractions on number lines*. Paper presented at the annual meeting of the American Educational Research Association, New Orleans.

Carpenter, T. P., Hiebert, J., & Moser, J. M. (1984). *The effect of problem structure and first graders' initial solution processes for simple addition and subtraction problems* (Technical Report No. 516). Madison, WI: Research and Development Center for Individualized Schooling.

Carpenter, T. P., & Moser, J. M. (1979). The acquisition of addition and subtraction concepts in grades one through three. *Journal for Research in Mathematics Education, 15,* 179–202.

Copeland, R. W. (1984). *How children learn mathematics* (4th ed.). New York: Macmillan.

Flavell, J. H. (1963). *The developmental psychology of Jean Piaget*. New York: Van Nostrand Reinhold.

Fuson, K. C. (1986). Teaching children to subtract by counting up. *Journal for Research in Mathematics Education, 17,* 172–189.

Fuson, K. C., Richards, J., & Briars, D. J. (1982). The acquisition and elaboration of the number word sequence. In C. J. Brainerd (Ed.), *Children's logical and mathematical cognition: Progress in cognitive development research* (pp. 33–92) New York: Springer-Verlag.

Ginsburg, H. P. (1983). *The development of mathematical thinking*. New York: Academic.

Harrison, M., & Harrison, B. (1986). Developing numeration concepts and skills. *Arithmetic Teacher, 33*(6), 18–21, 60.

Immerzeel, G., & Thomas, M. (1982). *Ideas from the ARITHMETIC TEACHER: Grades 1–4, primary*. Reston, VA: NCTM.

Kamii, C., & DeVries, R. (1976). *Piaget, children, and number*. Washington, DC: NAEYC.

Kulm, G. (1985). *Counting and early arithmetic learning*. Washington, DC: National Institute of Education.

Mueller, D. W. (1985). Building a scope and sequence for early childhood mathematics. *Arithmetic Teacher, 33*(2) 8–11.

Nelson, D., & Worth, J. (1983). *How to choose and create good problems for primary children*. Reston, VA: NCTM.

Price, S. S., & Price, M. E. (1978). *The primary math lab*. Santa Monica, CA: Goodyear.

Schoenfeld, A. (1987). Cognitive science and mathematics education: An overview. In A. H. Schoenfeld (Ed.), *Cognitive science and mathematics education* (pp. 1–31). Hillsdale, NJ: Lawrence Erlbaum Associates.

Steffe, L. P., von Glasersfeld, E., Richards, J., & Cobb, P. (1984). *Children's counting types: Philosophy, theory, and application*. New York: Praeger.

Thornton, C. A., Tucker, B. F., Dossey, J. A., & Bazik, E. F. (1983). *Teaching mathematics to children with special needs*. Menlo Park, CA: Addison-Wesley.

Troutman, A. P., & Lichtenberg, B. K. (1987). *Mathematics: A good beginning* (3rd ed.). Monterey, CA: Brooks/Cole.

5

Addition and Subtraction of Whole Numbers

VOCABULARY FOR TEACHERS

Children learn many new ideas and procedures when they begin the study of addition and subtraction. Many of the new terms associated with these ideas and procedures are for teacher use only. Some of the most demanding terminology relates to properties of numbers under specific operations. This section discusses the most important and relevant terminology for teachers to know before teaching addition and subtraction of whole numbers.

Sum and **addend** are terms that have replaced **minuend** and **subtrahend.** In the example $7 - 2 = 5$, the minuend is 7 and the subtrahend is 2. The number 5 is called the **difference.** Now, these terms are called **sum** for 7 and **addend** for 2 as well as for 5.

$$\text{sum} \quad - \quad \text{addend} \quad = \quad \text{addend}$$
$$\text{(minuend)} \quad \text{(subtrahend)} \quad \text{(difference)}$$

Algorithm refers to the step-by-step procedure for performing an operation such as addition or subtraction. The algorithm isn't taught until after initial work on the concept of the operation has been completed in the first grade and after children have been introduced to the basic facts.

Addition, subtraction, multiplication, and division are examples of **binary operations.** Binary operations can only be performed on two numbers at a time. For example, no matter how many numbers are to be added, they can only be added two at a time.

The **commutative property** for addition of whole numbers refers to the fact that whole number addends may be interchanged without changing their sum. The expressions $2 + 3 = 5$ and $3 + 2 = 5$ or $3 + 2 = 2 + 3$ are examples of the commutativity of whole number addition. On the other hand, subtraction of whole numbers is not commutative. For example, the expression $6 - 4$ does not equal $4 - 6$. Although the teacher has a formal understanding of the commutative property, children only have an intuitive understanding of the property by kindergarten or first grade.

The **associative property** for addition of whole numbers refers to changing the grouping (but not order) of three addends without affecting the sum. For example, the expressions $(2 + 1) + 4$ and $2 + (1 + 4)$ both yield 7 as the sum. The parentheses indicate that addition is to be done first, since addition is a binary operation. At first, this property is used in situations that require regrouping in addition—such as in the following example.

$$\begin{array}{cc} & 1 \\ 27 & 27 \\ \underline{+44} & \underline{+45} \\ & 72 \end{array}$$

When the "1" group of ten is written above the "2," the tens-place addition becomes a three-addend situation. The student must add 1, 2, and 4.

As with commutativity, the teacher should have a formal understanding of the associative property. The student should understand the property informally as early as the first grade.

The example $(6 - 2) - 1$ shows that the subtraction of whole numbers is not associative.

$$(6 - 2) - 1 = 6 - (2 - 1)$$
$$4 - 1 = 6 - 1$$
$$3 = 5$$

The **identity element** for addition is zero. In simple terms, zero added to any number will result in that number. A number doesn't "lose its identity" when zero is added to it.

Inverse operation is a term that refers to the relationship between addition and subtraction (and in chapter 6 to the relationship between multiplication and division). The property of inverse operations is illustrated by the examples $5 + 3 = 8$ and $8 - 3 = 5$ or $8 - 5 = 3$. Children learn about this relationship between the operations informally.

The **closure property** for addition of whole numbers acknowledges that the sum of two whole number addends is also a whole number. This property is not taught during the early childhood level. Teachers should observe that subtraction of whole numbers is not closed. For example, the expression $7 - 10$ does not yield a whole number solution. Middle school teachers should recognize that this property can be used to motivate students to go beyond whole numbers so that problems like $7 - 10 = $ _____ can have a solution. The system of integers—positive and negative whole numbers—is usually introduced this way.

Although the terms presented in this section are labeled *vocabulary for teachers,* the concepts the terms represent are to be learned by the children. Emphasizing concepts instead of terminology is challenging. Remember that words without meaning are useless to children.

VOCABULARY FOR CHILDREN

Generally, the new terms children will learn can be classified into two types. The first type includes terms that have probably not been used in any other context before. Some terms of this type are *addition, sum, subtraction, addend, minus, number line,* and *regrouping.* All of these terms have special mathematical meanings as presented in this chapter.

Terms of the second type have probably been encountered before but in contexts that were not necessarily mathematical. Some examples of this type of term are addition and subtraction *facts* or *basic facts,* addition *table, operation, difference,* and *sign* of an operation. Children might be familiar with the expressions "facts of life," "baseball facts," or "That's a fact," so they might have a generalized notion of the word *fact.* However, when the term *addition facts* is first used, the teacher needs to take time to discuss this use of the word *facts.* An addition fact refers to two whole numbers between 0 and 9 and their sum, such as $5 + 9 = 14$. Likewise, a subtraction fact would be a related inverse expression, such as $14 - 5 = 9$. The term addition *table* (and later multiplication table) needs some explanation. Up to this point, children associate the word *table* with the kitchen table, the dining room table, the end table, etc. In the new context, a table is an organized list of addition facts. Children believe the term *operation* means "a surgical procedure." In mathematics, *operation* is a general term applied to addition, subtraction, multiplication, and division. The term *difference* might also be a source of confusion to children since most likely it has been used and understood on a social or personal level. Young children are interested in whether or not they are different or like their friends in the clothes they wear, the things they do, or the toys they have. In a mathematical context, *difference* refers to a sum minus an addend. For example, the difference between 10 and 8 is 2 (i.e., $10 - 8 = 2$). Finally, when introducing the *signs* of addition (+) or subtraction (−) in first and second grade, an explanation might help to keep the children's minds from imagining a street sign or from thinking of the expression "to sign your name." The signs + and − are symbols that indicate addition and subtraction, respectively. The terms *plus sign* and *minus sign* are also used. Until children are able to use these terms successfully, the terms *add* and *take away* are used.

The vocabulary for students defines the core of what children will learn about addition and subtraction in the first and second grades. The words *add, subtract, addend, minus, take away,* and so on constitute the children's working vocabulary. These words need to become meaningful for children.

READINESS AND CONCEPT FORMATION

Children's readiness for learning addition and subtraction is very important. Even more important are the teacher's efforts to find out how and in what ways his or her students are ready to move into operating with whole numbers. All children begin formal learning of the operations with previously developed frames of reference. The challenge of teaching is to help children identify what they already know. Then, the teacher can facilitate the construction and reconstruction of higher levels of understanding.

The earliest kind of activity associated with learning to add and subtract includes joining and separating sets of discrete and continuous materials. Discrete materials include such things as sticks, bottle caps, or straws. Continuous materials include such things as water, a region, a solid, sand, or a string. Many objects can be both discrete or continuous depending on the way they are used. For example, three bananas can be considered to be three whole objects. On the other hand, when a banana is cut into several pieces, each piece is considered part of one whole (See Figure 5–1). Since the child lives in a world of both discrete and continuous materials, both are natural media to be used by the child in this learning process. During early preschool, it is not necessary for children to be able to count the objects or partitions; what is important is the children's physical manipulations of the materials and their development of the corresponding language and concepts. Figure 5–2 shows a kindergarten student joining and separating bottle caps.

The next step would be to count orally by ones to ten using discrete or continuous materials. This would be followed by counting backwards by ones from ten.

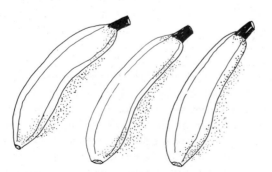
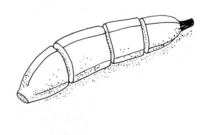

Three discrete bananas   Banana as continuous object

FIGURE 5–1
Discrete and Continuous Materials

FIGURE 5–2
Lisa joins and separates bottle caps.

Figure 5–3 illustrates the thinking models discussed for addition and subtraction. The thinking model used for addition is *joining* or *putting together* either discrete or continuous materials. For subtraction, the *take away* thinking model is separation of either discrete or continuous materials. Another thinking model frequently used to teach the concept of subtraction is *comparison*. Comparing is a process that children have been experiencing in the very early years of their lives. They are concerned with whether they can build blocks taller than the last try or whether they have as much juice as their sibling. Therefore, it is appropriate to encourage children to answer questions such as "How many more blocks does your tower have than mine?" or "How many more steps did Joan take than Jonathan?"

A third thinking model for subtraction is the *missing addend*. It is critical for the teacher to understand this thinking model thoroughly before using it to teach the concept of subtraction. This model is the most difficult of the subtraction thinking models to teach. The teacher must recognize that the process involved is trial and error addition. For example, if there are seven children in all and four are girls, to find out how many are boys a child might think as follows: "Four and *one* are five. No, try again."; "Four and *two* are six. No, that's not quite right."; "Four and *three* are seven. It must be three."

Therefore, a child should not be encouraged, at first, to interpret situations such as $7 = 4 +$ _____ as subtraction ($7 - 4 =$ _____). This subtraction interpretation should be made only *after* the child has had several experiences with the written representations of missing addends (i.e., $7 = 4 +$____). The child should be led to discover that the answer to 7 = 4 + _____ can be found by subtracting 4 from 7. The missing addend thinking model describes common situations met as early as preschool and, therefore, should be included in the process of teaching the concept of subtraction. The teacher is encouraged to provide enough Type 2 activities before moving to Type 3 activities.

For most students, addition and subtraction are abstract mathematical processes by the end of first grade. In the beginning stages of learning these operations, however, the child can relate to addition and subtraction only in so far as the information or situation presented makes sense to him or her. The child learns from *personal experience* in the here and now. For example, if the

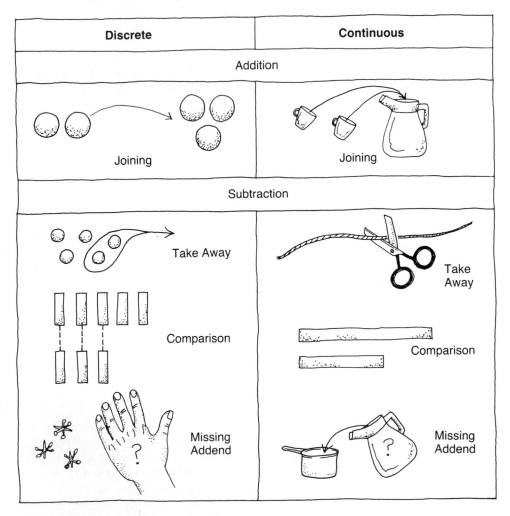

FIGURE 5–3
Concrete Manipulative Experiences

child is prematurely told that "subtraction is the opposite of addition," it will take longer to understand that fact than if the child personally experienced the joining and separating of objects.

Understanding abstract processes requires a certain level of cognitive sophistication. While it is possible to teach operations to children before they understand the underlying concepts, they will not be able to independently apply the operation to various situations. Therefore, it is critical for the teacher to know the child's level of functioning. Then, the teacher can structure the experience so that meaningful learning, rather than rote memorization, occurs.

BASIC ADDITION FACTS

Those children who are able should commit the facts to memory. Teaching should be aimed at facilitating memorization for immediate recall. Research has shown that children go through developmental stages of learning the facts and that they learn to memorize best through systematic exposure to all the facts that exist. Varied practice should precede repeated practice to maximize understanding and recall. This section covers these key points.

Learning the Addition Facts

The teacher must be aware of the developmental steps children take to reach the goal of memorization of addition facts. When children think through an addition problem at the least efficient level, they *count*. At an intermediate level, the children *count on*. At the most efficient level, children *memorize* the answer. For example, three hearts and two hearts can be added in the following ways.

Counting:	"One, two, three, four, five."
Counting on:	"Three, four, five."
Memorization:	"Three and two are five."

The same holds true for problems in the abstract form. For the problem 3 + 2, addition occurs according to the following:

Counting:	"One, two, three, four, five."
Counting on:	"Three, four, five."
Memorization:	"Three plus two are five."

While the previous developmental steps are being taken in the first grade, children should be introduced to the need to memorize facts. Varied practice should precede repeated practice (Brownell, 1973). Be aware that children might be asked to memorize facts before they understand what it means to memorize. It may be necessary for the teacher to model memorization for the child. That is, children need to practice the facts by varied involvement with concrete manipulatives, pictures, and combinations of these representations with their written symbols. *Varied practice* emphasizes understanding of the underlying concepts. *Repeated practice* refers to the drill designed to establish efficiency at the highest level of understanding and performance the learner has attained. If the learner is required to carry out repetitive practice at a level beyond his or her ability to understand, then that learner will lapse into a way of performing that makes sense to him or her, but is usually limiting and inefficient. A classic example is using counting on fingers to find sums during an exercise designed for higher level performance.

When children are given drill and practice (repeated practice) too soon, they will often rely on lower level thinking to obtain the answer. Because this lower level thinking requires counting or counting on, it takes more time for children to process the information. When the problem is presented in abstract form too soon for them, children typically resort to counting with their fingers. Older children (or even adults!) who still need fingers to count might have experienced repeated practice too early in their development of the understanding of addition facts. They were forced into a compromising situation— they had to use the only process available to them to establish some success.

Order of Teaching Basic Addition Facts

Teachers should consider the order in which facts are to be generated. An organized plan is better than a haphazard introduction. It is useful to think of first developing the sums to 10—starting with the sums to 2, then 3 and 4, and so on. Introduce 0 as an addend after introducing several nonzero addends. For example, addition facts that sum to five are shown in the following displays. Although these facts are presented in sentence form, they might not be presented to children in this form. The facts should be presented in concrete and pictorial forms first.

Examples of Addition Facts Without Zero

$1 + 1 = 2$	$2 + 1 = 3$	$3 + 1 = 4$	$4 + 1 = 5$	$5 + 1 = 6$	$6 + 1 = 7$
	$1 + 2 = 3$	$2 + 2 = 4$	$3 + 2 = 5$	$4 + 2 = 6$	$5 + 2 = 7$
		$1 + 3 = 4$	$2 + 3 = 5$	$3 + 3 = 6$	$4 + 3 = 7$
			$1 + 4 = 5$	$2 + 4 = 6$	$3 + 4 = 7$
				$1 + 5 = 6$	$2 + 5 = 7$
					$1 + 6 = 7$

Examples of Addition Facts Including Zero Addends

$0 + 0 = 0$	$0 + 1 = 1$	$0 + 2 = 2$	$0 + 3 = 3$	$0 + 4 = 4$	$0 + 5 = 5$	$0 + 6 = 6$	$0 + 7 = 7$
	$1 + 0 = 1$	$1 + 1 = 2$	$1 + 2 = 3$	$1 + 3 = 4$	$1 + 4 = 5$	$1 + 5 = 6$	$1 + 6 = 7$
		$2 + 0 = 2$	$2 + 1 = 3$	$2 + 2 = 4$	$2 + 3 = 5$	$2 + 4 = 6$	$2 + 5 = 7$
			$3 + 0 = 3$	$3 + 1 = 4$	$3 + 2 = 5$	$3 + 3 = 6$	$3 + 4 = 7$
				$4 + 0 = 4$	$4 + 1 = 5$	$4 + 2 = 6$	$4 + 3 = 7$
					$5 + 0 = 5$	$5 + 1 = 6$	$5 + 2 = 7$
						$6 + 0 = 6$	$6 + 1 = 7$
							$7 + 0 = 7$

An alternative approach is to use 1 as an addend with 1, 2, 3, . . . , 9; then 2 as an addend with 1, 2, 3, . . . , 9; and so forth. Remember, 0 as an addend should be avoided initially.

One as an Addend

$1 + 1 = 2$	$2 + 1 = 3$
$1 + 2 = 3$	$3 + 1 = 4$
$1 + 3 = 4$	$4 + 1 = 5$
$1 + 4 = 5$	$5 + 1 = 6$
$1 + 5 = 6$	$6 + 1 = 7$
$1 + 6 = 7$	$7 + 1 = 8$
$1 + 7 = 8$	$8 + 1 = 9$
$1 + 8 = 9$	$9 + 1 = 10$
$1 + 9 = 10$	

With either approach, consider teaching families of facts. For example, the family of facts for 1, 4, and 5 is as follows:

$$1 + 4 = 5 \qquad 5 - 1 = 4$$
$$4 + 1 = 5 \qquad 5 - 4 = 1$$

Properties

While students are learning the basic facts in first grade, the teacher should guide them to an intuitive understanding of the commutative property of addition by having them observe the results when the order of addends is changed.

Learning the commutative property of addition is helpful to the child who has trouble remembering rote facts. When a student realizes that the order of addends doesn't change the sum of the addends, the number of facts to be memorized decreases.

Using zero as an addend should be introduced after other nonzero addends have been used since zero is harder to understand as an addend. The identity element of addition is zero.

Horizontal and Vertical Forms for Addition Facts

Certain models are very convenient for facilitating the transition to horizontal and vertical forms for recording the facts. Some suggestions for the horizontal form, sometimes called the concept form because it is generally used at the concept formation stage, are shown in Figure 5–4. With imagination and available materials, the teacher can find other appropriate models.

Some of the models in Figure 5–4 can be adapted for teaching the vertical form, sometimes called the computational form (since computation is performed vertically). The models that are adaptable are shown in Figure 5–5 along with other examples of models that are in vertical form.

The child with a learning problem or developmental delay may benefit if the horizontal form is eliminated. The vertical or computational form will predominate in the student's studies over time. By requiring the child to learn two forms, the teacher may increase the time needed for the slow learner to achieve the objective. Two forms may also confuse the child or add unnecessary stimulation to an overly stimulated child. However, since both vertical and horizontal forms are on standardized tests and often such tests are mandated for all children, it might be worth the time to include both forms in instruction.

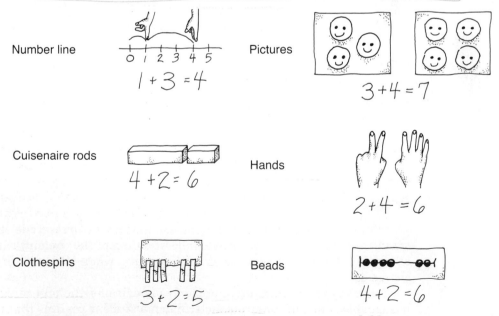

FIGURE 5–4
Horizontal Form for Addition

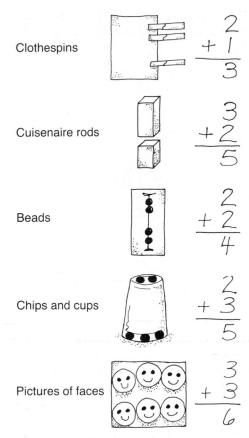

Clothespins	$\begin{array}{r} 2 \\ +\ 1 \\ \hline 3 \end{array}$
Cuisenaire rods	$\begin{array}{r} 3 \\ +\ 2 \\ \hline 5 \end{array}$
Beads	$\begin{array}{r} 2 \\ +\ 2 \\ \hline 4 \end{array}$
Chips and cups	$\begin{array}{r} 2 \\ +\ 3 \\ \hline 5 \end{array}$
Pictures of faces	$\begin{array}{r} 3 \\ +\ 3 \\ \hline 6 \end{array}$

FIGURE 5–5
Vertical Form for Addition

The Addition Table

In the beginning stages, the child will be working with sums to 10, later the sums will be increased to 18—determined by addends from 0 to 9. Sums to 18 will occur in the first grade. Children will have a better understanding of the inclusion of 0 as an addend or difference after they have worked with nonzero addends and differences—as discussed earlier in this chapter.

Early in the first grade, introduce the idea of making an organized list of all the sums by starting with a numberless addition table. The term *addition table* should be carefully introduced later in the year as the name for this organized list. Figure 5–6 shows the beginning stages of this table.

To construct the numberless addition table, the teacher can place masking tape or yarn on the floor to mark the boundaries for the organized list. Using a supply of red and blue plastic chips, painted bottle caps, or cutout paper pieces, the teacher can demonstrate the patterns of placing one blue chip with as many red chips as can be seen in groups across the top line of tape. This

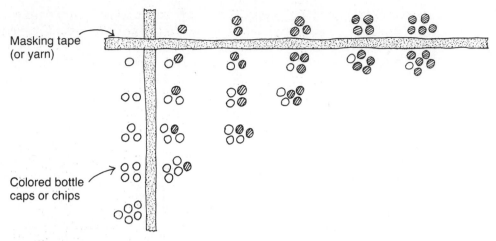

FIGURE 5–6
The Numberless Addition Table

pattern would continue for two blue chips and three blue chips, etc. Because children need to participate as much as possible, more than one addition table could be set up in the room. Teachers must guide children to replace the chips with number cards.

A transition process from the concrete to the abstract using two intermediate steps might be helpful for the average learner and essential for the problem learner. Chips could be replaced with pictures of chips, such as those

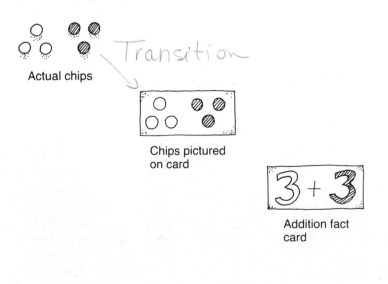

FIGURE 5–7
Moving from the Concrete to the Abstract

shown in Figure 5–7, then with addition fact cards, and, finally, with actual sums. These materials enable the teacher to provide Type 1, 2, and 3 learning activities. When constructing the addition table with children, all stages that the teacher feels are necessary should be demonstrated on the table.

Because the addition table has been constructed by the children, it is useful for more than just organizing the information obtained from studying the addition facts. The following are other observations to make.

1. *Using zero as an addend.* When zero has been adequately introduced as an addend, it can be recorded in the addition table as shown in Figure 5–8. The model used for generating the table is helpful for showing zero as an addend. For example, the expressions 0 chips + 3 chips and 3 chips + 0 chips are shown in Figure 5–8.

2. *Properties.* Arranging the basic addition facts in the form of a table facilitates both teaching and learning. Interesting patterns can be recognized leading to an intuitive knowledge of the identity property of addition and the commutative property of addition. Figure 5–9 illustrates how this observation reduces the number of addition facts that children must memorize. Seeing the patterns with equal addends is also helpful. If students are guided to discover these special characteristics, they are more likely to understand them and use them to their advantage. This guidance should occur through all stages of learning the facts—from concrete to abstract.

In Figure 5–9, the sums not classified as either identity property or equal addends are repeated on either side of the equal addend sums, which cut the table diagonally. This repetition occurs because of the commutative property.

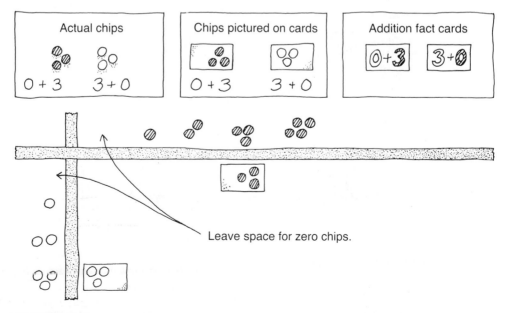

FIGURE 5–8
Representing 0 on the Addition Table

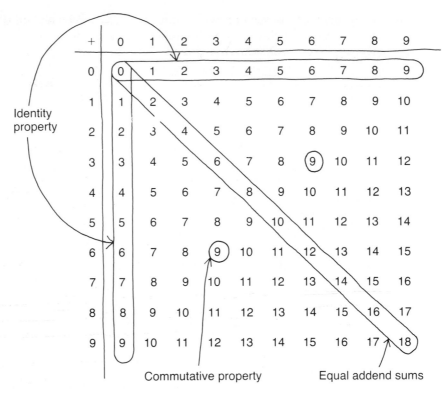

FIGURE 5–9
Properties and the Addition Table

If the table were to be physically folded along the diagonal of sums determined by equal addends, the remaining numbers would match up. For example, the sum for 6 + 3 and 3 + 6 (circled) would coincide. Students would only need to memorize the equal addend facts and the facts on one side of the fold—not including the identity property facts, which are looped in the diagram.

3. *Horizontal and vertical notation for addition.* The addition table doesn't allow for any transition to either the horizontal or vertical forms. The teacher could, however, judiciously arrange chips to facilitate either horizontal or vertical "reading" of chips inside the table. See Figure 5–10.

The Number Line and Addition

The previous explanation represents a thorough development of the basic addition facts through the systematic use of a discrete model. Despite the problems with using number lines (see chapter 4), they can be a useful continuous model for the teaching and learning of the addition process. The number line is best understood and used by children if they first see it as a *numberless* line. Children should begin their exposure to this model by constructing a line with marked segments. Their participation in the construction will pay off! Count segments, not the markers that designate the

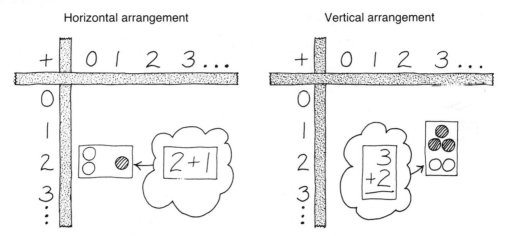

FIGURE 5–10
Horizontal and Vertical Arrangements on the Addition Table

beginnings and endings of segments. Later, numerals can be placed on the line, but only after careful attention has been paid to the equal segments. Initially, the arrows at the beginning and end of a number line are unnecessary. See Figure 5–11 for examples of the numberless line and the number line.

The student's physical encounter with addition on the number line is helpful in understanding the process. Walking on a number line marked on the floor is sometimes confusing because of the child's easily changed visual perspective.

It is important to reinforce the movement from left to right. The child's orientation can be lost by turning around or watching someone else "operate" from behind or to the right or left side of the line. For example, if you face a child and point to the left side on your number line, a young child will match your action by pointing to the right side of his or her number line.

Another alternative is to follow the advice given by the Yellow Pages slogan, "Let your fingers do the walking," as shown in Figure 5–12. For example, walk for two blocks, rest, then walk for two more blocks. How many blocks have you walked altogether? Encourage children to act out many such situations.

In summary, teaching and learning the basic addition facts are very involved processes. The properties play a large role in reducing the number of facts students must memorize. The addition table is an extremely useful organizational plan for recording facts as they are introduced. Attention given to the difficulties children have when moving back and forth between horizon-

FIGURE 5–11
The Numberless Line and the Number Line

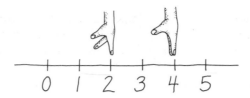

FIGURE 5–12
Let Your Fingers Do the Walking!

tal and vertical forms can prevent future problems. Students who have the ability should memorize the facts. Memorization will facilitate easier mastery of algorithms and estimation.

BASIC SUBTRACTION FACTS

Basic subtraction facts are defined as the related subtraction for all basic addition facts where the sum (minuend) is greater than the addend (subtrahend). For example, the equation $8 - 0 = 8$ is a subtraction fact related to $8 + 0 = 8$. The expression $0 - 8 = \_\_\_\_$ is not considered a basic subtraction fact; neither is $21 - 3 = \_\_\_\_$. However, for $3 + 6 = 9$, the related subtraction facts are $9 - 3 = 6$ and $9 - 6 = 3$.

Children truly understand addition when they are learning subtraction. Figure 5–13 shows a kindergartner matching two sets of Cuisenaire rod

FIGURE 5–13
This kindergartner is learning sums to ten intuitively.

stairsteps, where the length of each horizontal arrangement equals 10. By continuing her play, the girl can learn the relationship between addition and subtraction intuitively. Textbooks usually present subtraction nearly simultaneously with addition because they are inverse operations. The following discussion suggests ways to include subtraction while teaching addition. The following topics correspond to the previous section on basic addition facts.

Learning the Subtraction Facts

By the time children are ready to begin memorizing subtraction facts in the second grade, they have already memorized the addition facts. The same principle of varied practice and repeated practice holds for subtraction as it did for addition.

Since there are three different thinking models for teaching the concept of subtraction, varied practice with subtraction is more diverse than with addition. The take away model and the comparison model lead more directly to the memorization of subtraction facts than the missing addend model. Consider $5 - 3 = 2$ and the levels of thinking needed for this problem. At the lowest level of thinking, children would either manipulate objects or at least make reference to some picture of objects to determine the solution. Children would then count the objects left to determine the solution. Figure 5–14 shows how to count the difference in the take away and comparison situations and how to "count on" in the missing addend situation.

The take away and comparison situations would eventually be memorized as "Five minus three is two." The missing addend situation would eventually be understood as "Three plus two is five." (The terms *plus* and *and* are used

Problem	Thinking Model	Action	Script	Level
5 − 3 = ____	Take Away	Physically take away three objects from five, then count those objects left over.	"One, two."	Counting
5 − 3 = ____	Comparison	Physically match or align one for one, then count those left over.	"One, two."	Counting
3 + ____ = 5	Missing Addend	Try various numbers of objects to find out how many are missing.	"One, two, three, four, five." or "Three, four, five."	Counting Counting on
5 − 3 = ____	None	None	"Five minus three is two."	Memorization

FIGURE 5–14
Counting and the Subtraction Thinking Models

interchangeably.) When given subtraction drill and practice, which will occur mostly in the second grade, the child is expected to operate at the abstract or highest level of thinking.

TOUCH
MATH

However, if children are not ready for memorization because they have not had enough varied practice, they will resort to a lower strategy by referring to some manipulation, typically by counting on their fingers. Generally, this strategy will be in response to a take away situation. Remember when a child sees an expression such as $7 - 4 =$ _____, no thinking model is suggested; the expression requires abstract mathematics. If this is too abstract (the child cannot elicit recall), a resourceful child will find a useful strategy to find the solution—usually by using fingers to count. This strategy is undesirable when you expect the child to perform at the Type 3 level since using fingers slows the child down considerably. Children in this situation need to be directed through the use of more varied practice.

Order of Teaching Basic Subtraction Facts

An organized plan for subtraction is encouraged. It is advisable to teach subtraction facts in conjunction with their related addition facts as illustrated earlier. Several other examples are as follows:

$$2 + 6 = 8 \qquad 3 + 6 = 9 \qquad 7 + 0 = 7$$
$$6 + 2 = 8 \qquad 6 + 3 = 9 \qquad 0 + 7 = 7$$

$$8 - 2 = 6 \qquad 9 - 3 = 6 \qquad 7 - 0 = 7$$
$$8 - 6 = 2 \qquad 9 - 6 = 3$$

The second best approach would be to show the related subtraction facts involving the same addend. An example using 2 as an addend follows.

Addition	Related Subtraction	
$2 + 0 = 2$	$2 - 2 = 0$	$2 - 0 = 2$
$2 + 1 = 3$	$3 - 2 = 1$	$3 - 1 = 2$
$2 + 2 = 4$	$4 - 2 = 2$	$4 - 2 = 2$
$2 + 3 = 5$	$5 - 2 = 3$	$5 - 3 = 2$
$2 + 4 = 6$	$6 - 2 = 4$	$6 - 4 = 2$
$2 + 5 = 7$	$7 - 2 = 5$	$7 - 5 = 2$
$2 + 6 = 8$	$8 - 2 = 6$	$8 - 6 = 2$
$2 + 7 = 9$	$9 - 2 = 7$	$9 - 7 = 2$
$2 + 8 = 10$	$10 - 2 = 8$	$10 - 8 = 2$
$2 + 9 = 11$	$11 - 2 = 9$	$11 - 9 = 2$

Children can learn facts more easily if they are presented in an organized way. An organized presentation is especially helpful for children with learning problems. The teacher should not assume that children understand the organization just because they verbalize it. The teacher can be sure of the child's understanding only when the child has demonstrated understanding through a concrete example.

Properties

Subtraction of whole numbers is not commutative. For example, $3 - 2$ does not equal $2 - 3$. Children should learn intuitively that subtraction is not commutative in order to make the transition from memorizing addition facts to memorizing subtraction facts. Since they know that $2 + 3 = 3 + 2$, they may be tempted to think that $3 - 2 = 2 - 3$. Of course, $2 - 3 =$ _____ is not a subtraction fact by definition. When using manipulatives, it will be obvious that three objects cannot be taken away from two objects.

There is no identity property of whole numbers under subtraction. It is true that when zero is subtracted from any number, that number is the solution. For example, note that $6 - 0 = 6$. However, the expression $0 - 6$ has no whole number solution. This information is useful for children who are at the stage of memorizing subtraction facts; it reduces the number of facts students must memorize by 19.

Horizontal and Vertical Forms
for Subtraction Facts

Applying the models used in addition to subtraction in order to show the relationship between the horizontal and vertical subtraction forms is not a simple process. Horizontal subtraction on the number line is illustrated in Figure 5–15. In order to subtract "2," a student will have to move backwards on the number line, unlike addition. Nevertheless, working on the number line is still horizontal because of the customary horizontal orientation of the line.

Clothespins on a piece of cardboard, beads on a string, a horizontally arranged picture, hands, and Cuisenaire rods are models that can be used for the take away, comparison, and missing addends thinking models. See Figure 5–16 for an illustration of each.

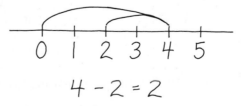

FIGURE 5–15
The Number Line and Horizontal Subtraction

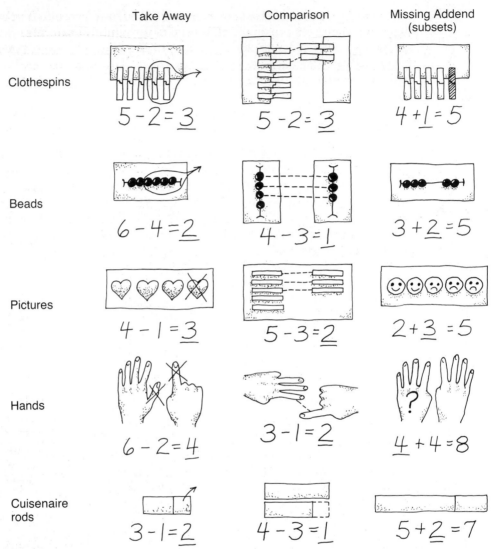

FIGURE 5–16
Other Horizontal Representations and the Subtraction Thinking Models

Using hands as a model can be done as illustrated; fingers are tucked under to represent subtraction for the take away situation. For the comparison model, it is inconvenient, if not impossible, to compare fingers physically since there are only 10 fingers.

Note that all models shown, except for the number line and Cuisenaire rods, represent discrete objects. Other continuous materials should be used as well.

Looking for the missing addend at this stage is *not* subtraction. When children see the plus sign (+), they expect to add! If the missing addend or parts are not in sight, trial and error addition should be used. If subsets of a set are used, the child can count objects to determine the solution.

Some of the same addition models can be adapted for teaching the vertical form or computational form for subtraction. Chips and cups are included as a new model. The missing addend examples shown in Figure 5–17 are subsets of sets.

As previously discussed, finding solutions for the missing addend problems can be done by covering the missing objects and using trial and error addition.

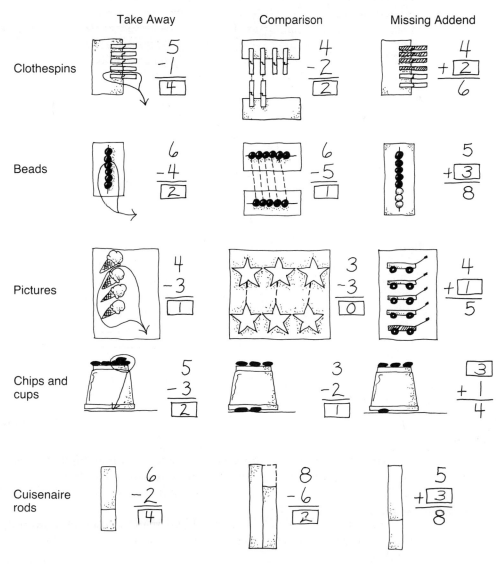

FIGURE 5–17
Vertical Representations and the Subtraction Thinking Models

Another method is to have the two addends be in two colors, in two positions, or to use some other means to separate them. Children can count objects to determine the solution.

The vertical arrangement of some situations pictured is cumbersome. For example, for the beads pictured in Figure 5–18, the "6" corresponds to all the beads shown and the solution is found at the top portion of the bead card. This arrangement is in this order to show the downward movement of the 4 beads. In other words, even though the physical arrangement of objects is vertical, the corresponding numbers in the problem are not necessarily aligned with the objects used. For the child who has learning problems, you might choose to use only the vertical form. However, as noted earlier in the discussion on addition, standardized tests include both horizontal and vertical forms. Therefore, advantages and disadvantages of presenting both forms must be considered.

The Addition Table and Subtraction Facts

The addition table is useful in the process of introducing and reinforcing the subtraction facts. Refer to Figure 5–9 to consider the family of facts for one, four, and five. Remember to make consistent use of the more appropriate subtraction thinking models. The "scripts" used for the take away, comparison, and missing addend models differ. Frequently, learners experience cognitive dissonance because they hear different explanations for the same abstract operation. In this situation, the best thinking model to use is the missing addend model. The question to ask is "What number plus four equals five?" This thinking model is most appropriate when an addend is covered up or missing in the addition table. When referring to an addition table, inappropriate questions are "How many more is five than four?" for the comparison thinking model or "Five take away four is what?" for the take away thinking model.

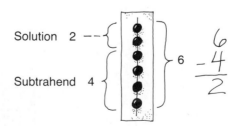

FIGURE 5–18
Difficulty Aligning Beads with Numerals

The Number Line and Subtraction

By the time children make use of the number line for subtraction, they should already have had experience with (a) constructing a numberless line, (b) constructing a numbered line, and (c) using the number line for addition. All of these experiences, which have been discussed earlier in this chapter, should have occurred in the first grade. Applying the number line to subtraction is straightforward for the three thinking models as shown in Figure 5–19.

In summary, teaching and learning subtraction facts is very involved. The relationship of subtraction to addition plays a key role in students' mastery of the subtraction facts. Therefore, the addition table becomes a powerful tool to facilitate the learning and memorization of subtraction facts. Students learn intuitively that the properties "don't work the same way" with subtraction as with addition. As with addition, emphasis should be on understanding first, then memorizing the facts.

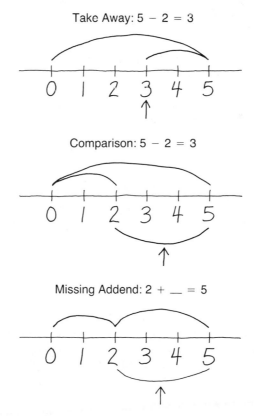

FIGURE 5–19
The Number Line and the Three Subtraction Thinking Models

LEARNING ADDITION AND SUBTRACTION ALGORITHMS

Learning the algorithm, the final step in learning addition and subtraction, begins toward the end of the first grade. This computational procedure uses the vertical notation form. It is imperative that children have a firm foundation in place value and regrouping prior to teaching the algorithm. Chapter 4 on numbers and numeration developed the use of several place-value and grouping models. Each model has its limitations. Teachers should be thoroughly familiar with each model they are using in order to make best use of the model's assets and to avoid problems inherent with its limitations. The addition algorithm is presented with bundles on place-value charts. This presentation of the addition algorithm will give a thorough treatment of the use of a grouping model.

Counting up and down by one with bundles was shown in chapter 4 to be readiness work for addition and subtraction algorithms as well as readiness work for the regrouping needed in computation. Remember that *regrouping* and *renaming* are two terms students will use when they perform algorithms in addition and subtraction and, later, in multiplication and division. *Regrouping* refers to the reorganization of objects. *Renaming*, on the other hand, refers to numbers.

Be aware of the need to identify prerequisite objectives when developing addition and subtraction skills. Refer to the Instructional Planner for Addition and Subtraction of Whole Numbers at the end of this chapter, where a list of objectives in hierarchical order is found. There is no perfect order for objectives. Some variability exists within most hierarchies found in current curricula. Of course, some objectives are best learned prior to certain objectives and after others. Good judgment is needed to determine the best order of mathematics concepts, facts, properties, procedures, and algorithms.

The following plan is recommended and illustrated.

1. Get children involved in reviewing basic addition and subtraction facts by having them use the concrete materials needed to develop the algorithm. After reviewing facts without regrouping, review those with regrouping. See the objectives in the Instructional Planner for Addition and Subtraction of Whole Numbers.

2. Initially, do each kind of problem using concrete models, accompanied by discussion, without the corresponding written work (Type 1). Follow this activity with a concrete representation and the corresponding written work (Type 2). Finally, the children will be prepared for drill and practice without any concrete models present (Type 3). See chapter 3 for a complete development of Type 1, 2, and 3 activities.

3. As the algorithmic process becomes more familiar to children, pictures of the concrete models may be substituted for the actual models. On the other hand, it might be better to de-emphasize the pictorial representations and

emphasize the concrete representations instead because of the complexity of the pictures needed to represent algorithms.

4. The use of intermediate algorithms can be used for teaching the regrouping process. These algorithms are called *intermediate* because they are learned as a transition to learning the standard algorithm. For example:

$$
\begin{array}{r} 23 \\ +\ 8 \\ \hline 11 \end{array}
\qquad
\begin{array}{r} 23 \\ +\ 8 \\ \hline 11 \\ 20 \\ \hline \end{array}
\qquad
\begin{array}{r} 23 \\ +\ 8 \\ \hline 11 \\ 20 \\ \hline 31 \end{array}
\text{ partial sums}
$$

Step 1   *Step 2*   *Step 3*

Step 1 sets up the problem and shows 3 ones plus 8 ones as a partial sum of 11. Step 2 shows 2 tens plus 0 ones, which is 20. Twenty is recorded as a second partial sum. The two partial sums are added in Step 3.

Correspondingly, a subtraction example is:

$$
\begin{array}{r} \overset{1}{\cancel{2}}3 \\ -\ 8 \\ \hline 5 \end{array}
\qquad
\begin{array}{r} \overset{11}{\cancel{2}}3 \\ -\ 8 \\ \hline 5 \\ 10 \\ \hline \end{array}
\qquad
\begin{array}{r} \overset{11}{\cancel{2}}3 \\ -\ 8 \\ \hline 5 \\ 10 \\ \hline 15 \end{array}
\text{ partial sums}
$$

Step 1   *Step 2*   *Step 3*

Step 1 sets up the problem and shows 8 ones from 13 ones as a partial difference of 5. Step 2 shows 0 tens from what is now 1 ten as a partial difference of 10. The two partial differences are then added in Step 3.

Every child, especially the child with learning problems, should be aware of place value when learning algorithms. The intermediate algorithms requiring the recording of partial sums and partial differences reinforce the understanding of place value.

When the addition algorithm is taught in the second grade it is probably the first time the young learner has been instructed to perform written work from right to left. For example, in the following problem the child is asked to add 5 and 3 first and then add 1 and 2.

$$
\begin{array}{r} 15 \\ +23 \\ \hline \end{array}
$$

Until now both reading and writing activities have been from left to right. The teacher should help the child with learning problems so the child feels comfortable changing directions when necessary. By using prompts and cues, the teacher can help the child feel more comfortable.

5. After learning how to add and subtract one-, two-, and three-digit

numbers using a concrete model (such as the model pictured in the following pages), the children need to start generalizing to any situation such as the following:

$$
\begin{array}{rrr}
149 & 4962 & 765 \\
+\ \ 9 & +\ 203 & +342 \\
\hline
70 & 324 & 7245 \\
-\ 5 & -\ 35 & -1596 \\
\hline
\end{array}
$$

Previous use of a concrete model to build a basic understanding of the algorithm should enable children to generalize at the abstract level needed for a Type 3 lesson.

An Overview of Teaching the Addition Algorithm

Three problems have been selected to illustrate how to teach the addition algorithm using Type 1, 2, and 3 learning activities with bundled sticks as the model. Figure 5–20 shows adding two-digit and one-digit numbers without regrouping. Figure 5–21 shows adding 2 two-digit numbers with regrouping to tens. And, Figure 5–22 shows adding 2 three-digit numbers with regrouping to hundreds. The Instructional Planner has a more comprehensive list of objectives for teaching the addition algorithm. Any of the listed objectives can be taught using the approach shown in the following three figures. Remember that when learning moves to a Type 3 level, do not overemphasize proficiency and efficiency. Emphasis should be on using the calculator and estimation. Children's knowledge of place value is critical, which is emphasized by repeated use of the place-value chart and place-value model in this text.

An Overview of Teaching the Subtraction Algorithm

This section gives an overview of how to teach the subtraction algorithm. As in addition, some intermediate problems are omitted but the teacher should consider them for use in the classroom.

Recall that the three thinking models for subtraction are take away, comparison, and missing addend. The most convenient to use with a concrete model is take away, although comparison also works reasonably well. The missing addend model is not suggested for use with concrete models because it is cumbersome. If comparison were used, both the minuend and subtrahend would be represented by bundles. Then, the two sets would be matched to determine how many more sticks were represented in the minuend than in the subtrahend. Figure 5–23 shows comparison in a Type 2 lesson. When the two bundles of ten and the single stick are matched (indicated by vertical dots), they can be removed as shown, leaving one bundle of ten and two single sticks

OBJECTIVE: Adding Two-Digit and One-Digit Numbers Without Regrouping
EXAMPLE: 23
                  + 4

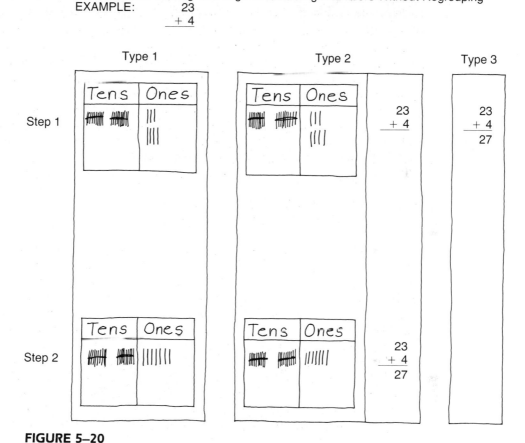

FIGURE 5–20

unmatched. These unmatched sticks represent the number 12—the difference between the minuend and the subtrahend.

Two problems have been selected to illustrate how to teach subtraction using the take away model. Figure 5–24 shows subtraction of a one-digit number from a two-digit number without regrouping, and Figure 5–25 shows subtraction of a two-digit number from a two-digit number with regrouping. As in addition, Type 1, 2, and 3 levels of instruction are shown. Type 3 also shows an intermediate algorithm. The Instructional Planner includes subtraction objectives sequenced among the addition objectives. Any of these objectives can be taught using the same approach shown in Figures 5–24 and 5–25. As with addition, emphasize understanding using a place-value chart and model. Show students how to subtract on the calculator and always have them estimate solutions before they determine final solutions.

OBJECTIVE: Adding Two Two-Digit Numbers with Regrouping to Tens
EXAMPLE: 35
                 + 17

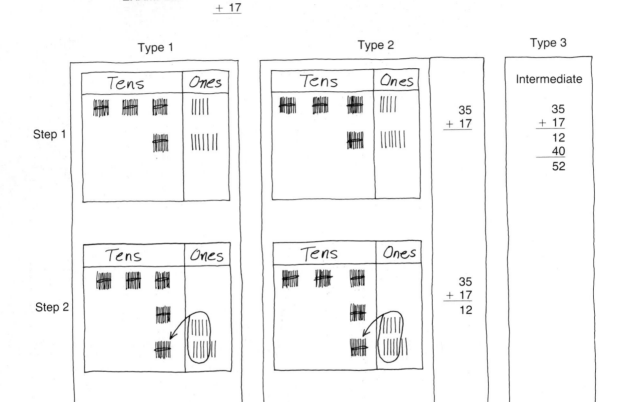

FIGURE 5–21

USING THE CALCULATOR TO LEARN ADDITION AND SUBTRACTION

Contrary to the belief that the calculator shouldn't be used until all concepts and procedures have been mastered, the following suggestions show how the

OBJECTIVE: Adding Two Three-Digit Numbers with Regrouping to Hundreds
EXAMPLE: 135
              + 292

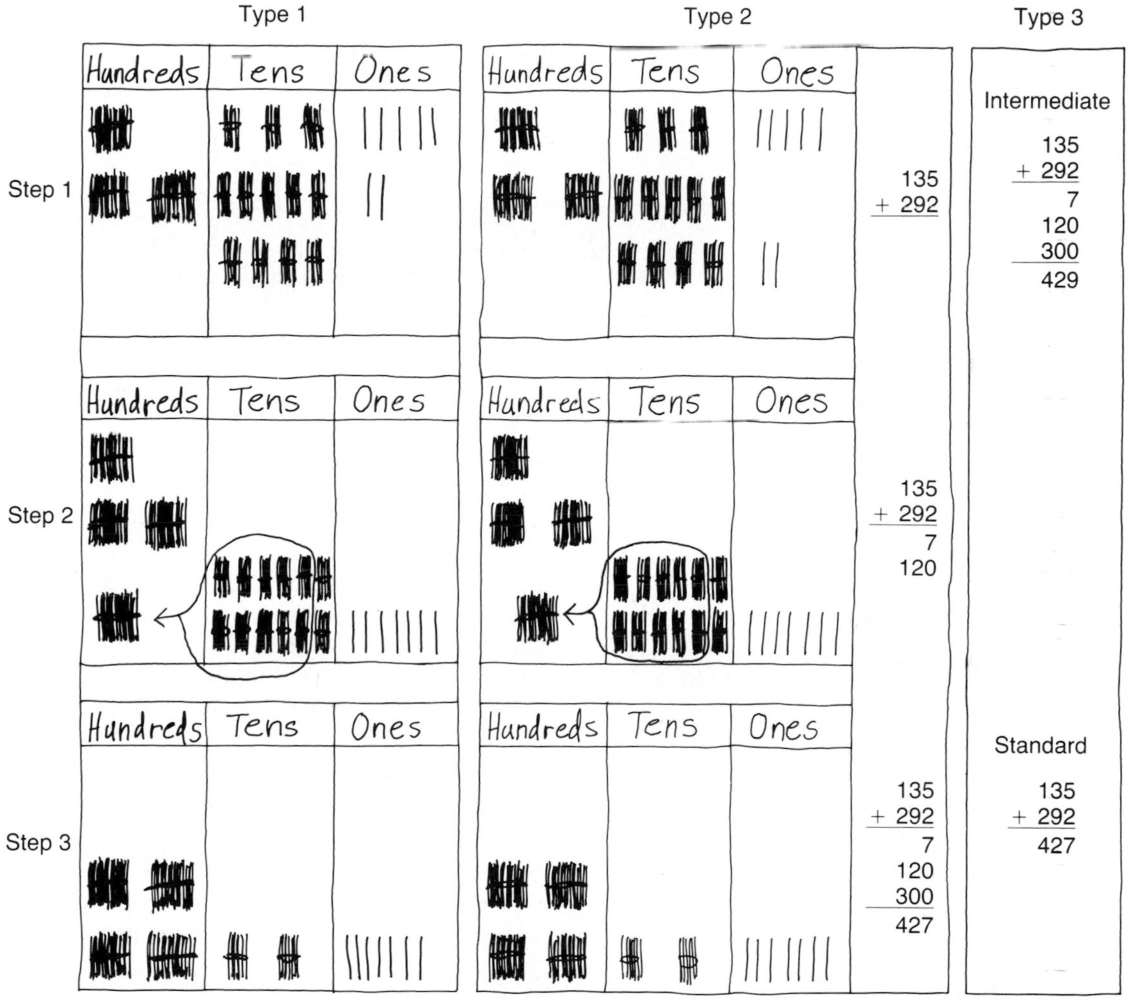

FIGURE 5–22

calculator can and should facilitate the learning of concepts and procedures. Children should grow up with the impression that the calculator can facilitate their thinking, not diminish it!

Concept Formation

In first grade, toward the end of the concept formation stage of learning addition and subtraction, the calculator adds a valuable dimension to the

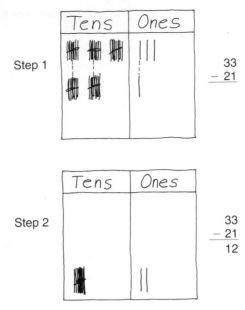

FIGURE 5–23
Comparison as Type 2

learning process. (At this time, the teacher is introducing written symbols.) First, the counting on and counting back procedures can be applied to addition and subtraction, respectively, as shown in Figure 5–26.

Another use of the calculator is with the missing addend thinking model for teaching subtraction. The teacher will use the children's knowledge of addition in this situation. As mentioned earlier, when using the missing addend thinking model, the strategy for finding a solution is trial and error addition. Preceding this strategy, though, is tallying. Figure 5–27 shows the strategies for 5 + _____ = 8 with a calculator having a constant function and then with a calculator not having a constant function. At first, children should not use the constant function. Although the constant key is more efficient, it requires a more sophisticated level of understanding than children have at this stage.

Basic Facts

If the calculator is going to be used for teaching basic facts, it should not be used in isolation but rather as part of a Type 2 experience. Calculator activities should not replace the learning activities previously described in this chapter. Calculator activities are intended to supplement and correspond with these activities. Figures 5–28 to 5–30 illustrate five special situations with respect to basic facts. The teacher should provide many problems like the ones shown so that children will notice patterns, where appropriate. Also, these problems provide necessary varied practice.

OBJECTIVE: Subtracting One-Digit Numbers from Two-Digit Numbers
Without Regrouping

EXAMPLE:
$$\begin{array}{r} 35 \\ -\ 3 \\ \hline \end{array}$$

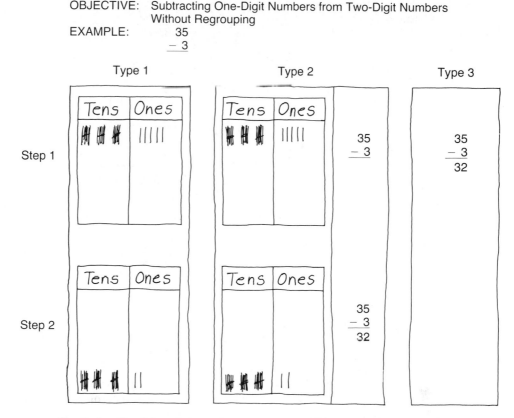

Reminder: The 3 is not shown because we are taking away, not comparing.

FIGURE 5–24

Algorithms

One of the best ways to use the calculator for learning the addition and subtraction algorithms is with intermediate algorithms. Figures 5–31 and 5–32 display examples with regrouping and without regrouping. Notice that in the following problems the displayed numbers on the calculator are not indicated for each substep. At this advanced stage of using the calculator, recording each display is no longer necessary. Only critical displays are now shown.

Problem Solving

The previous discussion and illustrations demonstrated using the calculator as a tool for learning algorithms. Learning algorithms could be considered

OBJECTIVE: Subtracting Two-Digit Numbers from Two-Digit Numbers with Regrouping
EXAMPLE: 53
                  − 29

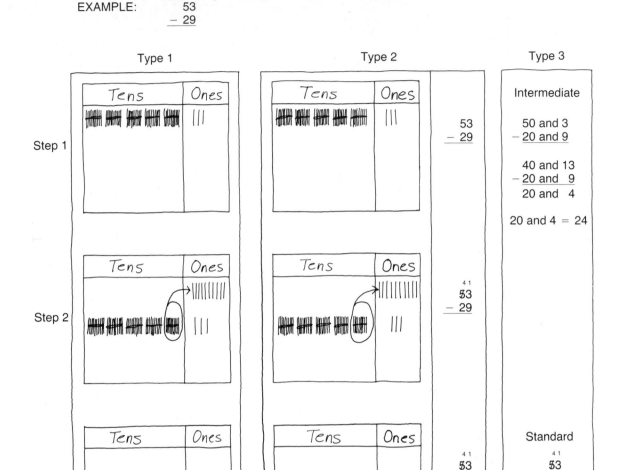

FIGURE 5–25

an outcome of problem solving since everything learned at this level is nonroutine. The teacher should encourage use of the calculator while the child is constructing an understanding of the concepts of operations and their corresponding algorithms. In the case of the special child, who is capable of learning the concept of operations but not capable of learning algorithms, the

Addition

Problem: 5 + 2 = _____	
Step 1	ENTER DISPLAY 5 5 + 5 1 1 = 6 + 6 1 1 = 7
Step 2	How many times did you add 1 to 5? 2
Step 3	ENTER DISPLAY 5 5 + 5 2 2 = 7
Step 4	Did you get the same answer? Yes

Subtraction

Problem: 6 − 3 = _____	
Step 1	ENTER DISPLAY 6 6 − 6 1 1 = 5 − 5 1 1 = 4 − 4 1 1 = 3
Step 2	How many times did you subtract 1 from 6? 3
Step 3	ENTER DISPLAY 6 6 6 3 3 = 3
Step 4	Did you get the same answer? Yes

FIGURE 5–26
Counting On and Counting Backwards by One

calculator becomes the only means of obtaining answers. This child should be taught precisely how to get answers using the calculator.

USING THE COMPUTER TO LEARN ADDITION AND SUBTRACTION

The computer has been more readily accepted than the calculator for classroom use. The irony is that the computer has the potential to do even *more* for the student than the calculator! The following suggestions are just some of the ways that the computer can facilitate the learning of concepts and procedures in addition and subtraction of whole numbers.

Problem: 5 + _____ = 8

	Tallying strategy		Trial and error strategy	
	ENTER	DISPLAY	ENTER	DISPLAY
With constant function	5	5	5	5
	+	5	+	5
	1	1	=	10
	=	6	2	2
	=	7	=	7
	=	8	4	4
			=	9
	Tally of equals ///		3	3
	5 + <u>3</u> = 8		=	8
			5 + <u>3</u> = 8	
Without constant function	ENTER	DISPLAY	ENTER	DISPLAY
	5	5	5	5
	+	5	+	5
	1	1	2	2
	=	6	=	7
	+	6	c	0
	1	1	5	5
	=	7	+	5
	+	7	4	4
	1	1	=	9
	=	8	c	0
			5	5
	Tally of equals ///		+	5
	5 + <u>3</u> = 8		3	3
			=	8
			5 + <u>3</u> = 8	

FIGURE 5–27
Missing Addend With and Without Constant Function

Programming

After children have mastered some simple BASIC programming statements in the second or third grade, they will be able to write simple programs

Adding Zero
Zero added to any number always equals that number.

With constant function	ENTER	DISPLAY	(PROBLEM)
	0	0	
	+	U	
	=	0	
	1	1	(1 + 0 = 1)
	=	1	
	2	2	(2 + 0 = 2)
	=	2	
	3	3	
	=	3	(3 + 0 = 3)
Without constant function	ENTER	DISPLAY	
	0	0	
	+	0	
	1	1	
	=	1	(0 + 1 = 1)
	c	0	
	0	0	
	+	0	
	2	2	
	=	2	(0 + 2 = 2)
	c	0	
	0	0	
	+	0	
	3	3	
	=	3	(0 + 3 = 3)

FIGURE 5–28

involving addition and subtraction. If children are not able to write programs, they can copy a given program to run. The following is an example of such a program.

```
10 PRINT "WHAT IS THE FIRST NUMBER?"
20 INPUT FIRST
30 PRINT "WHAT IS THE SECOND NUMBER?"
40 INPUT SECOND
50 PRINT "THE SUM IS"
60 PRINT FIRST + SECOND
```

Subtracting Zero
Zero subtracted from any number always equals that number.

With constant function	ENTER	DISPLAY	(PROBLEM)
	0	0	
	−	0	
	=	0	
	1	1	(1 − 0 = 1)
	=	1	
	2	2	(2 − 0 = 2)
	=	2	
	3	3	(3 − 0 = 3)
	=	3	
Without constant function	ENTER	DISPLAY	
	1	1	
	−	1	
	0	0	
	=	1	(1 − 0 = 1)
	c	0	
	2	2	
	−	2	
	0	0	
	=	2	(2 − 0 = 2)
	c	0	
	3	3	
	−	3	
	0	0	
	=	3	(3 − 0 = 3)

FIGURE 5–29

Programs that add a constant to an input number, programs that compare numbers, and programs that find differences can also be written. Using the computer in an interactive mode offers students an opportunity to explore very large numbers (larger than a calculator display will accommodate). An example of using the interactive mode in this fashion is as follows:

```
enter:   PRINT 11111111 + 22222222
enter:   <RETURN>
display: 33333333
```

Commutativity of Addition
Changing the order of addends does not change the sum.

ENTER	DISPLAY		ENTER	DISPLAY
2	2		3	3
+	2		I	3
3	3		2	2
=	5		=	5
c	0			

Vertical Form

	Addition				Subtraction	
PROBLEM	ENTER	DISPLAY		PROBLEM	ENTER	DISPLAY
3	3	3		7	7	7
	+	3			−	7
+4	4	4		−3	3	3
7	=	7		4	=	4

Horizontal Form

	Addition				Subtraction	
PROBLEM	5 + 6 = 11			PROBLEM	11 − 6 = 5	
ENTER	5 + 6 =			ENTER	11 − 6 =	
DISPLAY	5 5 6 11			DISPLAY	11 11 6 5	

FIGURE 5–30

Commercial software producers have developed many interesting and innovative programs that help to teach the basic facts and provide Type 2 and 3 activities for addition and subtraction. Often these programs have "animated" graphic displays that demonstrate the addition and subtraction facts with objects on the screen. As with any software purchase, you should take into consideration your children's level of development.

Problem Solving

Young children who have learned the concepts of addition and subtraction but have not worked extensively with symbols can be encouraged to solve problems. Two simple examples are problems such as "Show me two groups of objects to add so their sum has three digits," and "Show me two groups of objects to compare so there are four objects left over." Until a child is confident with symbolic algorithms, concrete models should be available any time he or she is engaged in problem solving.

Addition Without Regrouping

	ENTER	ENTER	ENTER	ENTER	PROBLEM
	c	c	c		462
	600	400	60	2	+215
	+	+	+	+	7
	70	200	10	5	70
	+	=	=	=	600
	7				677
	=				
DISPLAY	677	600	70	7	
	Step 4	Step 3	Step 2	Step 1	

Addition With Regrouping

	ENTER	ENTER	ENTER	PROBLEM
	11	50	3	53
	+	+	+	+28
	70	20	8	11
	=	=	=	70
DISPLAY	81	70	11	81
	Step 3	Step 2	Step 1	

Subtraction Without Regrouping

	ENTER	ENTER	ENTER	PROBLEM
	c	c		34
	2	30	4	−12
	+	−	−	2
	20	10	2	20
	=	=	=	22
DISPLAY	22	20	2	
	Step 3	Step 2	Step 1	

FIGURE 5–31

At all levels, children should be encouraged to look for patterns. One pattern that many children discover on their own is that adding 9 is the same as adding 10 and then subtracting 1. For example, to add 7 + 9, the child thinks 7 + 9 is 17 take away 1 or 16.

Subtraction With Regrouping

	ENTER	ENTER	ENTER	PROBLEM
	c	c		144
	2	140	4	$-$ 72
	+	$-$	$-$	100 and 40 and 4
	70	70	2	$-$ 70 and 2
	=	=	=	140 and 4
				$-$ 70 and 2
DISPLAY	72	70	2	70 and 2
	Step 3	Step 2	Step 1	144
				$-$ 72
				2
				70
				72
				or
				144
				$-$ 72
				72

FIGURE 5–32

The child must use a trial and error strategy to arrive at the correct answer for the missing addend model. At a more advanced level, problem solving may be used in problems such as the following:

$$\begin{array}{r} 203 \\ - 2 \\ \hline \end{array}$$

A teacher who analyzes error patterns in students' work can encourage students to use problem-solving strategies to help correct the errors. For example, a student who consistently misses addition problems where 8 is an addend should be encouraged to use the "make it simpler" strategy. Using this strategy the student can represent problems with concrete objects. Children can also be encouraged to act out problem situations. Saying, "Show me how you know" will encourage children to engage in problem-solving behaviors.

ESTIMATION

For any arithmetic problem there are two types of answers. One type is the exact answer; the other type is an estimated answer. As soon as a child starts learning the addition and subtraction concepts, estimating answers should be encouraged. An example of how to encourage estimation would be to ask the child if the sum of two numbers, such at 5 and 8, will be greater than 10 or less than 10. At a higher level, sums such as 23 + 59 and 138 + 247 should be estimated. An important part of students' estimation skills is not only to guess, but also to examine the guess in terms of the actual computational result, and to draw a conclusion about the "accuracy" of the guess. Teachers should emphasize to students that estimates and exact answers are two different types of answers and that one type is not better than the other—unless the situation demands just one type. A situation such as estimating the number of students and the number of chairs available and deciding whether more chairs are needed is an example of estimation in everyday life. Estimating the amount of money needed for a purchase is another example. Estimating the result of adding or subtracting when using a calculator is also a very useful strategy. By estimating the result, a child can determine whether he or she made an error while keying in a problem. Estimation should be encouraged at all times, even when teaching sophisticated computational algorithms.

For multi-digit computation, such as 405 + 698, the "front ends" of each number can be added. This problem changes to 400 + 600. For greater accuracy, the numbers can be rounded to the nearest hundreds place, changing the problem to 400 + 700. In each case, but especially in the first, compensation might need to be done. That is, when the sum of 1000 is obtained in the front-end approach, a quick review of 698 transformed to 600 should show that the final solution is nearly 100 less than it should be.

In conclusion, great care should be taken to provide thorough and careful instruction when children are learning the first operations on whole numbers. Concept formation for addition and subtraction is vital. Without the concepts, basic facts are meaningless. The algorithms for addition and subtraction should be carefully developed, with maximum attention given to place-value concepts. Calculators and computers can be valuable tools for the teacher to use when helping children explore the processes of addition and subtraction. The benefits of incorporating estimation skills, even at this early stage, cannot be overstated.

SUMMARY

In this chapter, we have focused on the foundations of learning addition and subtraction. Attention was given to readiness and concept formation. Without clearly developed concepts, the basic facts and algorithms for adding and subtracting are not very useful to the child. Suggestions for teaching basic facts were given along with strategies for teaching the traditional algorithms. The teacher should be aware of the important role that place-value concepts play in this process. Estimation, computers, and calculators can all be used to aid concept and algorithm development. At the end of this chapter, all the concepts and skills discussed are organized into an instructional planner.

PLANNING FOR INSTRUCTION

The Instructional Planner for Addition and Subtraction of Whole Numbers follows. Its purpose is to guide the teacher in selecting teaching activities and in determining a hierarchy of learning— from the concrete to the abstract and from the verbal to the written.

The hierarchy of mathematical objectives summarizes the general order of which topics should be taught. For addition and subtraction four major categories of objectives or types of learning are listed: concepts, facts, properties, and algorithms. Each objective is divided into sub-objectives. Approximate ages are suggested for teaching these objectives.

The hierarchy of learning behaviors focuses on three types of activities: those in the concrete and pictorial form (Type 1); those in the transitional form (Type 2), where concrete or pictorial models are combined with corresponding written work; and those in abstract form (Type 3).

Type 1 The **concrete** and **pictorial** form emphasizes manipulation of concrete models followed by pictorial models. This form also emphasizes language development through listening and speaking.

Type 2 **Transitional** form emphasizes interaction with concrete or pictorial representations and abstract symbols. This form is a transitional step from the concrete to the abstract. Student participation through listening and speaking continues with the addition of reading and writing.

Type 3 The **abstract** form places emphasis on interaction with ideas through listening and speaking as well as reading and writing. With this form there is no interaction with concrete or pictorial models.

The following activities are examples of learning experiences appropriate for the mathematical objectives listed in the Instructional Planner for Addition and Subtraction of Whole Numbers. Each activity is classified by approximate age, mathematical objective, and type of learning behavior. Other similar materials could be substituted for the materials suggested for Type 1 and 2 activities. Where there are no activities designated, the teacher may develop some. The activities at the end of this chapter are examples of what can be done to teach the objectives covered in this chapter. The teacher is encouraged to go beyond these ideas!

Estimation is important to emphasize throughout all activities in order to prepare children for real world mathematics. Therefore, you will see instructions to "guess first" in some of the activities.

A vertical column could be added to the left side of the Instructional Planner to record students' names, which could be placed on the Planner to correspond with the mathematical objectives currently being studied. Clusters of names on a given Planner could suggest possible groupings in the class for instructional purposes. At different times, a student might need to work individually, with a small group, or with the large group. The Instructional Planner can be helpful for grouping decisions based on level of mathematical objective and level of learning behaviors, rather than just test scores.

Addition and Subtraction of Whole Numbers

Age	Types of Learning	Mathematical Objectives	Types of Behavior and Experiences			
			Type 1 Concrete	Type 1 Pictorial	Type 2 Transitional	Type 3 Abstract
2–6	Concept formation	Joining and separating	1, 2, 3 4, 6	5	3, 4, 6	3, 4, 6
		Take away	7		7	7
		Comparison	8	8	8	8
		Missing addend	9		9, 10	9
5–6	Facts				3, 4, 6	3, 4, 6
					7, 8, 9	7, 8, 9
5–6	Properties	Commutativity for Addition	11		11	11
		Identity for Addition	12		12	
		Associativity for Addition	13		13	
		Addition Table	14		14	14
						See pages 108–110.
7–8	Algorithms	Addition (multiples of 10) without regrouping				
		Subtraction (multiples of 10) without regrouping				
		Addition of two-digit numbers and one-digit numbers without regrouping				Figure 5–20
		Addition of two-digit numbers and one-digit numbers with regrouping				
		Subtraction of one-digit numbers from two-digit numbers without regrouping				Figure 5–24
		Subtraction of one-digit numbers from multiples of 10 < 100				
		Subtraction of one-digit numbers from two-digit numbers with regrouping				

Age	Types of Learning	Mathematical Objectives	Types of Behavior and Experiences			
			Type 1 Concrete	Type 1 Pictorial	Type 2 Transitional	Type 3 Abstract
		Addition of 2 two-digit numbers without regrouping				
		Addition of 2 two-digit numbers with regrouping				Figure 5–21
		Subtraction of 2 two-digit numbers without regrouping				
		Subtraction of two-digit numbers from multiples of 10 < 100				
		Subtraction of 2 two-digit numbers with regrouping				Figure 5–25
		Addition of 2 three-digit numbers without regrouping. Then, with regrouping				Figure 5–22
		Subtraction of 2 three-digit numbers without regrouping. Then, with regrouping				
		Subtraction of one-digit numbers from multiples of 10 < 1000				
		Subtraction of two-digit numbers from multiples of 100 < 1000				
		Subtraction of three-digit numbers from multiples of 100 < 1000				
		Subtraction with 0 as a placeholder				
		Generalize addition and subtraction				

ACTIVITY 1

Type 1: Concrete

Age: 2–3

Objective: Joining and separating continuous materials

Materials: Sand or water, containers

Instructions: Provide each child with one container of sand (or water) and two or three empty containers. Show how to pour sand (or water) from large containers into empty containers and then back into the larger ones. Encourage children to discuss what they are doing.

ACTIVITY 2

Type 1: Concrete

Age: 2–3

Objective: Separating continuous materials into parts

Materials: Strips of ribbon or paper, scissors, two or three containers

Instructions: Show the children how to cut ribbon or paper into pieces and how to place pieces into the containers. Encourage children to discuss what is happening to the ribbon or paper. You can ask them if there was more ribbon before it was cut and similar questions. Accept all answers, even those that do not indicate an understanding of conservation.

ACTIVITY 3

Type 1: Concrete

Age: 2–6

Objective: Joining and separating discrete materials

Materials: Wooden blocks with two 3-inch finishing nails driven into their top surfaces, beads in a box, number cards

Instructions: Show children how to take beads from the box one by one and how to place the beads on two nails on the wooden block. Then, show children how to join the beads again by removing the beads from the nails and replacing them in the box. Let children repeat this process. Encourage discussion.

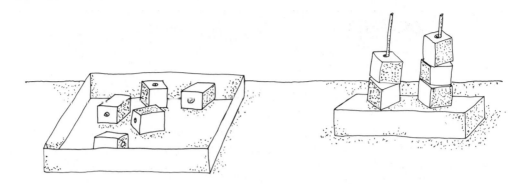

Type 2: Transitional Perform the same activity as the previous one except include labeling the beads with number cards. Ask the children questions about the number of beads in the box and on the nails.

Type 3: Abstract Tell a story about having some beads that are placed on nails. These materials are not present. As children listen, they record what they hear. Children should be encouraged to repeat the story and to make up their own stories.

Say: "I have five beads in a box. I put two on a nail and three on another nail. If I put all the beads back in their box, I have five beads in the box." Have students record the numbers with number cards. Eventually, children will use operation and relationship symbols. Another approach would be to initiate the story with beads already on the nails.

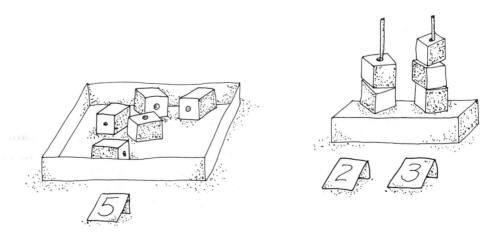

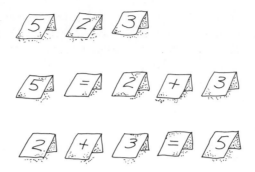

ACTIVITY 4

Type 1: Concrete

Age: 3–6

Objective: Joining and separating discrete materials

Materials: Unifix cubes, box, number cards

Instructions: Demonstrate how to remove the cubes from the box and make two stacks of cubes. Then, dismantle the stacks, replace the cubes in the box, and repeat the process. Let the children perform this task. Encourage the children to discuss what they are doing. (Notice that this activity is more difficult than Activity 3, because the stacks to build are not designated by containers, posts, or other structures.)

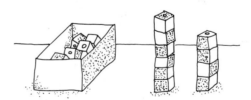

Type 2: Transitional This time, have children label each stack with an appropriate number card (such as in the previous activity). For the very young child, keep the total number of cubes under five or six.

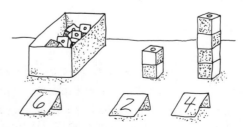

Type 3: Abstract   Without unifix cubes present, tell a story about having a box of unifix cubes and making two stacks with them. As children listen, they record what they hear. Children should be encouraged to repeat the story and make up their own stories.

Say: "I have seven cubes in a box. I made one stack with four of them and another stack with three of them. If I put all the cubes together in one stack, I have seven (or if I put them all back in the box I have seven)." Each student records the story using number cards. Eventually, students will use operation and relationship symbols. Sometimes, initiate this activity with the cubes stacked first.

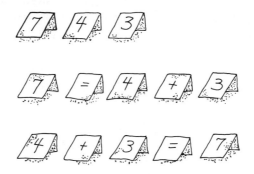

ACTIVITY 5

Type 1: Pictorial

Age: 3–5

Objective: Joining continuous material

Materials: Chalk, outside pavement or chalkboard

Instructions: Show the children how to draw a series of connecting lines to make one long line. Have each child take chalk and add another segment to the line. Ask them how their actions are changing the line.

ACTIVITY 6

Type 1: Concrete

Age: 3–6

Objective: Joining and separating discrete materials

Materials: Bead cards and number cards

Instructions: Give each child more than one bead card, where each bead card has a different number of beads on it. Show the children how to separate the

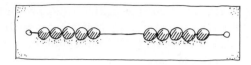

beads into two parts. Ask them how many beads are in each part. Encourage children to perform this same activity by themselves. Ask them if they can separate the beads another way.

Type 2: Transitional   Next, have children lable each set of beads with the appropriate number cards. For the very young child, keep the total number of beads under five or six. Occasionally, show the bead card arranged vertically instead of horizontally. Discuss the new arrangement.

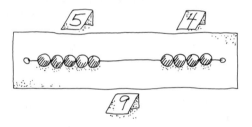

Type 3: Abstract   Without bead cards present, tell a story about having a bead card and separating the beads into parts. As the children listen, they should record what they hear. Children should be encouraged to repeat the story and make up their own stories.

Say: "I have a bead card with four beads on it. I moved the beads so there was one bead on one side and three beads on the other side. If I move the beads together I will have four in all." Encourage the students to record the story using number cards. Eventually, have them use operation and relationship symbols. Sometimes, initiate the story with the beads already arranged in separate groups.

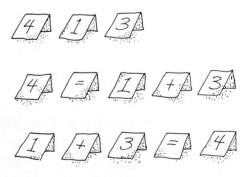

ACTIVITY 7

Type 1: Concrete

Age: 4–6

Objective: Take away and subtraction facts

Materials: Toy cars, box for a garage, number cards

Instructions: Tell the children how many cars you have in all. Then, "drive" 1, 2, or 3 of the cars into the box garage, explaining what you are doing as you perform the activity. Then, count how many cars are left. Then, reverse the process. Each child should do the same activity. Encourage them to use different numbers of cars (not to exceed 9 or 10 cars in all). Have them explain how many cars they had at the start of the activity, how many drive into the garage, and how many are left. Encourage students to tell a story about the cars.

Type 2: Transitional   This time, have children label each set of cars with the appropriate number cards (as in previous activities). Keep the total number of cars under 9 or 10. Consider showing the related addition facts.

Type 3: Abstract   Without the cars and garage present, tell a story about the cars and garage and have the children record the numbers while they are listening. Say: "Five cars were parked in a driveway. Somebody drove two of the cars into the garage. Three cars were left in the driveway." Have the students record the story using number cards.

   Consider presenting the related addition facts: "Three cars were parked in a driveway. Somebody drove two cars out of the garage and parked them with the other three cars. Now there are five cars again in the driveway." Have students record this story using number cards.

ACTIVITY 8

Type 1: Concrete

Age: 5–6

Objective: Comparison and subtraction facts

Materials: Little pieces of paper, crayons, number cards, paper with columns, prepared worksheets

Instructions: Arrange pieces of paper and crayons on a table. Ask children if there are more pieces of paper or more crayons. Then, depending on their responses, ask how many more pencils than crayons or vice versa. Ask children to place one crayon on each piece of paper. Then, ask if there are more pieces of paper or more crayons. Ask how many more. Repeat this activity using varying amounts and varying materials.

Type 1: Pictorial   Give each child a worksheet with unequal numbers of pieces of paper and crayons pictured. Ask if there are more pieces of paper or more crayons. Have children show which items could be matched by drawing lines between them. Ask if there are any extra pieces of paper or crayons. Ask how many extras there are.

Type 2: Transitional   Have children take pieces of paper and crayons and place them in spaces provided on a worksheet. Then, children can respond to questions on the bottom of the worksheet as shown. Repeat using varying materials in varying amounts.

Type 3: Abstract   Without objects or pictures present, tell a story while the children listen and record the numbers in the story using number cards. Say: "Joe has six crayons and five pieces of paper. He wants to match each crayon to one piece of paper. Are there enough crayons? Too few? Too many? How many more crayons are there?" Students record the numbers using number cards.

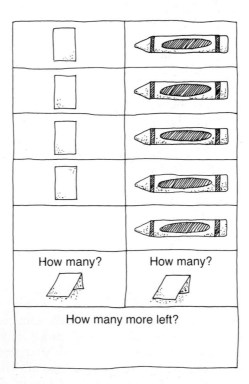

ACTIVITY 9

Type 1: Concrete

Age: 5–7

Objective: Missing addend and addition facts

Materials: Box with small hole on the top, bottle caps, number cards

Instructions: Tell the children that you have eight bottle caps. Three are on the table and the rest are in the box. Ask: "How many caps are in the box?" Have children guess some numbers until the right number is guessed. When a number is guessed, have the children start with that number and "count on" three more. When they find the correct number have them check the box to verify their answer. Repeat using different numbers. Encourage discussion.

Type 2: Transitional   Do the same activity as before, but this time have the children label each set of bottle caps with number cards.

Type 3: Abstract   Give the children a worksheet like the one shown. Show that the problems on the right of the worksheet are shortcuts for finding the missing addends in the problems on the left.

Name _____

$2 + \underline{} = 6$	$6 - 2 = \underline{}$
$3 + \underline{} = 9$	$9 - 3 = \underline{}$
$7 + \underline{} = 8$	$8 - 7 = \underline{}$
$9 + \underline{} = 11$	$11 - 9 = \underline{}$
$\underline{} + 5 = 8$	$8 - 5 = \underline{}$
$\underline{} + 3 = 5$	$5 - 3 = \underline{}$
$\underline{} + 1 = 8$	$8 - 1 = \underline{}$
$\underline{} + 3 = 10$	$10 - 3 = \underline{}$

ACTIVITY 10

Type 2: Transitional

Age: 5–7

Objective: Missing addend

Materials: Walk-on number line

Instructions: Tell children that someone jumped twice to get to the number 5. The first jump covered two spaces. How many spaces did the second jump cover? Repeat this activity using other numbers. Encourage discussion and acting out.

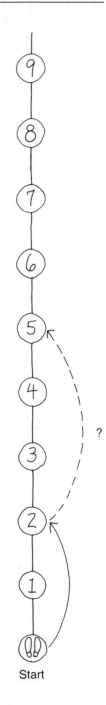

ACTIVITY 11

Type 1: Concrete

Age: 6

Objective: Commutative property

Materials: Clothespins on cards, worksheets, pencils

Instructions: Show a card with two clothespins on top and four on the bottom and ask children how many clothespins there are in all. Then, turn the card over (top to bottom) to show four clothespins on top and two on the bottom. Show that there are still six clothespins in all. Have children repeat this process using different numbers. Encourage the children to generalize.

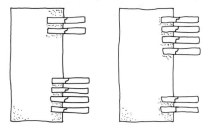

Type 2: Transitional Have children record their work on worksheets while they solve various problems using the clothespins on a card.

Type 3: Abstract Assign a worksheet on the commutative property. Encourage children to make up their own examples by remembering their previous activities with clothespins on cards.

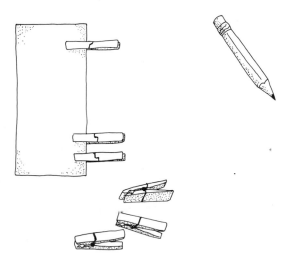

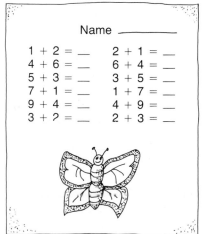

Name _____

1 + 2 = __   2 + 1 = __
4 + 6 = __   6 + 4 = __
5 + 3 = __   3 + 5 = __
7 + 1 = __   1 + 7 = __
9 + 4 = __   4 + 9 = __
3 + 2 = __   2 + 3 = __

ACTIVITY 12

Type 1: Concrete

Age: 6–7

Objective: Identity property of addition

Materials: Two cups, flowers (pencils or sticks), number cards, worksheets

Instructions: Place two flowers in one cup and no flowers in the other cup. Ask how many in each. Then, ask how many in all. Repeat this activity using combinations of zero and other nonzero numbers. Encourage discussion.

Type 2: Transitional   Do the same as the previous activity, but this time have children place number cards by each cup. Then, tell, and also label, how many there are in all. Repeat this activity using combinations of zero and other nonzero numbers. Encourage discussion.

This activity can be extended by assigning a worksheet with pictures of flowers and cups where children must complete a number sentence for each picture.

ACTIVITY 13

Type 1: Concrete

Age: 6

Objective: Associative property of addition

Materials: Clothespins in three colors, paper, pencils

Instructions: Start with two sets of three groups of clothespins. Attach the clothespins in each color group end to end.

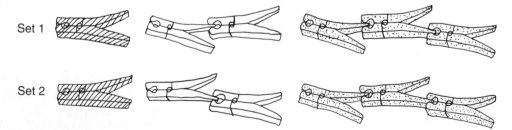

Set 1

Set 2

Connect the first two groups in the first set and the second two groups in the second set. Discuss how many there are in each group and how many there are in each set. Discuss what is different and what is the same about each set.

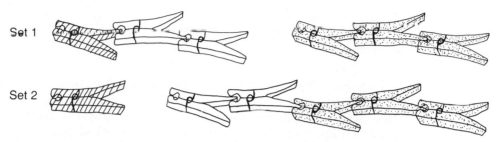

Set 1

Set 2

Connect the two groups in each set. Compare and discuss.

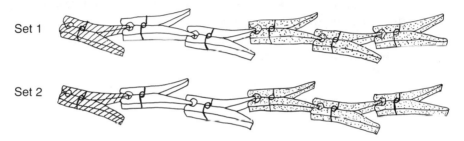

Set 1

Set 2

Repeat this activity using different numbers of clothespins.

Type 2: Transitional Have children label each group of clothespins accordingly. Encourage both horizontal and vertical arrangements. Have children draw pictures to represent the real clothespins.

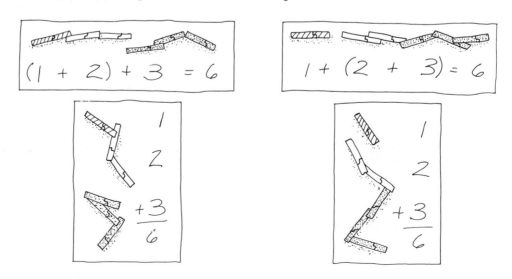

$$(1 + 2) + 3 = 6$$

$$1 + (2 + 3) = 6$$

$$\begin{array}{r} 1 \\ 2 \\ +3 \\ \hline 6 \end{array}$$

$$\begin{array}{r} 1 \\ 2 \\ +3 \\ \hline 6 \end{array}$$

ACTIVITY 14

Type 1: Concrete

Age: 6–7

Objective: Addition table, facts

Materials: Yarn, tape, bottle caps, large table or floor area, addition
fact cards

Instructions: Start a numberless addition table for children to finish. Encourage discussion and cooperation. Look for patterns. Gradually complete the entire table of facts. This activity could extend over several days. (See the Addition Table section of this chapter on pages 95-98 for more discussion.)

Type 2: Transitional Next, have children replace the bottle caps with fact cards. Have them do this gradually as facts are studied. As a last step, add zero as an addend.

Type 3: Abstract After the previous activities have been completed have children replace the rest of the bottle caps with numbers. Use the answer sides of the fact cards to make the table. Include zero. Look for patterns. Reinforce children's intuitive understanding of the commutative and identity properties.

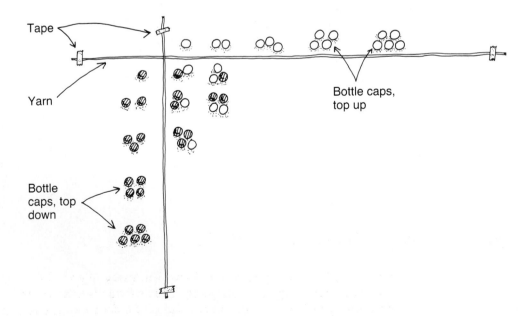

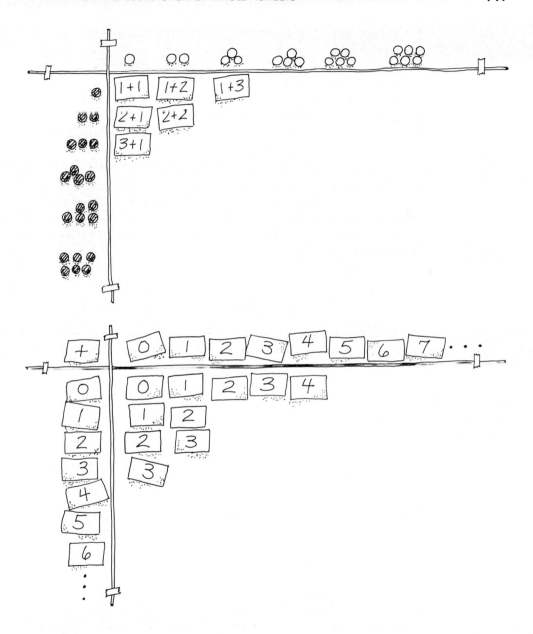

STUDY QUESTIONS AND ACTIVITIES

1. Describe a Type 1, Type 2, and Type 3 activity where the objective is to construct a bar graph that shows children's favorite outdoor activities. List three interpretive questions about the graph that would elicit addition or subtraction.

2. Reflect on what children might think when they hear the following expressions.
   a. Show me two plus three in the addition table.
   b. Borrow one from the seven.
   c. Watch your signs!

3. Observe a preschool class for about an hour and make note of the opportunities there are to informally add or subtract with the children. How many of these opportunities are used? If possible, videotape this class and play it back for further review with others. Compare your findings.

4. Ask a first grade teacher to administer a practice set of exercises in addition and/or subtraction that you can collect and grade. (These could be basic facts or higher order addition or subtraction exercises). Look for error patterns. Give the children in the class the opportunity to explain or show how they arrived at their solutions for one of the error patterns you identified. (a) Justify from the children's perspective their reasons for this error pattern. (b) Describe instruction that might make use of this information in order to help children reconstruct their thinking.

5. Children's existing understandings of mathematics should be an integral part of a mathematics lesson. The suggested activities for the previous question encourage this view. Open any first through fourth grade teacher's edition to a lesson where addition or subtraction is addressed. Identify directions to the teacher that encourage this view.

REFERENCES AND RESOURCES

Baratta-Lorton, M. (1976). *Mathematics their way*. Menlo Park, CA: Addison-Wesley.

Beattie, I. D. (1986). Modeling operations and algorithms. *Arithmetic Teacher, 33*(6), 23–28.

Bright, G., & Behr, M. (1984, April). *Identifying fractions on number lines*. Paper presented at the annual meeting of the American Educational Research Association, New Orleans.

Brownell, W. A. (1973). The progressive nature of learning mathematics. In F. J. Crosswhite, J. L. Higgins, A. R. Osborne, & R. J. Shumway (Eds.), *Teaching mathematics: Psychological foundations* (pp. 60–71). Worthington, OH: Charles A. Jones.

Carpenter, T. P., Hiebert, J., & Moser, J. M. (1984). *The effect of problem structure and first graders' initial solution processes for simple addition and subtraction problems* (Tech. Rep. No. 516). Madison, WI: Research and Development Center for Individualized Schooling.

Carpenter, T. P., & Moser, J. M. (1983). The acquisition of addition and subtraction concepts. In R. Lesh & M. Landau (Eds.), *Acquisition of mathematical concepts and processes* (pp. 7–44). New York: Academic Press.

Dickinson, J. C. (1986). Gather, organize, display: Mathematics for the information society. *Arithmetic Teacher, 34*(4), 12–15.

Hosmer, P. C. (1986). Students can write their own problems. *Arithmetic Teacher, 34*(4), 10–11.

Immerzeel, G., & Thomas, M. (1982). *Ideas from THE ARITHMETIC TEACHER*. Reston, VA: NCTM.

Kulm, G. (1985). *Learning to add and subtract: Learning activities and implications from recent cognitive research*. Washington, D.C.: National Institute of Education.

Reys, B. J. (1986). Estimation and mental computation: It's "about" time. *Arithmetic Teacher, 34*(1), 22–23.

Reys, R. E., & Reys, B. J. (Eds.). (1986). Estimation and mental computation. *Arithmetic Teacher, 34*(1), 24–25.

Reys, R. E., Suydam, M. N., & Lindquist, M. M. (1984). *Helping children learn mathematics*. Englewood Cliffs, NJ: Prentice Hall.

Spiker, J., & Kurtz, R. (1987). Teaching primary-grade mathematics skills with calculators. *Arithmetic Teacher, 34*(6), 24-27.

Steffe, L. P., VonGlasersfeld, E., Richards, J., & Cobb, P. (1984). *Children's counting types: Philosophy, theory, and application*. New York: Praeger Press.

Thornton, C. A., Tucker, B. F., Dossey, J. A., & Bazik, E. F. (1983). *Teaching mathematics to children with special needs*. Menlo Park, CA: Addison-Wesley.

6

Multiplication and Division

MULTIPLICATION AND division are usually introduced as concepts after addition and subtraction are well established and most addition and subtraction facts are committed to memory. The introduction of these operations often begins with multiplication at the end of second grade. It is not absolutely necessary to follow this particular sequencing. Readiness activities for multiplication may be incorporated into addition activities in the first grade. Similarly, readiness for division may be incorporated in subtraction activities in the second grade. Since children have a tendency to compartmentalize their learning, teachers need to use as many bridges as possible to help children connect what they already know. Multiplication and division are easily developed in this way—by connecting them to addition and subtraction.

Multiplication and division can be seen as a more efficient means of adding and subtracting. The relationship of these operations to addition and subtraction is not the only relationship that needs careful development. The inverse relationship between multiplication and division should also be carefully developed. Mathematics should be seen by children as interrelated concepts and it should "make sense" to them.

This chapter is organized in a similar way as chapter 5 on addition and subtraction. The key terms for teachers and students and the relationships between addition and multiplication as well as the relationships between subtraction and division are very important. Every teacher should thoroughly familiarize him- or herself with the different thinking models and algorithms for division. Division has traditionally been the most difficult operation to teach.

VOCABULARY FOR TEACHERS

Repeated addition and **repeated subtraction** are terms teachers should know. Although the concepts may be understood by children, the terms have the potential to create confusion. Repeatedly adding or repeatedly subtracting the same addend are the most frequently used thinking models for introducing the concepts of multiplication and division, respectively.

Another common model used to introduce multiplication is the **array.** However, at the age of 7 or 8, when children are introduced to multiplication through arrays, it is not necessary for them to understand the term *array.* Later, in middle school, the use of the term will be expected. Teachers should know the meaning of the term and its use. An array is an arrangement of discrete objects in rows and columns that form a rectangular shape. Repeated addition of discrete objects can be represented in arrays. Generally, the first factor in a multiplication problem represents the number of rows and the second factor represents the number of columns of the array. For example, in the expression 3×2, there are 3 rows of 2 each. The instructional materials and the teacher should be consistent.

The least used model for multiplication in the primary classroom is called **cross products** or **Cartesian products.** Neither term is necessary for children to use even if the concept is considered in a lesson. A Cartesian product is the total number of ordered pairs possible between two given sets. For example, if one set consisted of three different t-shirts and the second set consisted of two different pairs of jeans, there would be six different outfits possible.

There are two terms that describe the types of interpretations used to introduce the concept of division: **measurement** (repeated subtraction) and **partitive division.** These terms are not important for children to master, especially since the meaning of the terms is not obvious. However, these concepts should be introduced at the end of third grade because they are extremely important. Measurement is the process of finding the number of sets when the number of elements per set is given. Partitive division is the process of finding the number of elements per set when the number of sets is given. In either case, the teacher should understand the meaning of the terms *divisor,* *dividend,* and *quotient* even though children have been using the terms *factor* and *product* instead. The quotient is the result obtained when dividing a dividend by a divisor. That is, in the equation $20 \div 5 = 4$, the number 20 is the dividend, the number 5 is the divisor, and the number 4 is the quotient. Children have been asked to use the terms *factor* and *product* so they will connect multiplication and division more readily.

Students will learn the properties of whole number multiplication in the early childhood grades, but without the associated terminology. These properties are the **commutative property,** where $a \times b = b \times a$; the **associative property,** where $(a \times b) \times c = a \times (b \times c)$; the **identity element** of 1, which states that $a \times 1 = 1 \times a = a$; and the **zero property,** where $a \times 0 = 0 \times a = 0$. Finally, the **distributive property** is learned, which involves the distribution of multiplication over addition. In this property, the expression $a \times (b + c) = (a \times b) + (a \times c)$. Division of whole numbers is right distributive in this expression where $(a + b) \div c = (a \div c) + (b \div c)$.

VOCABULARY FOR STUDENTS

During their study of multiplication, beginning in the second grade, students will encounter the terms *factor, product, multiplication,* and *division.* The use of the term *factor* at the age that children learn multiplication is not likely. If the term is used, it will be the first time the term has held any meaning for students. However, the term *product* might already be understood as something made by nature or industry. In this case, children will have to learn the mathematical meaning, which is "the number obtained by multiplying two or more numbers together." Some classroom materials might still use *multiplier* and *multiplicand.* In the equation $2 \times 3 = 6$, the factor 2 is the multiplier and the factor 3 is the multiplicand. These terms, though commonplace to teachers, are new and difficult for youngsters to master. The terms *multiplication* and *division* are new terms for children. These terms are "big" words and the teacher should appreciate the difficulty children might have learning them. Children will learn the meaning of multiplication and division intuitively through hands-on activities.

READINESS

In chapter 4 on numbers and numeration it was suggested that second grade children count up and down by ones, twos, fives and tens. Counting with the calculator makes it possible to count by other numbers as well, such as threes, sevens, and elevens. These activities, done with or without representational models, enrich the children's readiness for multiplication and division.

There are many real-world situations that the teacher should take advantage of to prepare children for multiplication and division. Some multiplication examples are counting by twos to determine how many children are lined up in pairs and counting by threes to determine how many pencils are in a box. Some sample division situations are determining how many game cards each player gets after dealing a deck and determining how many children get a certain number of crayons after passing them out. Of course, activities can be created as shown in Figure 6–1, where the child is filling each cup with three straws as a readiness activity for multiplication.

FIGURE 6–1
Using cups and straws to make groups of three is a readiness activity for multiplication.

CONCEPT FORMATION

As with addition and subtraction, children must learn the concepts of multiplication and division before being taught to memorize basic facts or algorithms. The following thinking models present the different ways the concepts are learned. Numerous problem-solving and concrete manipulative experiences must be offered to children to assist them in constructing their understandings of these operations.

Multiplication

Three situations or thinking models require multiplication. As mentioned, the easiest model to understand is *repeated addition*. In this model the same addend is added over and over. The activity of counting children in pairs, which was previously mentioned, is an example of this model. Emphasize how many twos have to be added. After a number of such problems, the teacher can introduce the multiplication symbol and explain that multiplication is a "shortcut" for repeated addition. "Finding shortcuts" will be done repeatedly during a child's study of mathematics.

Arrays also present situations that can be simplified by multiplication. Recall that an array is an arrangement of discrete objects in rows and columns. Examples would be musicians in a marching band or, as shown in Figure 6–2, cans of juice in a carrying pack.

The number of objects arranged in an array can always be found by repeated addition. However, not all repeated additions can be arranged in an array. For example, if musicians are marching in a 4 by 5 array, then the total number of musicians can be found by adding 5 + 5 + 5 + 5. On the other hand, an array cannot be used to show that a child practiced the piano 4 hours every week for 3 weeks, because hours and weeks cannot be physically or pictorially arranged.

Consistency in labeling arrays is recommended. Most instructional materials show rows as horizontal and columns as vertical. The symbolic expression shows the number of rows first and the number of columns second.

Cross products can also be used to teach the concept of multiplication. However, since this model is the most difficult to use, it is used the least. Consider having a choice of three different flavors of frozen yogurt with two different toppings. The six possible combinations are found through the cross product as illustrated in Figure 6–3.

Division

There are two situations that require division. Both of these situations occur naturally in the real world. The *measurement* situation is generally thought of as repeated subtraction. For example, if someone had 12 crackers and wanted to put 3 crackers on each plate, how many plates are needed? In this case, 3 crackers at a time are "subtracted" from the 12 crackers until there are 0 crackers left. The children would count the number of plates with 3 crackers to find the answer. The children in Figure 6–4 are modeling this same

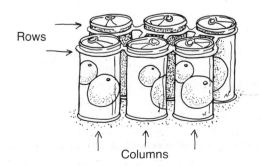

FIGURE 6–2
An Array

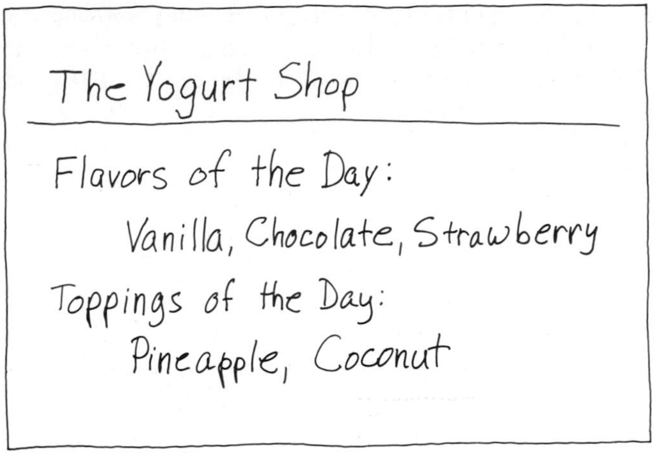

The Yogurt Shop

Flavors of the Day:
    Vanilla, Chocolate, Strawberry
Toppings of the Day:
    Pineapple, Coconut

	Pineapple	Coconut
Vanilla	Vanilla with Pineapple	Vanilla with Coconut
Chocolate	Chocolate with Pineapple	Chocolate with Coconut
Strawberry	Strawberry with Pineapple	Strawberry with Coconut

FIGURE 6–3
Cross Product

situation with bottle caps. The number of elements in the set divided by the number of elements equals the number of sets (N ÷ E = S).

The other division situation is called *partitive* (actually, a better term would be *distributive*). To use the crackers and plates example again, if someone had 12 crackers and wanted to place the same number of crackers on each of 3 plates, how many crackers would there be on each plate? The teacher would distribute 1 cracker to each plate and continue to distribute the 12 crackers by placing them one at a time on each of the 3 plates until all of them are used. Third grade children in Figure 6–5 are modeling this situation by using bottle caps. The number of elements in the set divided by the number of sets equals the number of elements in each set (N ÷ S = E).

Initially, children should be directed to solve each of these types of problems by modeling them with counters. Along with acting out the repeated subtraction problems by using objects, children should eventually be able to perform repeated subtraction with number sentences, as shown in these figures. You will notice that the number sentences for each are the same! However, the thinking required to act out the problems is different.

Division could be presented in terms of multiplication, that is, in terms of a missing factor. What number would you need to multiply by 3 to get 12? Even though this situation can be dealt with concretely, it is more difficult than with other models. Therefore, it is not advisable to use this situation during the earliest stages of learning division. Some teachers prefer to avoid this approach altogether when initially teaching division.

Division is usually introduced in the third grade; readiness activities can occur in second or third grade. When introducing division, it is recommended that the teacher not start out with large numbers of objects (Kamii, 1976). Make sure to present repeated subtraction situations until the children feel comfortable with them. Be careful! Not all textbooks are consistent. Some textbooks introduce division through repeated subtraction, but then intermix repeated subtraction problems, missing factor problems, and partitive problems all in the same set of exercises! Since this practice can confuse students, it is important to always look ahead for consistency.

Children need to be conceptually and operationally knowledgeable of the repeated subtraction model of division. One important way to determine students' understanding is to observe them demonstrate what they are thinking by using concrete models. To introduce the partitive situation, point

FIGURE 6–4
By using bottle caps, these children are showing how many groups of 3 there are in 12.

FIGURE 6–5
These children are modeling a division situation by showing how many bottle caps there are in each of three groups.

out that instead of looking for how many times a number can be subtracted from a given number, now children will know how many times a number can be subtracted. What they will be finding instead is the number being subtracted. The way to find that number out is to distribute the objects until they are all gone. Then, count out how many objects are in each part. A familiar example is dealing cards in preparation for a card game.

You can use "repeated subtraction" for both measurement and partitive division. If a number of objects is to be partitioned into a given number of sets, consider repeatedly subtracting the number of objects according to the number of sets across which the objects are to be distributed. Figure 6–6 shows this type of repeated subtraction using $8 \div 2 = 4$. The first situation is one in which the child is given eight crackers and a stack of plates. The child puts two crackers on the first plate and sets it aside, then puts two crackers on the second plate and sets it aside, and so forth until all eight crackers are used. Then, the child determines how many plates were required.

The second situation requires that eight crackers be placed on two plates. The child puts one cracker on the first plate and one cracker on the second plate. A second cracker is put on each plate and a third and so on until all eight crackers are used. Then, the child determines how many crackers are on each plate.

Usually, when children are doing an activity like this one, they are not particularly concerned with "how many plates have three crackers," unless they're concerned that they won't receive a plate with crackers themselves!

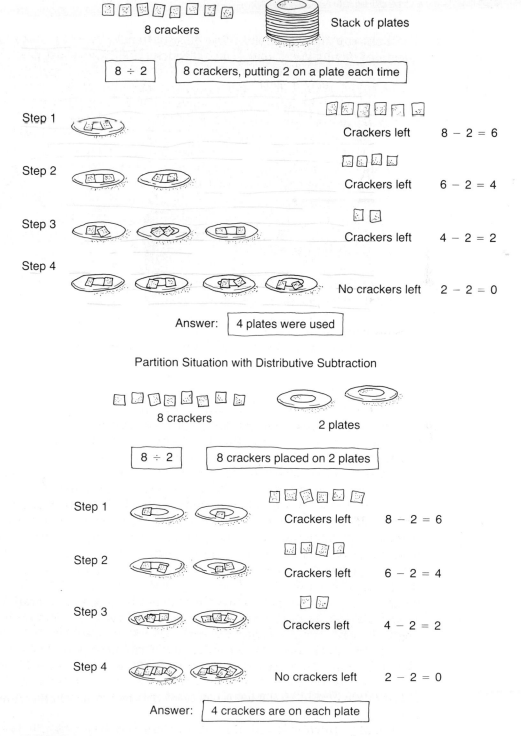

FIGURE 6–6
Measurement Situation with Repeated Subtraction

Teachers can maximize this type of situation by talking about it, raising questions, acting it out, and so on. Of course, the activity just described would be easy to implement at snack time.

Children do not form concepts in a meaningful way without careful preparation and planning by the teacher. Natural situations can be used for conveying concepts as well as carefully planned "lessons." Wise teachers will use natural situations to their best advantage. Carefully relating new concepts to well-established ones should be done through questioning. Questions such as "Is this like something we've done before?" and "How is it different?" help children construct and reconstruct their understandings.

BASIC MULTIPLICATION FACTS

A basic multiplication fact is an arithmetic sentence with the numbers zero through nine in which the two factors equal a resulting product. At an optimal point in the child's experience, these facts should have had enough use to become part of long-term memory. However, conceptual development is essential before any "memorization" is appropriate.

Learning Multiplication Facts

Children should be given many opportunities to use real objects to model and act out multiplication situations as well as word problems created by the teacher. The basic facts of multiplication need not be emphasized until the concepts and the models of multiplication have been mastered in the third grade. That is, children should be able to recognize situations that will require "multiplication" and be able to obtain results through repeated addition, arrays, or cross products without having answers memorized. Eventually, the basic multiplication facts should be learned well enough for instant recall, but only after children have had many experiences that do not emphasize the recall of answers. Games are far more conducive to dispelling math anxiety than timed tests. Often, the simpler facts will be learned without specific attention to memorization—just through constant use. The basic multiplication facts can be presented in several ways, similar to the presentation of addition facts. The "old fashioned" way is to have children learn them as tables such as the fours table, which is 4×1, followed by 4×2, followed by 4×3, etc. Another way is to study facts by families. The families method focuses on all the combinations of factors whose product is a specific number, such as 12. The 12 family would have the facts 1×12; 2×6; 3×4; 4×3; 6×2; and 12×1 as members. The sentences $3 \times 4 = 12$ and $4 \times 3 = 12$ are *related facts*. The "doubles," such as 2×2; 3×3; 4×4; and so forth can also be highlighted to facilitate learning. Neither method is more advantageous than the other. You might wish to emphasize the method most emphasized in the textbook, but use the other method to reinforce the children's learning and to encourage mastery of the facts.

Some children have a very difficult time memorizing specific nonmeaningful facts that require rote memorization skills. While it is important for these students to learn facts to the best of their ability, it is also important that mathematics not become frustrating and unpleasant for them. Therefore, emphasis should be placed on the application and execution of multiplication. These students may need to use the calculator or multiplication fact sheets in order to solve problems while attempting to memorize facts. Some students may never learn all the multiplication facts.

Order of Teaching Multiplication Facts

The simpler facts should be taught first, starting with the twos and threes. These facts will give children an opportunity to use repeated addition or arrays to model problems. Starting with one as a factor will confuse students. The factor of one can be easily modeled. However, it is difficult for children to understand that the number is only added once or that there is only one row in the array. To avoid this confusion, teach some other facts first so that using one as a factor will seem more logical to children. Concrete examples help in illustrating one as a factor as can be seen in Figure 6–7.

The introduction of the symbolic representations of basic multiplication facts should be delayed until the children's concept of multiplication is established. This teaching approach cannot be overemphasized. The "connecting" (Baratta-Lorton, 1976) of symbols with models and concrete representations should be done gradually—starting with facts that are most familiar to children. The term for connecting activities is *transitional activities*.

For some children, the nines table is sometimes easier to learn than the others, with the exception of the twos and threes. The learner can be led to discover that the answer to a nines fact has digits that add to nine. Children can also discover that the products of 9, 18, 27, 36, 45, 54, 63, 72, 81 are the most symmetric products in the multiplication table. Number theory discoveries can enhance the process of learning these tables and provide some fun for students.

One of the Type 2 activities that intrigues children and helps them to remember the answers to multiplication facts is to have them skip count on a hundreds chart. In this activity, they color the products of a certain table. A detailed description of this activity follows in the Activity section of this chapter.

Children need to have the opportunity to see and have a feel for larger products, such as 9 × 9. Arrays are one method of ensuring that children have well-established concepts of the magnitude of the numbers involved instead of just an instant answer learned by rote.

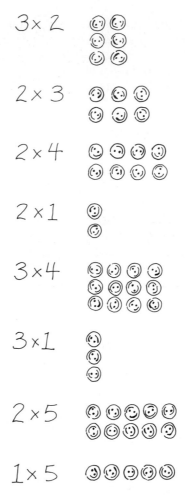

FIGURE 6–7
Multiplication Facts and Arrays

Properties

As children work with multiplication situations, they will learn intuitively that the order of the factors does not influence the product. The fact that the order of factors does not change the product describes the commutative property of multiplication. Usually, the teacher only has to ask children whether finding 5 × 4 is any different than finding 4 × 5 to see if they understand. This property is the most obvious one for multiplication and it does not need to be formally named. Children simply need to have an awareness of the property so they can put it to use in their thinking. As seen in Figure 6–8, the 3 × 2 and 2 × 3 arrays are clearly equivalent in numbers of objects.

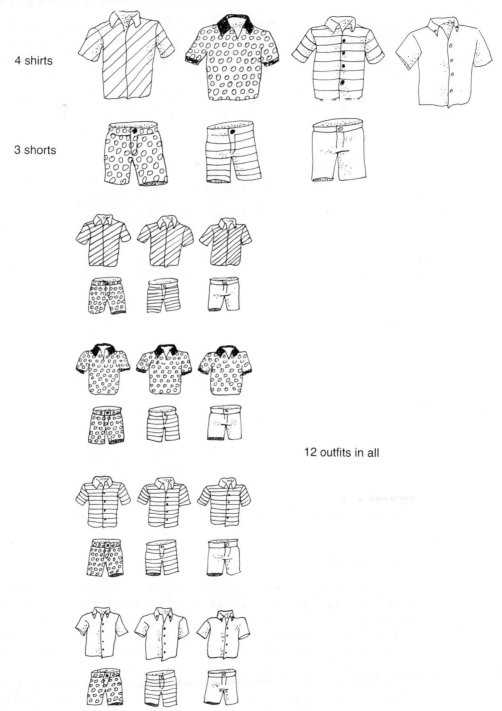

4 shirts

3 shorts

12 outfits in all

FIGURE 6–8
Cross Product for 4 × 3: Getting Ready for the Associative Property

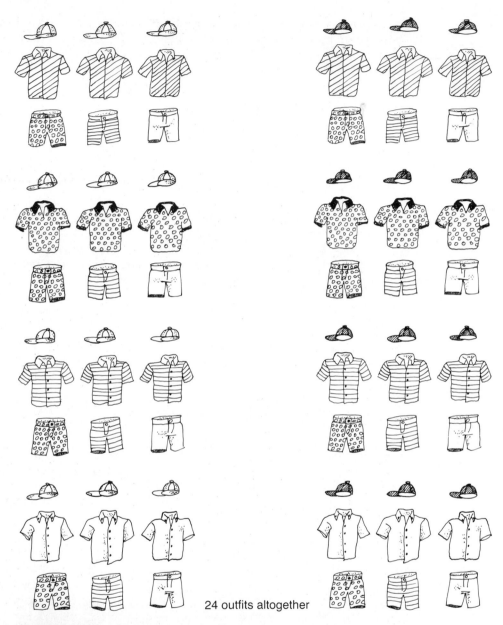

24 outfits altogether

FIGURE 6–9
Associative Property: (4 × 3) x 2 = 4 × (3 × 2)

Another property is the associative property of multiplication, which states that when multiplying three factors, the order of operating does not affect the outcome. Once again, it isn't necessary for children to know the name of this property. However, they should have Type 1 experiences with this property. Some natural situations for exploring the associative property might arise out of a multi-level cross products problem. An example would be to figure out how many outfits can be made using 4 shirts and 3 pairs of shorts (12 outfits). This example can be seen in Figure 6–8.

After children have determined that 12 outfits can be put together, the teacher could ask how many different outfits could be put together if there were 2 different hats from which to choose. There would be 24 outfits as shown in Figure 6–9.

Now, the teacher can ask what would happen if children had started with 2 different hats and 3 pairs of shorts first (6 outfits) and then selected from the 4 shirts (24 outfits). Children will have great fun figuring out that this change doesn't make any difference in the result! A Type 2 example is presented using arrays of chips in Figure 6–10. See Activity 7 for another Type 2 interpretation of the associative property.

When children are ready to consider the associative property symbolically, the teacher should be aware that this is probably their first experience with parentheses, which can create visual confusion. Therefore, it is critical that children understand from an intuitive, hands-on perspective. If children are asked to represent products with three factors, these products are usually of the form, $a \times (b \times c) = (a \times b) \times c$.

The distributive property is illustrated using arrays in Figure 6–11. This is the only property that combines two operations—multiplication and addition. The teacher needs to explain very carefully in order for the child's eyes to "see" the two interpretations using the same arrangement of markers. In the figure, two groups of $3 + 4$ are shown on the left. The result is 14. On the right, a group of two 3s and a group of two 4s are added. The result is also 14.

This property requires special attention since it is used widely in mathematics for the rest of the students' school experience. The distributive property forms the basis of most of the vertical algorithms for multi-digit multiplication. Symbolically, when one factor is expressed as the sum of two numbers such as in the expression $a \times (b + c)$, the expression is rewritten as the sum of two products in the form $(a \times b) + (a \times c)$. Typically, the first symbolic experience children have with this property is in the horizontal form just stated. The application of the property is in problems such as 4×12, where 12 is rewritten as the sum of 10 and 2. This problem is written as $4 \times (10 + 2)$ and solved by rewriting it as $(4 \times 10) + (4 \times 2)$. Unfortunately, the parentheses, again, are a source of extra "visual noise." Also, unless the right distributive property is used, as in $(10 + 2) \times 4$, the child has to multiply 4 by the tens column first then the ones column—the exact opposite of the algorithm used in the vertical form. It might be best to avoid the horizontal form. The vertical form

$$\begin{array}{r} 12 \\ \times\ \ 4 \end{array}$$

can be rewritten as   .

$$\begin{array}{r} 10 \text{ and } 2 \\ \times\ \ \ \ \ \ \ \ \ \ 4 \\ \hline 40 \text{ and } 8 \end{array}$$

or 48

The use of "and" is better than "+," since it avoids the use of two operational signs. This is an example of the need for ample exposure to

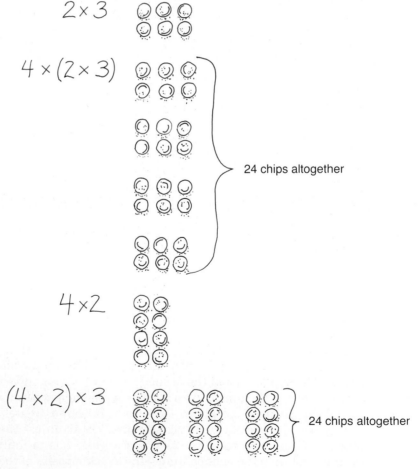

FIGURE 6–10
Associative Property: 4 × (2 × 3) = (4 × 2) × 3

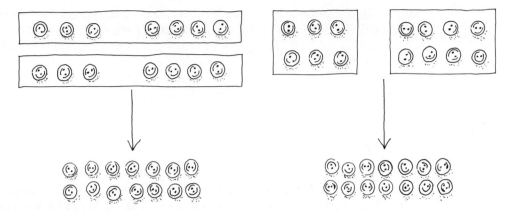

FIGURE 6–11
Distributive Property: 2 × (3 + 4) = (2 × 3) + (2 × 4)

physical models (like the place-value models in chapters 4 and 5) to help children construct an intuitive understanding that keeps their minds on track.

Horizontal and Vertical Forms for Multiplication Facts

There are two forms for symbolic multiplication, just as there are two forms for symbolic addition as well as for subtraction. When the horizontal form is used, a mathematical sentence such as 3 × 5 = 15 is the result. When children are first connecting symbols with multiplication situations, the teacher should clearly show "3" as the "grouping" or "row" value, as shown in Figure 6–12.

The vertical form, which does not appear as a mathematical sentence, should be introduced about the time that children are learning multiplication

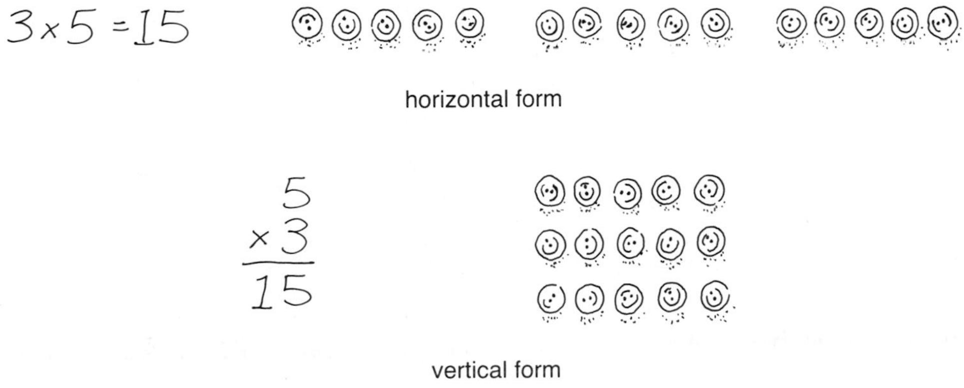

$3 \times 5 = 15$

horizontal form

$$\begin{array}{r} 5 \\ \times 3 \\ \hline 15 \end{array}$$

vertical form

FIGURE 6–12
Show the Groupings in Multiplication

of two-digit numbers. The timing of this introduction makes sense because the standard algorithm for two-digit multiplication uses the vertical format.

The vertical form will happen naturally when using a place-value chart for showing multiplication. Chips or beans can be used on a place-value chart to show repeated addition—one of the models for multiplication. Two examples are shown in Figure 6–13. The procedure shown will be developed later in the chapter.

Multiplication Table

The first multiplication table that children see should be numberless and should be constructed by them as early as the end of second grade. Using the numberless table, arrays of counters can be displayed and the properties of multiplication can be explored.

Figure 6–14 shows the concept of a numberless multiplication table.

Children should be thoroughly familiar and comfortable with the number-less multiplication table. They should have many experiences using it to find basic multiplication facts. Then, they can replace the bottle cap arrays with pictures of arrays and, later, factors expressed as the product $a \times b$ (where a represents the number of rows and b represents the number of columns). These gradual changes of the numberless table offer the opportunity to learn and

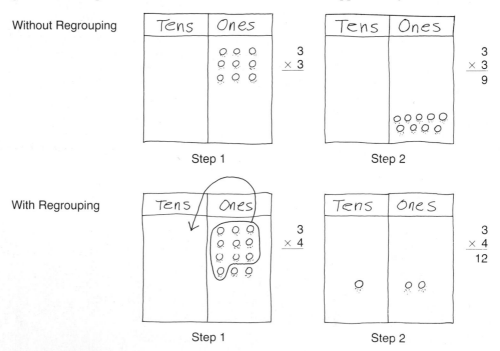

FIGURE 6–13
Vertical Multiplication on Place-Value Chart

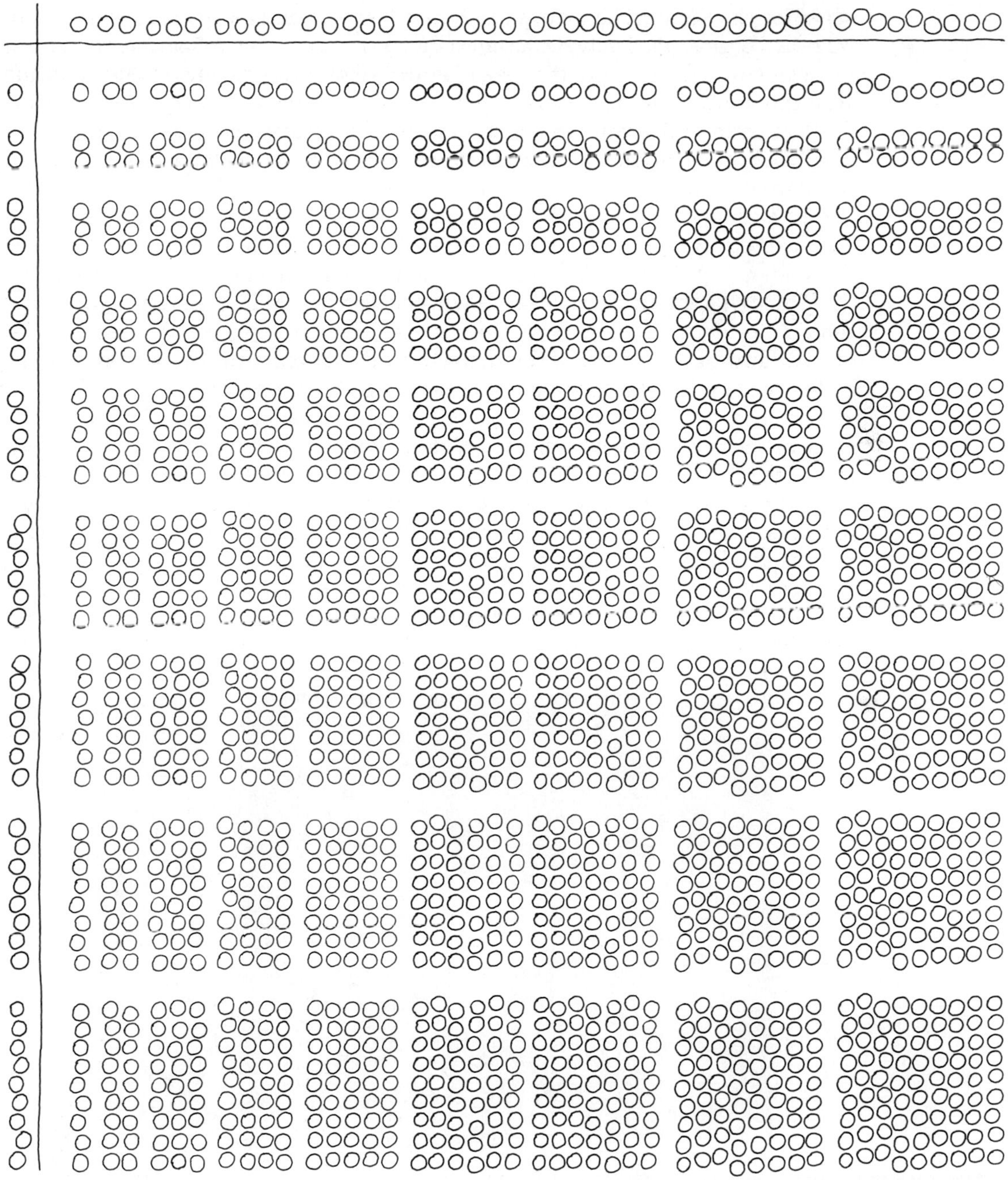

FIGURE 6–14
Numberless Multiplication Table

organize the facts through Type 1, 2, and 3 experiences. This progression will increase children's understanding of how to use a multiplication table, the meaning of arrays, and the basic multiplication facts. The second grade children in Figures 6–15, 6–16, and 6–17 have constructed a numberless multiplication table and are using it in various stages of abstraction.

After the facts from factors of two and greater are developed, then one can be used as a factor, and later zero. It isn't necessary to develop all the facts through nine as factors before introducing one and zero. The point is that one and, especially, zero are far more difficult to understand as factors than are numbers greater than one. Teachers should consider not entering zero in the table as a factor until children have had considerable experience with the table.

At any stage of the development of the table, the properties can be explored. The annotated table in Figure 6–18 shows how the properties can be studied in this form. The zero property of multiplication is shown by zero bottle caps in the first row and the left column. The identity property for multiplication is shown by the observation that the second row and second column are identical to the factors across the top and down the side of the table. The commutative property is shown by the circled products: the expression 4×3 is the same as 3×4, the expression 2×3 is the same as 3×2, etc.

The property of zero should carefully be explored. As mentioned earlier, zero as a factor is difficult for children to understand. This is especially true for children who do not have a solid grasp of the concept of zero. Therefore, it is

FIGURE 6–15
These second grade children are making a numberless multiplication table by using bottle caps.

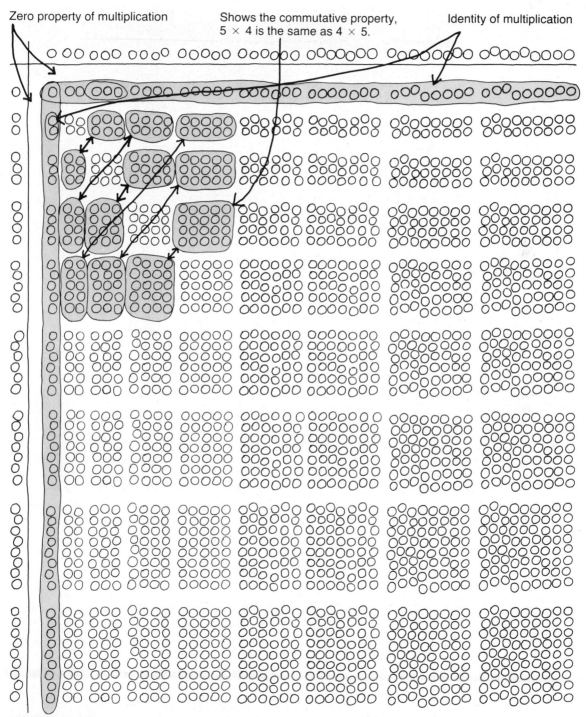

FIGURE 6–18
Exploring Properties on the Numberless Multiplication Table

With three, two,
one, and zero
groups of 5

With three, two, one,
and zero groups of 4

FIGURE 6–19
Property of Zero

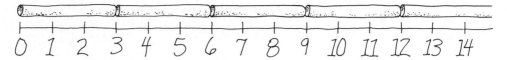

FIGURE 6–20
Using Straws for Skip Counting on the Number Line

Straws or popsicle sticks cut to a specified multiple of the "unit" length can be laid along the number line to show skip counting as repeated addition. See Figure 6–20.

Sometimes arrows are used to show skip counting on the number line, but this is not recommended for young children. Arrows can have different meanings and are a possible source of confusion for children. The arrows at the end of the number line mean that it continues indefinitely. Arrows shown on "jumps" have a completely different meaning. Consider showing the jumps without arrows, as in Figure 6–21.

A suggested alternative to using a number line is to use a number strip. To make a number strip numbers are written in blocks of a uniform size and placed end to end. A classroom-size strip could be made from index cards and taped together; an individual strip could be made from strips of graph paper that were cut and taped end to end.

When children skip count they can be helped to imagine a strip much longer than the finite one being used. In fact, a class project might be to make a very long number strip.

Since multiplication is the inverse operation of division, the information presented in the previous sections can be applied to the teaching and learning of division.

BASIC DIVISION FACTS

Since division is the most difficult operation for children to learn, the division facts are the hardest for them to understand and memorize. The following sections bring attention to the critical factors about teaching and learning division facts. Emphasis should be placed on helping the child recall and use already constructed understandings in subtraction and multiplication. Building on previous understanding will facilitate the child's construction of a

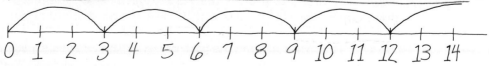

FIGURE 6–21
The Number Line Without Arrows

stable understanding of division as well as the child's memorization of division facts. As always, encourage children to take time to think and reflect.

Learning Division Facts

The basic division facts can be derived from the basic multiplication facts. For example, $12 \div 3 = 4$ is related to the basic multiplication sentences of $4 \times 3 = 12$ and $3 \times 4 = 12$. Similarly, $30 \div 5 = 6$ has $5 \times 6 = 30$ and $6 \times 5 = 30$ as related multiplication sentences.

Although it isn't appropriate for children to consider zero immediately at the beginning of their study of division, it is important that the teacher be prepared to discuss division by zero if the question arises. Consider $4 \div 0 = ?$ and its related multiplication sentences: $? \times 0 = 4$ and $0 \times ? = 4$.

The problem with these sentences is that there is no number to replace "?" with to make the sentences true. Consider the number sentence $0 \div 0 = ?$ Does $0 \div 0 = 1$? If so, the related multiplication sentences would be $0 \times 1 = 0$ and $1 \times 0 = 0$, which are true. Further exploration would show that *any* number would make the sentence true, that is, $0 \div 0 =$ any number. Unfortunately, this discovery is inconsistent with the way operations are defined! That is, there is supposed to be only one answer to this type of problem. Therefore, division by zero is meaningless and should be avoided.

Order of Teaching Division Facts

The best order for teaching basic division facts will probably parallel the order in which the basic multiplication facts were taught. Let's look at the choices. Basic division facts can be taught using division tables or families of facts. A family of basic division facts is composed of pairs of factors whose products are the same. For example, the family of facts for 12 are 2×6; 6×2; 3×4; and 4×3. Of course, 1×12 and 12×1 represent two other pairs of factors. Since multiplication is commutative, the commuted pair for each pair of factors does not need to be emphasized but should be included when basic division facts are first introduced.

One method of teaching division facts is to present them in the form of missing factor problems. For example, the sentence $3 \times ? = 12$ is a missing factor problem. The child must determine what number times 3 yields 12. As previously mentioned, the missing factor approach is very abstract. However, there are two thinking situations that can be used to determine the missing factor. The first situation is the measurement situation discussed earlier in this chapter. The child starts with 12 objects and subtracts groups of 3 objects, then counts the number of groups subtracted.

The other possibility is the partitive situation. For this situation, the child needs to have 3 locations or partitions into which 12 objects would be placed. Then, the number of objects at each location would be the missing factor—now the "found factor."

The missing factor model for division is a very attractive choice because it is tied so closely with multiplication and should, presumably, be easier for teachers to teach and for students to learn. However, there are some difficulties with this model that are not readily apparent. Most of the difficulties occur at the time children are learning the standard long division algorithm in the third and fourth grade. Sometimes if the missing factor model for division is the only model taught, it hampers the student's effectiveness at performing long division.

Properties

The commutative property and the associative property do not hold for the operation of division. Children can be led to understand this fact with some simple examples. For example, ask a child to find $12 \div 4$. Then, ask if the same result is obtained by finding $4 \div 12$. If the child is asked to model the two situations, the outcome should be especially clear. Similarly, modeling two simple problems such as $(24 \div 6) \div 2$ and $24 \div (6 \div 2)$ will show that division is not associative.

What about the distributive property? Consider the expression $12 \div (2 + 3)$. This expression can be rewritten as $(12 \div 2) + (12 \div 3) = 6 + 4 = 10$. The expression $12 \div (2 + 3)$ does not equal $12 \div 5$. However, the right distributive property will work—consider $(6 + 4) \div 2$, where $(6 \div 2) + (4 \div 2) = 10 \div 2$.

Horizontal and Vertical Forms for Division Facts

There are three forms for division, two horizontal forms and one vertical form. The expression $8 \div 4$ is read "eight divided by four," which corresponds to the way sentences are read—from left to right. However, the other horizontal form $4\overline{)8}$ is read either "four into eight" or eight divided by four," (which is right to left). Great care must be exercised to provide practice translating from one form to the other and to make sure the language of each is correct. A child who must learn the long division algorithm does not need to become confused about terminology! For instance, the problem $849 \div 23$ should be translated into $23\overline{)849}$ so that the problem can be solved. A child who has been taught to carefully translate $849 \div 23$ to $23\overline{)849}$ will be more successful translating the problem back to its original form $849 \div 23$.

The form $a \div b = c$ is generally presented during concept formation. Although the form

$$\frac{c}{a\overline{)b}}$$

is not in the form of a sentence, it is also used during concept formation. This second form is used for the long division algorithm, where the numbers involved take the student beyond the basic division facts.

The long form for this notation is initially read from right to left ("*b* divided by *a*"). However, when numbers appear below the initial problem statement, the child's eyes are scanning from top to bottom, even though the grouping in the dividend is done from left to right (for example, from 100 to 10 to 1). So, even though children are trained to read and write from left to right, here they are being asked to use a form that requires right-to-left reading as well as top-to-bottom writing. The vertical form

$$\frac{a}{b} = c$$

is clearly a number sentence, but it is sometimes read without indicating division; that is, it is read "*a* over *b* equals *c*." This form is useful when teaching rational numbers and should be introduced after the two other forms have been well established.

Multiplication Table and Division Facts

The multiplication table, beginning with the numberless form in the second grade, can be useful for learning the basic division facts. Children should be given a product (dividend) and a factor (divisor) and asked to find the other factor (quotient). For example, given the problem $24 \div 8$, the students should be shown how to find the factor 3 from the table by first locating the 8 row and the product 24. Then, the 3 is found at the top of the table, above the product of 24, as marked in Figure 6–22.

Because division by 0 is undefined, there are fewer division facts for children to learn than multiplication facts.

The division facts $8 \div 4 = 2$ and $0 \div 3 = 0$ can be found on the multiplication table. However, so can $3 \div 0$ and $0 \div 0$, which are not to be considered division facts. For this reason, the teacher should use the multiplication table very carefully. Consider covering part of the table with paper strips to avoid such difficulties.

Number Line

Just as the number line was used to introduce multiplication through repeated addition, a number line can also be used to model division as repeated subtraction. Where the multiplication model moved from left to right on the number line, division moves from right to left. By this time, students have had ample opportunity to understand the number line as a model; there shouldn't be a need to start with a numberless line. Figure 6–23 shows that the bunny takes 5 hops that are 3 units each to go from the number 15 to the origin. Figure 6–24 shows the turtle going 3 blocks at a time (before resting!). So the turtle must make four 3-block trips to go from 12 to the origin.

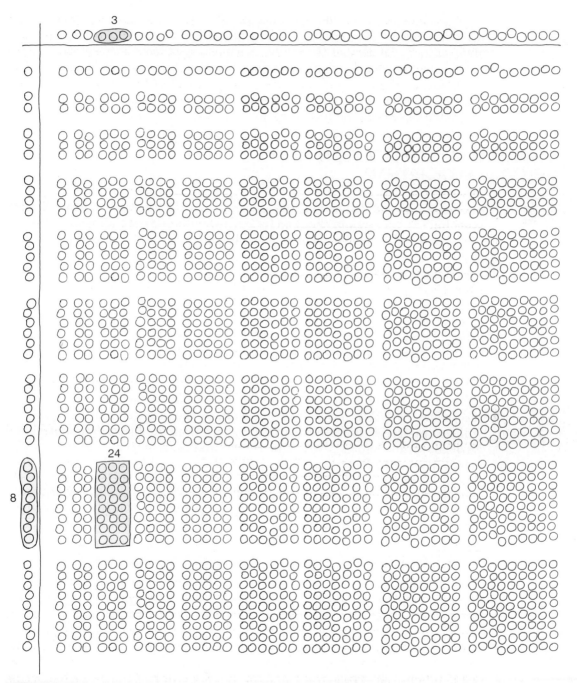

FIGURE 6–22
The Division Fact 24 ÷ 8 = 3 on the Numberless Multiplication Table

Remember that children's understanding of what division means and where the division facts come from supports their efforts to memorize the basic division facts. Remember that children's mastery of facts is one of the keys to their learning the division algorithm. The teacher must be aware of the difficulties children might have when switching from the horizontal to the vertical division forms. Teachers should also know how to use the multiplication table in order to help children discover the division facts.

LEARNING MULTIPLICATION AND DIVISION ALGORITHMS

The standard multiplication and division algorithms can be learned in a meaningless, rote way or they can be learned with understanding and insight. Children need to understand how such long, involved procedures lead to correct results. In multiplication and division, particularly at first, place-value charts can be just as helpful as they were when children were learning the addition and subtraction algorithms. Place-value charts support the use of vertical notation for learning the algorithms. For both algorithms, as with addition and subtraction, a working knowledge of place value is critical. There is no point in teaching the meaning behind these algorithms if the learners are not proficient with place-value concepts. If learners are not proficient, it is necessary to review and reteach place-value concepts.

There is no perfect representational model to use to demonstrate these procedures—each has its strengths and weaknesses. What is important is that the teacher be so familiar with the model he or she chooses, that the end result will be children's successful learning experiences. Addition and subtraction were shown in chapter 5 with the use of bundles, a proportional place-value model. By the time multiplication and division have been learned, children should be able to progress to a nonproportional model, such as chips, when working with larger numbers. Depending on its location on a place-value chart, one chip would represent 10 or 100. Recall that a bundle of 10 sticks looked like 10 and a bundle of 100 sticks looked like 100. In contrast, a chip does not look like 10 or 100. (Reread the section on proportional and nonproportional models in chapter 4.) For children with special needs, the

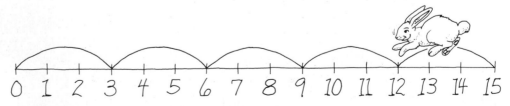

FIGURE 6–23
The Division Fact 15 ÷ 3 = 5 on the Number Line

proportional models may be best for modeling the early development of the multiplication algorithm. A nonproportional model would be less clumsy, but the teacher needs to be certain that children have really grasped the meaning of the nonproportional model before he or she develops algorithms using it.

As with addition and subtraction, the teacher should identify prerequisite objectives when developing multiplication and division algorithms. (See the Instructional Planner at the end of this chapter for the multiplication and division objectives.) As with addition and subtraction, there is some variability within the hierarchies of objectives. Teachers must exercise good judgment to determine the best order of concepts, facts, properties, procedures, and algorithms. The following plan is recommended:

1. Get the children involved in reviewing basic multiplication and division facts with the manipulative materials that will be used to develop the algorithm. Chips are used in the illustrations that follow. First, review the facts that do not require regrouping of chips, then review those that do require regrouping.

2. Initially, do each kind of problem manipulatively. Your demonstration should be accompanied by discussion, but without the corresponding written work (Type 1). The discussion should concern a meaningful situation, in the form of a verbal problem, for which chips can be used to act the situation out.

Next, use the corresponding written work to accompany the concrete representation of the problem (Type 2). Finally, the children will be prepared for drill and practice without any manipulatives present (Type 3). Fourth grade topics can be taught in earlier grades if limited to Type 1 or Type 2 activities. For a review of the Type 1, 2, and 3 experiences, see chapter 3.

3. As the process becomes familiar, pictures of the manipulatives may be shown. The disadvantage in using pictures is that it eliminates any interaction with the model. Another disadvantage is that the model can be quite complex to show in picture form. In particular, it is difficult to represent the action on a model in picture form. Showing action on models is often attempted in textbook and workbook pages and is, in many cases, very confusing. Perhaps the best pictures are those in children's minds obtained from the actual action

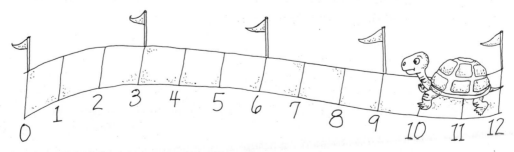

FIGURE 6–24
The Division 12 ÷ 3 = 4 on the Number Line

on the model! Instead of using pictures that are labeled with symbols, have children express their concrete interpretation of a problem with symbols. Or, as in Figure 6–25, give children a problem and have them express it on a place-value chart using a place-value model. These third-grade boys are solving 2 × 16 with bottle caps on a place-value chart. They called it their "bottle cap computer."

4. The use of intermediate algorithms is suggested for each operation. These algorithms are "intermediate" to learning the standard algorithm. The following problem shows the use of an intermediate multiplication algorithm.

Problem: There are 23 cards with 5 seashells glued on each card. How many seashells are there altogether?

$$
\begin{array}{ccc}
23 & 23 & 23 \\
\underline{\times\ 5} & \underline{\times\ 5} & \underline{\times\ 5} \\
15 & 15 & 15 \quad \text{partial} \\
 & \underline{100} & \underline{100} \quad \text{products} \\
 & & 115 \\
\textit{Step 1} & \textit{Step 2} & \textit{Step 3}
\end{array}
$$

In *Step 1*, the number of shells on 3 cards is found.
In *Step 2*, the number of shells on the remaining 20 cards is found.
In *Step 3*, the number of shells on 23 cards is found.

Step 1 sets up the problem and shows the partial product of 15—derived from 5 times 3. (Some authorities recommend starting with an expanded form.) Step 2 shows the other partial product of 100—derived from 5 times 20. Use of this intermediate algorithm draws more attention to place value than the standard algorithm. Notice that 5 times 20 was computed, not 5 times 2. Another advantage of the intermediate algorithm is that it corresponds to children's previous experiences with finding products. That is, whenever children were asked to record a product, they placed the product below the problem statement, as shown in Step 3. The standard algorithm, which is more efficient and uses shortcuts, permits a small notation above the problem to help keep track of partial products.

$$
\begin{array}{c}
1 \\
23 \\
\underline{\times\ 5} \\
115
\end{array}
$$

A "little" 1 is "carried" to the tens place in the standard algorithm. To an adult who is familiar with the standard algorithm, that procedure seems "natural and easy." To a child, it seems unnatural.

Two intermediate algorithms suggested for preparing children for the standard algorithm for division are the *scaffold* and the *stacking* algorithms.

Both algorithms represent repeated subtraction, which is the measurement thinking model. First, consider the scaffold algorithm. The version on the left of the following example shows the work of a child who estimates and on the right is the work of a child who shows exact values. Notice that both solutions are correct.

Problem: If you had 137 seashells that you wanted to display on cards in groups of 4 seashells per card, how many cards would you need?

$$
\begin{array}{ll}
4\overline{)137} & \\
\underline{80} & 20 \times 4 \\
57 & \\
\underline{56} & 14 \times 4 \\
1 & 34 \qquad \text{R } 1
\end{array}
\qquad\qquad
\begin{array}{ll}
4\overline{)137} & \\
\underline{120} & 30 \times 4 \\
17 & \\
\underline{16} & 4 \times 4 \\
1 & 34 \qquad \text{R } 1
\end{array}
$$

The problem is now shown in step form.

$$
\begin{array}{l}
\textit{Step 1} \\
4\overline{)137} \\
\underline{120} \quad 30 \times 4
\end{array}
\qquad
\begin{array}{l}
\textit{Step 2} \\
4\overline{)137} \\
\underline{120} \quad 30 \times 4 \\
17 \\
\underline{16} \quad 4 \times 4 \\
1
\end{array}
\qquad
\begin{array}{l}
\textit{Step 3} \\
4\overline{)137} \\
\underline{120} \quad 30 \times 4 \\
17 \\
\underline{16} \quad 4 \times 4 \\
1 \quad 34 \quad \text{R } 1
\end{array}
$$

FIGURE 6–25
These third graders are solving 2 × 16 by using bottle caps on a place-value chart.

The answer is 34 cards will be needed or 35 cards will be needed, depending on what is decided about the remaining shell.

Step 1 showed how many seashells can go on 30 cards. Step 2 showed how many shells can go on 4 more cards. Step 3 showed how many cards are needed with 1 shell left over. The teacher and students can decide if they want to put the extra shell on a separate card, for a total of 35 cards, or to put the extra shell on one of the 34 cards, thus giving one card a total of 5 shells instead of 4. This decision-making process can be an opportunity for lively discussion by the whole group.

The other intermediate division algorithm, which also uses the measurement situation, is the stacking algorithm. This algorithm works essentially the same way as the scaffold algorithm does, but instead stacks the partial factors in the same location as the answer in the standard algorithm. The following is an illustration of the stacking algorithm using the same problem with seashells.

$$
\begin{array}{r}
34 \\
4 \quad \text{partial} \\
30 \quad \text{factors} \\
\hline
4\overline{)137} \\
120 \\
\hline
17 \\
16 \\
\hline
1 \quad \text{remainder}
\end{array}
$$

given factor

Step 1 sets up the problem and shows 30 as the first partial factor. The number 120 is recorded as the product of the given factor 4 and the first partial factor 30. Step 2 shows the difference between 137 and 120 and the next partial factor 4. Step 3 shows the sum of the partial factors, 34, and the remainder of 1. The answer is 34 with a remainder of 1.

Notice on the left of the following display how both the scaffold and stacking algorithms can be combined into one algorithm, and how the stacking algorithm can be abbreviated as shown. However, be careful not to make things too complicated for the young learner!

$$
\begin{array}{r}
4 \\
30 \\
\hline
4\overline{)137} \\
120 \quad 30 \times 4 \\
\hline
17 \\
16 \quad 4 \times 4 \\
\hline
1 \quad 34 \quad \text{R } 1
\end{array}
\qquad
\begin{array}{r}
34 \\
\hline
4\overline{)137} \\
120 \quad 30 \times 4 \\
\hline
17 \\
16 \quad 4 \times 4 \\
\hline
1 \quad 34 \quad \text{R } 1
\end{array}
$$

Combination of stacking and scaffolding   Shorter version of stacking in combination with scaffolding

The result is 34 with remainder 1. The following is the standard form.

$$\begin{array}{r} 34 \quad \text{R } 1 \\ 4\overline{)137} \\ \underline{120} \\ 17 \\ \underline{16} \\ 1 \end{array}$$

Notice the attention given to place-value by the placement of the 0 as well as the position of the 34.

Now, consider a partitive situation that uses the same basic information and the standard form.

Problem: How many seashells can be displayed in each of four posters if there are 137 shells in the collection? The same number of shells should be on each card.

Step 1	*Step 2*	*Step 3*
$\begin{array}{r}0\\4\overline{)137}\end{array}$	$\begin{array}{r}3\\4\overline{)137}\\\underline{120}\end{array}$	$\begin{array}{r}34\\4\overline{)137}\\\underline{120}\\17\\\underline{16}\\1\end{array}$

Step 1

Question: How many groups of 100 shells are on *each* of the 4 posters?
Answer: Zero.
Record: Write 0 in the hundreds place. (Zero can eventually be eliminated.)

Step 2

Question: How many groups of 10 shells are on *each* of the 4 posters?
Answer: Three.
Record: Write 3 in the tens place.

Step 3

Question: How many groups of "individual" shells are on each of the four posters?
Answer: Four with one remaining.
Record: Write four in the ones place and make a note that one is the remainder.

5. Eventually, children should learn the standard multiplication and division algorithms to complete work more efficiently and to solve more generalized problems. Which thinking situation is used in the standard algorithm? Rapid application of the division algorithm should be done without

having to refer to a particular thinking model. However, reasonableness of results could be checked using either model.

An intermediate algorithm without a problem context

$$
\begin{array}{r}
12\overline{)156} \\
120 \quad 10 \times 12 \\
\overline{36} \\
\underline{36} \quad \underline{3 \times 12} \\
13
\end{array}
$$

A standard algorithm without a problem context

$$
\begin{array}{r}
13 \\
12\overline{)156} \\
\underline{12} \\
36 \\
\underline{36}
\end{array}
$$

OVERVIEW OF TEACHING THE MULTIPLICATION ALGORITHM

The place-value chart was used in addition and subtraction of whole numbers and is a familiar format for children. Therefore, it is wise to start the multiplication algorithm with a place-value chart. In order to use a place-value chart, the thinking model of repeated addition is needed. Please see the overview of the addition algorithm given in chapter 5.

Three objectives for teaching the multiplication algorithm have been selected to illustrate this overview. Each objective is shown in the context of Type 1, 2, and 3 experiences. Figure 6–26 illustrates multiplying a multiple of 10 less than 100 times a one-digit number without regrouping. Figure 6–27 illustrates multiplying a multiple of 10 less than 100 times a one-digit number with regrouping. Figure 6–28 illustrates multiplying a two-digit number and a multiple of 10 less than 100. Notice the intermediate algorithm used in Figure 6–28. The Instructional Planner for Multiplication and Division includes other objectives that do not have accompanying figures.

In Figure 6–28, notice that since 20 is a multiple of 10 both digits of the first factor of 43 are "shifted" one column to the left. The result is 430, which shows that 43 has been multiplied by 10. Then, the 430 is doubled to show that it is multiplied by 2. The digit 2 comes from the 20, which equals 10×2. This procedure should not be rote but instead it should develop out of showing the complete arrays as in Figure 6–27. After children understand the underlying reason for the movement of chips or bottle caps, they can take the shortcut of shifting the multiplicand to indicate when it is multiplied by 10 or 100.

OBJECTIVE: Multiplying Multiples of 10 Less than 100 by One-Digit Numbers
Without Regrouping
EXAMPLE: 40
                 $\times$ 2

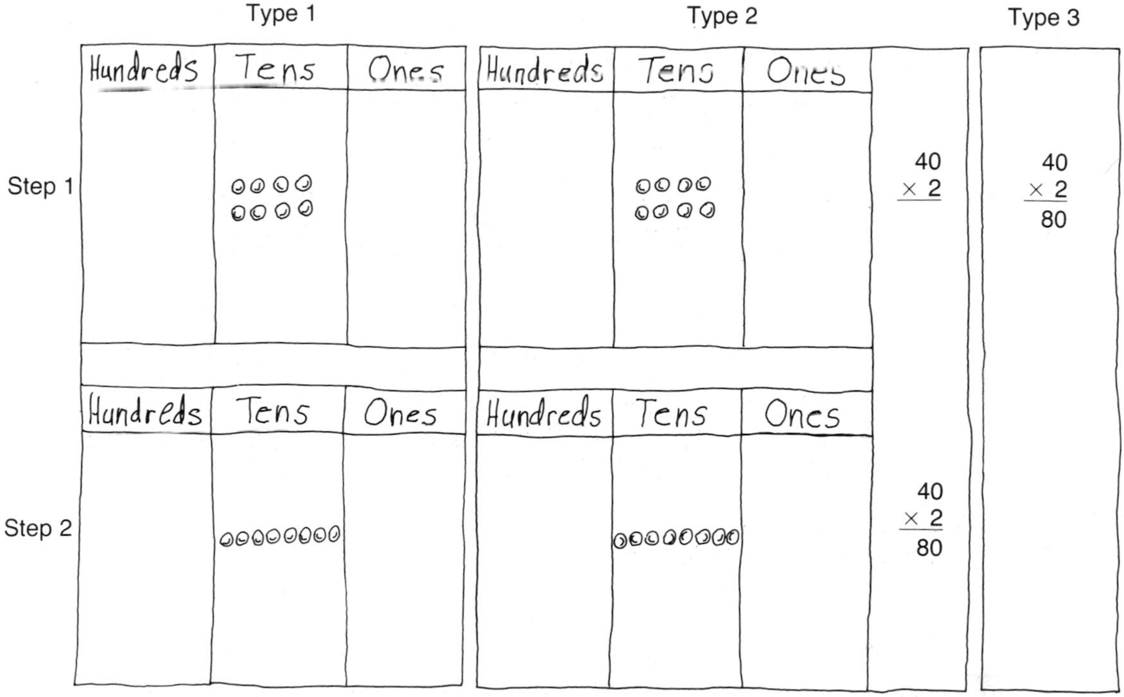

FIGURE 6–26

At this point, the concrete representations of multiplication situations are rapidly becoming too cumbersome for extended use. The connection between real objects and symbols should be well established before proceeding. With this connection established it is an appropriate time to start emphasizing intermediate algorithms as a means of bridging the gap between the concepts of multiplication and the standard algorithm. Place-value concepts are also reinforced by these intermediate algorithms. (See the discussion of intermediate algorithms earlier in this chapter.)

OVERVIEW OF TEACHING THE DIVISION ALGORITHM

Since multiplication has been learned using a place-value chart, one way to start the division process is in the same familiar setting. The emphasis that the chart gives to place value is important for the children's understanding of the positioning of symbols in both intermediate and standard algorithms.

OBJECTIVE: Multiplying Multiples of 10 Less Than 100 by One-Digit Numbers
with Regrouping

EXAMPLE: 40
                $\times$ 4

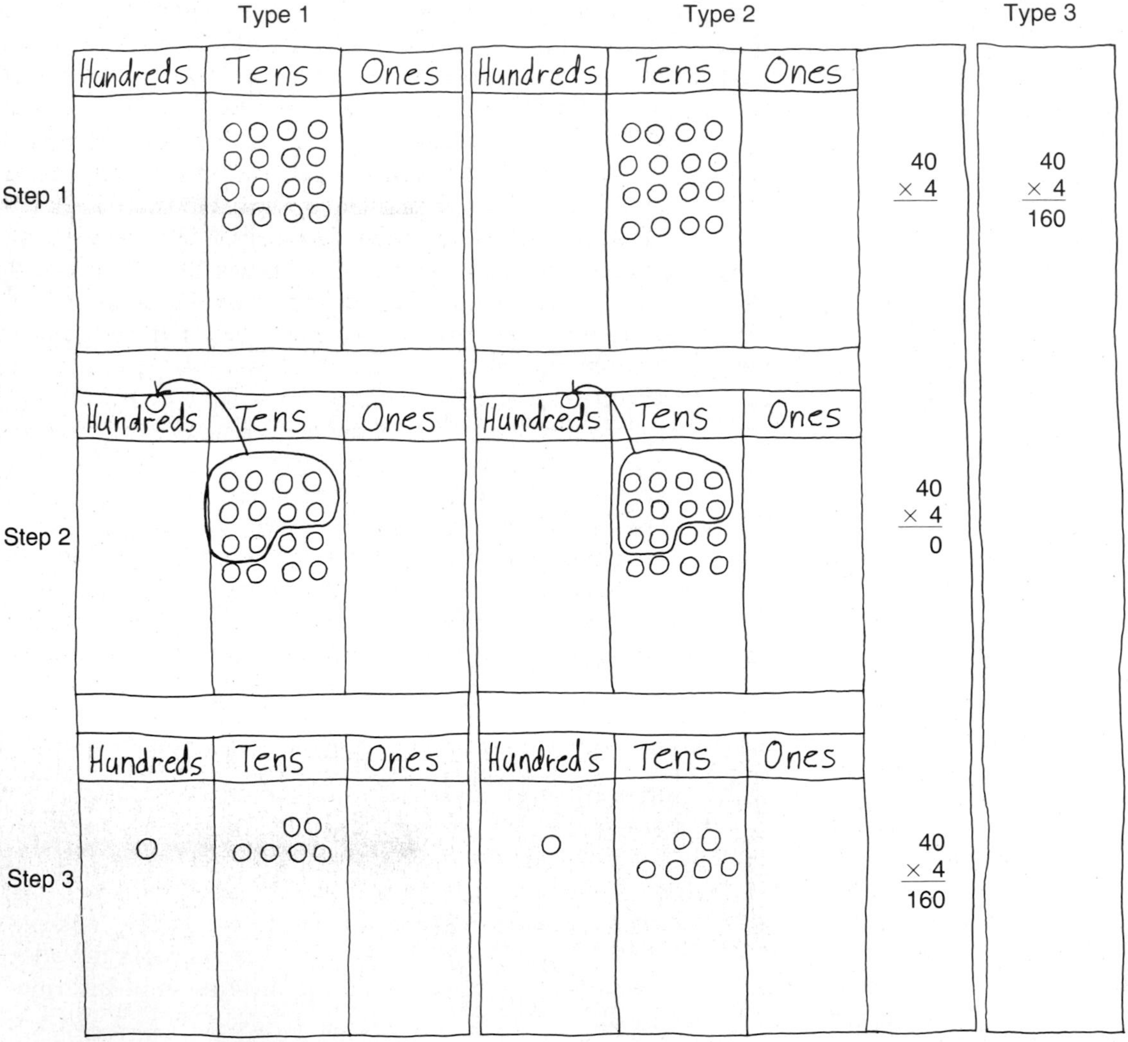

FIGURE 6–27

Two objectives for teaching the division algorithms have been selected to illustrate this overview. As with multiplication, both are shown in the context of Type 1, 2, and 3 experiences. Figure 6–29 illustrates a basic division fact and Figure 6–30 illustrates dividing a three-digit number by a two-digit number. Explanation of the intermediate algorithm shown in Figure 6–30 can

OBJECTIVE: Multiplying Two-Digit Numbers by Multiples of 10 Less Than 100
Without Regrouping

EXAMPLE: 43
           × 20

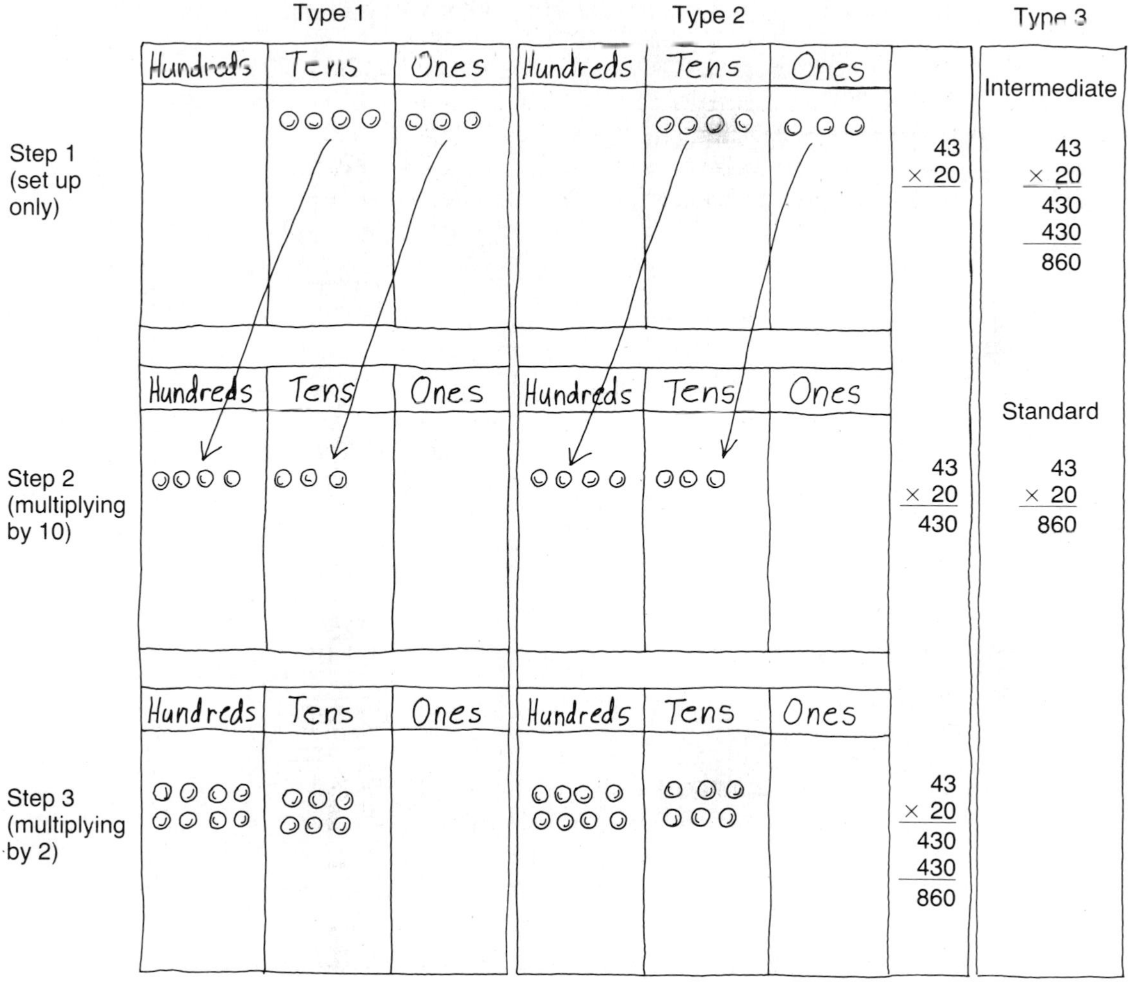

FIGURE 6–28

be reviewed in the section *Learning Multiplication and Division Algorithms*. The measurement thinking model is used in these examples, which asks the question "Given a certain number of elements in each group, how many groups are there?" The Instructional Planner includes some other objectives that do not have accompanying figures.

OBJECTIVE: Starting with Basic Division Facts to Learn the Division Algorithm
EXAMPLE: 5)‾35‾

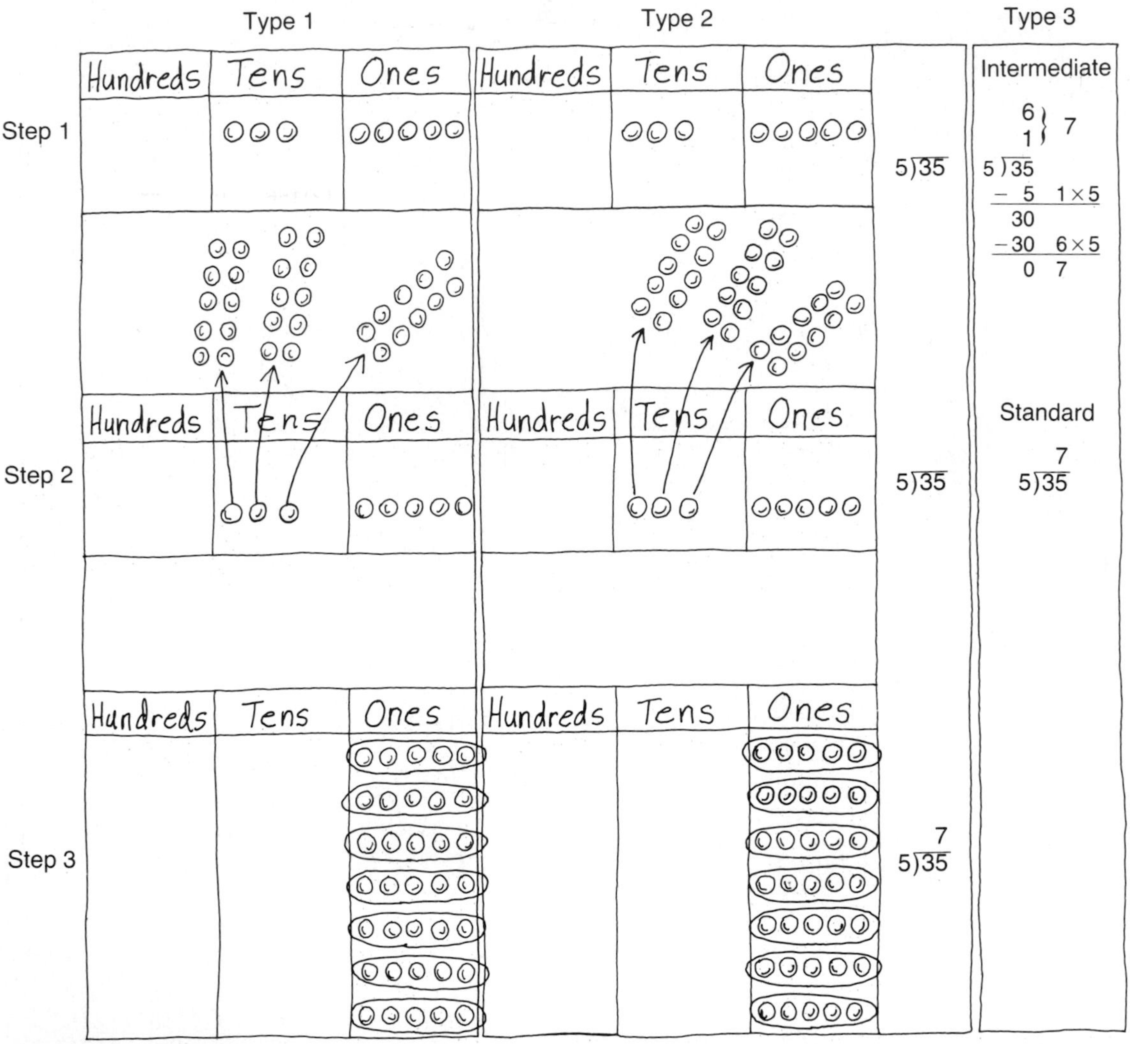

FIGURE 6–29

USING THE CALCULATOR TO LEARN MULTIPLICATION AND DIVISION

The calculator is even more useful in teaching the concepts of multiplication and division than it is with addition and subtraction. At this point, the children know so much more both about numbers and the calculator. The teacher should capitalize on the use of this tool as much as possible—especially

OBJECTIVE: Dividing a Three-Digit Number by a Two-Digit Number
EXAMPLE: 12)156

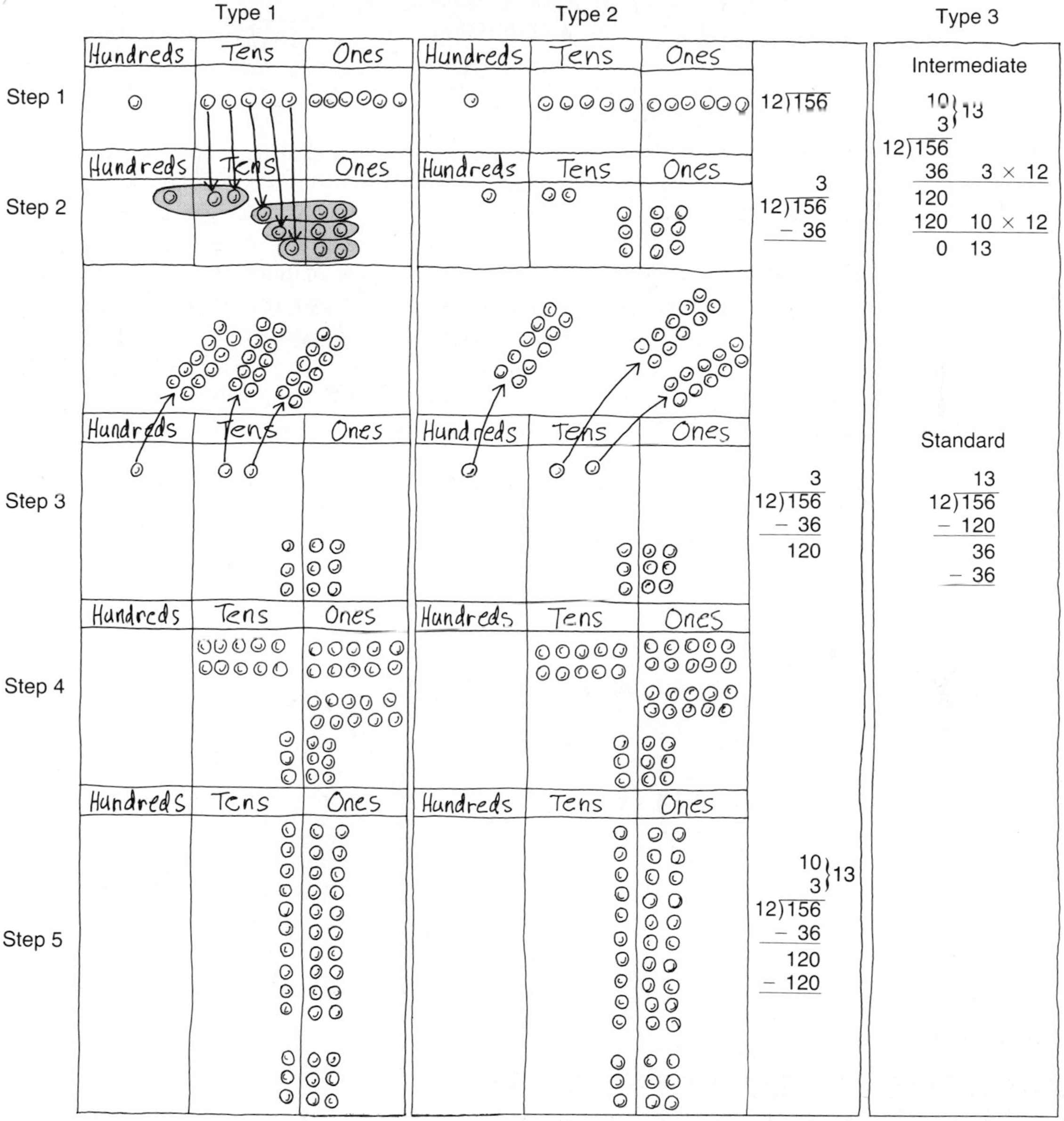

FIGURE 6–30

Note: This model lends itself to the intermediate algorithm, but not the standard algorithm.

since using the calculator and estimating will be the primary means of obtaining solutions in the real world. The following section looks at how the calculator can be used in concept formation, with basic facts, and with algorithms in multiplication and division.

Concept Formation

Starting in the first and second grades, the calculator can be used as a means of showing repeated addition for multiplication or repeated subtraction for division. By adding a constant and counting the number of times it is entered, children can find the results of problems that would not otherwise be reasonable for them to try. Early in the process of learning multiplication, children can demonstrate 2×30 with manipulatives and/or pencil and paper algorithms. However, some students might like to explore by finding 20×30. This problem can be done with repeated addition of a constant number using a calculator. Similarly, division can be explored by using repeated subtraction of a constant number from a dividend that has been entered into the calculator. The number of times that the constant is added or deducted will yield the answer. By this time, children will be able to use the constant function as shown in the following example. Children should be assisted in interpreting the procedure if the last "deduction" results in any number other than 0.

Problem: $3 \times 17 = ?$			*Problem:* $24 \div 8 = ?$		
ENTER:	DISPLAY:		ENTER:	DISPLAY:	
17	17	once	24	24	
$\times$	17		$-$	24	
17	17		8	8	
$=$	34	twice	$=$	16	once
$=$	51	three times	$=$	8	twice
			$=$	0	three times

Answer: $3 \times 17 = 51$ *Answer:* $24 \div 8 = 3$

Problem: $24 \div 7 = ?$		
ENTER:	DISPLAY:	
24	24	
$-$	24	
7	7	
$=$	17	once
$=$	10	twice
$=$	3	three times

Answer: $24 \div 7 = 3$, R 3

Basic Facts

Using a calculator to drill and practice the basic multiplication facts and basic division facts is often beneficial. Children can be encouraged to guess a product or quotient and verify their results using the calculator. In this way, estimation and basic facts can be reinforced concurrently.

Algorithms

The calculator can be invaluable as a tool for helping children master the standard and intermediate algorithms for multiplication and division. For example, if a child is asked to compute 28×136, the result of multiplying 136 by 8 can be verified as correct or incorrect using the calculator. Then, the result of multiplying 136 by 20 can be verified thereby reinforcing the place-value concepts upon which the standard algorithm is based. These products can also be added to verify that the final results of the pencil-and-paper algorithm are correct. Using a calculator when exploring long division can be especially helpful. Consider the following example.

```
  19)2368          19 into 2400 can be estimated and checked
      124
  19)2368
     1900
      468          19 into 468 can be estimated and checked
      380
       88          19 into 88 can be estimated and checked
       76
       12
```

In this problem, 19 into 2368 can be estimated by using rounding to the nearest 10 and 1000, respectively. The estimated results can be checked using the calculator, which reinforces estimation skills. Checking long division problems or long multiplication problems using the inverse procedures is time-consuming, whereas, using a calculator to check results is much easier and is more likely to be done. It is important to use calculators to build understanding, not just to verify paper-and-pencil work. Children quickly learn the futility of using calculators *only* to check results and they resent it.

USING THE COMPUTER TO LEARN ABOUT MULTIPLICATION AND DIVISION

Criteria used to select and use computer software for multiplication and division should be no different than the criteria used to select and use other instructional materials. A piece of software that fits well with the objectives in the Instructional Planner for Multiplication and Division of Whole Numbers should be sought. You also need to consider the level of sophistication of vocabulary and symbols as well as the appropriateness of the pace. In addition, as mentioned in chapter 3, it is important to consider how meaningful and how concrete the software's manipulative activities are. An overriding concern when selecting computer software should be whether it helps make mathematical thinking purposeful and helps commit the learner to the pursuit of understanding (Pea, 1987).

There are numerous commercially prepared programs that offer exciting and thorough practice for multiplication and division facts. Also, there are programs that give children opportunities to practice the long multiplication algorithm and the long division algorithm. When selecting software, the teacher needs to preview it carefully to ensure that the programs are demanding enough—but not too demanding—for the level of the children. Few teachers would be able to write programs that are more effective or more fun than those available on the market. However, for a special situation, children might benefit from teacher-written programs that directly address their special needs. For example, you might want to write a short program to help some children practice specific multiplication facts.

When exploring the concept of multiplication, children can become confused by the scientific notation used by most calculators to handle results that "overflow" the display. The computer can then be used as a calculating tool to display products (or any other results) that require more display digits than are available on hand-held calculators.

ESTIMATION AND PROBLEM SOLVING

At this stage, the primary emphasis of problem solving should be teaching children to identify a multiplication or division situation from other situations. Emphasis on children's ability to act out and to model situations is important. The teacher should be aware that the word problems at the end of the multiplication and division sections in standard textbooks are "problems" only for awhile. These word problems soon become exercises whose purpose is practicing the algorithms instead of problem solving. To answer these exercises children quickly develop a group of set responses that hinder them greatly in future problem-solving situations. Problems that can be solved by multiplication and division should be intermixed, so that children can choose an appropriate method of solution. For example, suppose a problem asks how many rows with 5 chairs per row are needed to seat 30 people. One child might go directly to division by writing the expression $30 \div 5 = 6$ rows of chairs.

Another child might solve the problem through multiplication by doing the following.

5 rows × 5 chairs per row is 25 chairs
6 rows × 5 chairs per row is 30 chairs, so 6 rows will be needed

Some nonstandard approaches might also be used:

3 rows × 5 chairs per row = 15 chairs
15 chairs + 15 chairs = 30 chairs, so 6 rows will be needed

Therefore, it will take 3 rows and 3 more rows or 6 rows to get 30 chairs. A wise teacher will not insist on only one "right" approach to a problem, but will give every child an opportunity to solve the problem in his or her own fashion. The teacher should watch for errors in concepts and help students make needed corrections without making them feel stupid! As long as children have concepts correct and are applying them creatively, their problem-solving approaches should not be "dictated" by the teacher. Students should be encouraged to discuss their methods of solution within groups so that all of the students' problem-solving abilities may be enriched. A positive teacher will openly recognize the validity of each correct approach to a problem, and will not make negative comments about slow or inefficient methods. In this way, students will feel comfortable in taking risks in problem solving.

In conclusion, the concepts and algorithms of multiplication and division that were presented in this chapter help form a basis for the child's higher mathematical reasoning and problem solving. The ideas presented are essential to real world living and problem solving as well as prerequisite to future mathematical learning. Children should be able to reflect and think about what they know and what they can do. They should be able to participate with the teacher in stabilizing and coordinating their understandings about the four operations presented in this and the previous chapters. Children should memorize their facts, know the algorithms, and be able to use the calculator and estimation to solve problems.

SUMMARY

This chapter covered multiplication and division concepts. Suggestions for helping children learn the basic facts and explore properties were presented. The development of transitional and traditional algorithms for multiplication and division was approached from a perspective of "meaningfulness." The role of place-value concepts in the understanding of algorithms was emphasized. Strategies for incorporating calculators and computers as well as for incorporating estimation and problem solving were discussed.

PLANNING FOR INSTRUCTION

The Instructional Planner for Multiplication and Division of Whole Numbers includes activities according to approximate age, type of learning, mathematical objective, and type of learning behaviors. These should be considered as possible examples of the kinds of experiences children should have while learning multiplication and division. Notice the heavy use of Type 1 and Type 2 activities. Emphasize *thinking*. Have children decide if they think their answers are right or wrong and why. Also, have small-group work where children share their ideas. Finally, encourage children to take their time with some activities. Too often, children think a good student is a fast student. Help them see by using these activities that a good student is a thinking student!

INSTRUCTIONAL PLANNER
Multiplication and Division of Whole Numbers

			Types of Behavior and Experiences			
Age	Types of Learning	Mathematical Objectives	Type 1 Concrete	Type 1 Pictorial	Type 2 Transitional	Type 3 Abstract
4–9	Concept Formation	Repeated Addition (for Multiplication)	1	1	1	1
		Arrays	2		2	3
4–9		Distributive Subtraction (for Division)	5		5	
4–9	Facts		2		2	
5–9		Repeated Subtraction (for Division)	4		4	
6–8	Properties	Commutative Property of Multiplication	6			
		Associative Property of Multiplication			7	
		Distributive Property of Multiplication over Addition	8, 9		8	
		Property of Zero				10
		Identity of Multiplication	11			

See pages 161–162

INSTRUCTIONAL PLANNER (continued)
Multiplication and Division of Whole Numbers

			Types of Behavior and Experiences			
Age	Types of Learning	Mathematical Objectives	Type 1 Concrete	Type 1 Pictorial	Type 2 Transitional	Type 3 Abstract
6–8	Algorithms	Multiplying a multiple of 10 less than 100 and a one-digit number without regrouping			Figure 6–26	
6–8		Multiplying a multiple of 10 less than 100 and a one-digit number with regrouping			Figure 6–27	
6–8		Multiplying a two-digit number and a one-digit number without regrouping				
6–8		Basic Division Facts			Figure 6–29	
6–9		Dividing a two-digit number by a two-digit number with a one-digit solution (factor)				
6–9		Dividing a three-digit number by a two-digit number			Figure 6–30	
6–9		Multiplying a multiple of 10 less than 100 by 10				
6–9		Multiplying a two-digit number and a multiple of 10 less than 100			Figure 6–28	

ACTIVITY 1

Type 1: Concrete

Age: 4–8

Objective: Concept formation for multiplication

Materials: Paper plates, saltine crackers

Instructions: The teacher and children put out one paper plate with four crackers on the plate. Discuss how many crackers there are. Then, the teacher asks for another paper plate with four crackers on it and discusses with the children how many crackers there are altogether. This procedure is continued until there are several plates with four crackers on each. Then, the teacher asks the students how many crackers were on each plate and how they found the total number of crackers each time. Repeat this same sequence with a different number of crackers on each plate.

Type 1: Pictorial Have students record the result of each successive addition by drawing pictures.

Type 2: Transitional Write the numbers for each addition to keep a record of multiples of the number of crackers on each plate.

Type 3: Abstract

$$4 = 4$$
$$4 + 4 = 8$$
$$4 + 4 + 4 = \underline{\hspace{1.5em}}$$
$$4 + 4 + 4 + 4 = \underline{\hspace{1.5em}}$$

ACTIVITY 2

Type 1: Concrete

Age: 4–9

Objective: Concept formation for multiplication and basic facts

Materials: String or tape, and counters such as beans or chips

Instructions: The teacher should mark the top and left borders of a "multiplication table" with tape or string. This activity can be done on a large table top or a marked-off portion of the floor (with plans to leave this portion of the floor as a display for some time). Then, the teacher arranges counters across the top of the upper border starting with one chip, two chips, three chips, . . . , nine chips as shown in Figure 6–14. The same procedure is used along the left border of the table. With some prompting from the teacher, children can take turns over a period of several days to "fill in" the rest of the table with arrays of chips or beans. This process continues until the table is filled with arrays of chips to form a numberless multiplication table.

Type 2: Transitional After the children have worked extensively with the numberless multiplication table, they can begin to use symbols with the table. Place cards on top of the arrays as shown. This activity can be done over a period of time. Do not remove the arrays of chips at this point because the children should be able to lift the cards to examine the arrays beneath as they do problems.

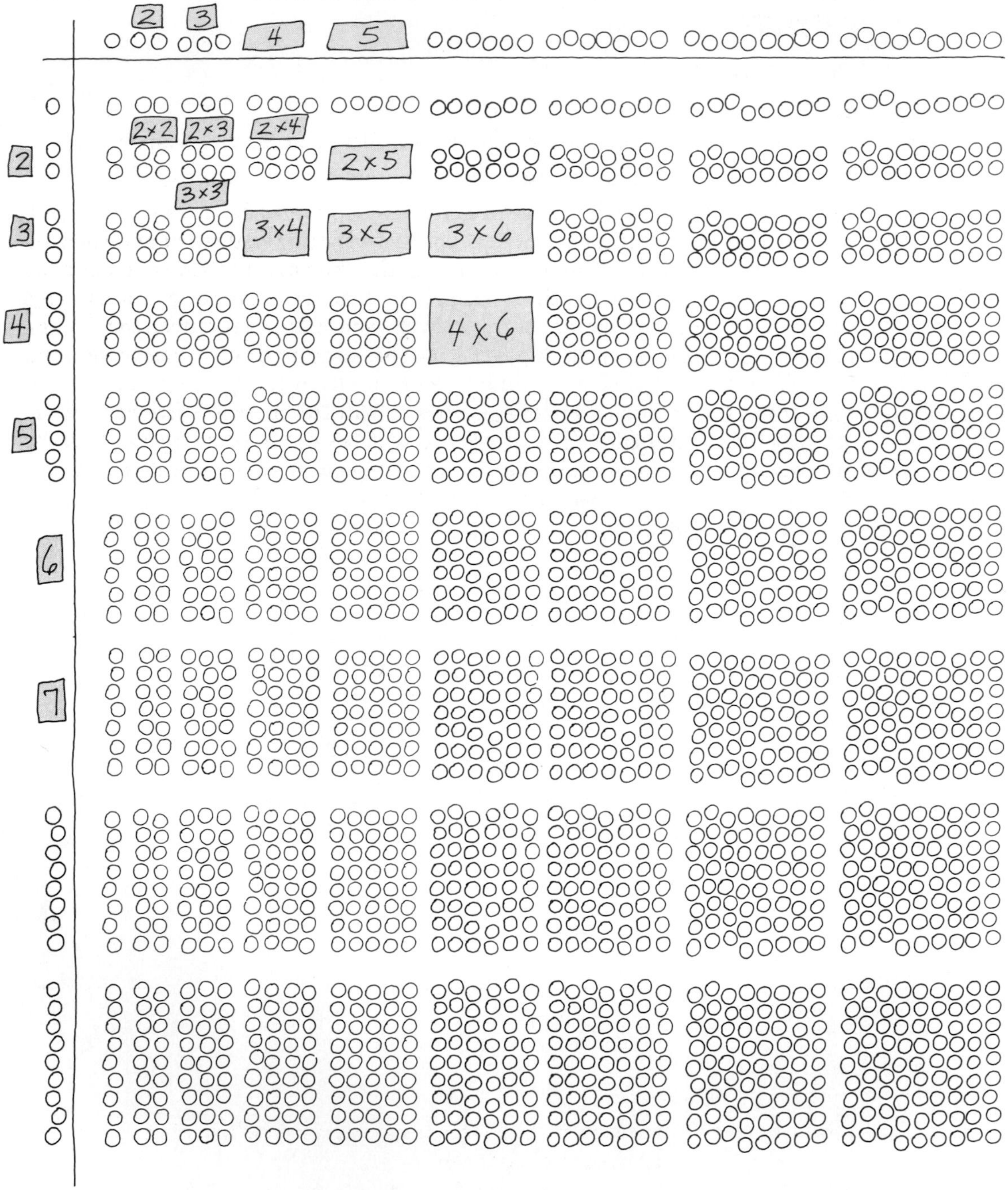
2
3
4
5
2×2
2×3
2×4
2×5
3×3
3×4
3×5
3×6
4×6
6
7

ACTIVITY 3

Type 3: Abstract

Age: 4–8

Objective: Concept formation for multiplication

Materials: Grid paper (2 cm squares)

Instructions: Have the children fill in the grid paper with numbers from 1 to 100, in rows of 10. Then have them count by twos (up to 10 twos) and color in each block they "land on." Have them examine the pattern that is forming on the grid. Ask questions like "Could this process be continued? If we counted by twos until we reached the end of the chart, how would the pattern look? What would these numbers be called? Are there any odd numbers that have been colored?"

This activity can be extended by using a new grid and coloring every three numbers (up to 30 or beyond), every four numbers (up to 40 or beyond), every five numbers (up to 50 or beyond), etc. Be sure to ask questions about the patterns formed by the colored number squares.

1	2	3	4	5	6	7	8	9	10
11	12	13	14	15	16	17	18	19	20
21	22	23	24	25	26	27	28	29	30
31	32	33	34	35	36	37	38	39	40
41	42	43	44	45	46	47	48	49	50
51	52	53	54	55	56	57	58	59	60
61	62	63	64	65	66	67	68	69	70
71	72	73	74	75	76	77	78	79	80
81	82	83	84	85	86	87	88	89	90
91	92	93	94	95	96	97	98	99	100

ACTIVITY 4

Type 1: Concrete

Age: 5–9

Objectives: Concept of division (using repeated subtraction) with and without remainders

Materials: Beans and soufflé cups

Instructions: Have the children count out 12 beans. Give them a stack of soufflé cups. Ask the children to take one soufflé cup and put 2 beans in it. Then, have them take another soufflé cup and put 2 beans in it, and so forth until all the beans are used. Ask the children how many soufflé cups were needed. Then, have the children try the same procedure with 9 beans. Discuss what can be done with the bean that is "remaining" or "left over." Ask them what they do when they are "dividing up" crayons or other objects and there are some "left over." Continue this activity with other amounts of beans and different numbers of beans in each soufflé cup. Encourage the children to guess how many cups will be needed. Also, encourage them to predict whether there will be any "left over." Comment on which amounts of beans would require 2 cups, 3 cups, 4 cups, and so forth.

Type 2: Transitional   Have the children keep a record similar to the following:

Number of Beans	Number in Each Cup	How Many Cups?	How Many Left?
5	3	1	2
6	3	2	0
7	3	2	1

ACTIVITY 5

Type 1: Concrete

Age: 4–9

Objective: Concept of division (using distributive subtraction) with and without remainders

Materials: Beans and soufflé cups

Instructions: Have the children count out eight beans. Give them two soufflé cups and demonstrate distributing the eight beans, one at a time, into the cups. Ask how many beans are in each cup. Help children focus on the fact that both cups contain the same number of beans. Then, have the children try the same procedure with nine beans. Discuss what can be done with the bean that is "remaining" or "left over." Ask them what they do when they are "dividing up" crayons or other objects and there are some "left over." Continue with other amounts of beans and different numbers of soufflé cups. Encourage the children to guess how many beans will be in each cup. Also, encourage them to predict whether there will be any "left over." Comment on which amounts of beans could be completely distributed among two cups, among three cups, among four cups, and so forth.

Type 2: Transitional   Have children keep a record similar to the following:

Number of Beans	Number of Cups	How Many in Each Cup?	How Many Left?
5	3	1	2
6	3	2	0
7	3	2	1

ACTIVITY 6

Type 1: Concrete

Age: 6–8

Objective: Commutative property of multiplication

Materials: A numberless multiplication table (see previous activities)

Instructions: Have the children find the array for 4 × 6 and compare it with the array for 6 × 4. They should notice that each array has the same number of chips, and that one array is a "sideways" arrangement of the other. Have the children compare several other pairs, such as 5 × 3 and 3 × 5 or 8 × 7 and 7 × 8. When the children have examined several such pairs, have them discuss what they found. Help them to generalize that the order in which the factors are given does not affect the answer. This generalization is called the commutative property of multiplication.

ACTIVITY 7

Type 2: Transitional

Age: 6–8

Objective: Associative property of multiplication

Materials: Square grid paper, scissors

Instructions: Have part of the class shade two 3 × 4 arrays of squares and another part of the class shade four 2 × 3 arrays. Then, have students work in pairs with one student from each part of the class in each pair. Have one student place his or her shaded regions on the other student's shaded regions (cut if necessary). After a few more examples, ask students to write mathematical sentences showing this relationship. Students do not have to arrange the numbers exactly as shown. Any meaningful expression that communicates the concept of associativity should be accepted. For example, a student's unfamiliarity with parentheses might make their use impossible. The student may not show the first expression.

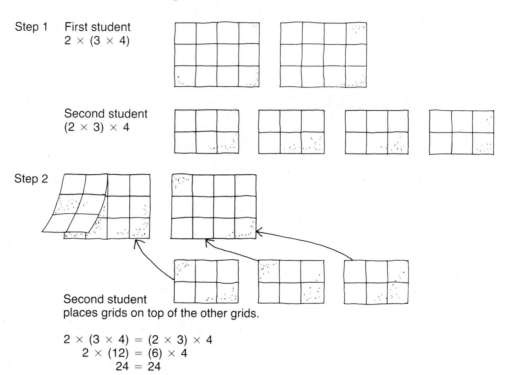

Step 1   First student
$2 \times (3 \times 4)$

Second student
$(2 \times 3) \times 4$

Step 2

Second student
places grids on top of the other grids.

$$2 \times (3 \times 4) = (2 \times 3) \times 4$$
$$2 \times (12) = (6) \times 4$$
$$24 = 24$$

ACTIVITY 8

Type 1: Concrete or Pictorial

Age: 6–8

Objective: Distributive property of multiplication over addition

Materials: Numberless multiplication table, calculators

Instructions: Have the children find the product of 5 × 7 on the numberless multiplication table. Then, have the children find the products of 5 × 3 and 5 × 4 and add these results. Do this with other pairs of addends and other factors. Ask children what they observed in each case. Ask them why they think they get the same results. Encourage discussion. It is not necessary to have children learn the name *distributive property of multiplication over addition*. Explore addends and factors that do not appear on the numberless multiplication table, such as 6 × (7 + 5). These expressions can be explored using a place-value chart and chips.

Type 2: Transitional Use the calculator to explore addends and factors. In this way, the child is focusing on the idea of what's being done rather than the computation involved. The calculator makes it possible to choose numbers not seen on the multiplication table.

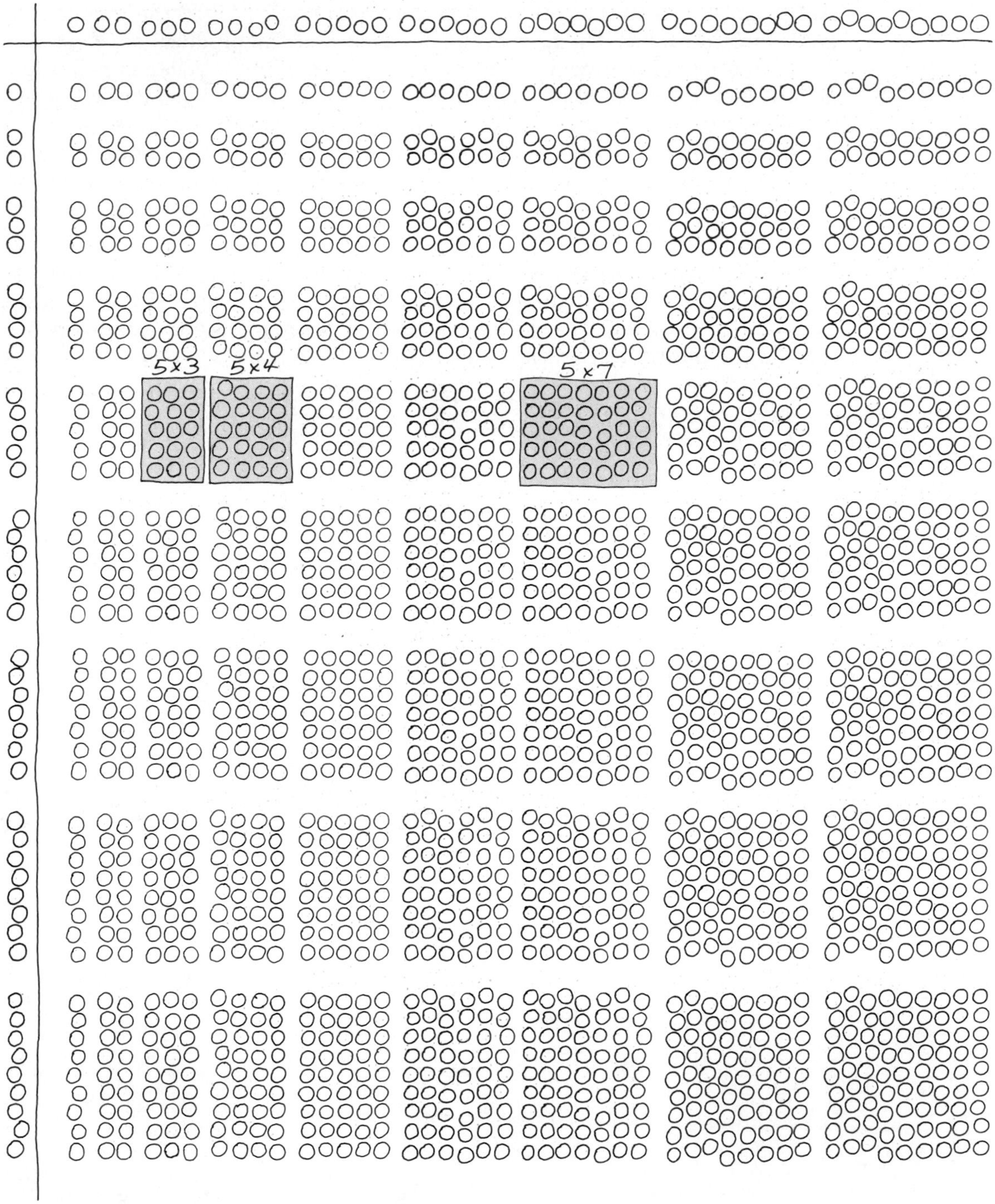
5×3
5×4
5×7

ACTIVITY 9

Type 1: Concrete

Age: 6–8

Objective: Distributive property of multiplication over addition

Materials: Index cards and chips or other small objects

Instructions: Have children use two index cards to show 3 + 4. They should put 3 chips on one card and 4 chips on the other. Next, have them put the sum (7) on another card to the side. Now, tell the children to show 3 + 4 multiplied by 5 by "copying" the card with 3 chips and the card with 4 chips five times. Then, have them "copy" the card with 7 chips five times. Ask the children what they observe. Have them count the chips on the sets of two cards and count the chips on the "sevens" cards. Ask them why the totals are the same. Repeat this activity with other sums and factors.

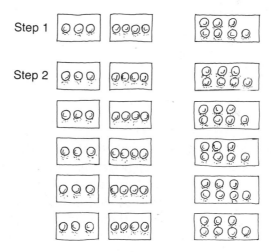

ACTIVITY 10

Type 3: Abstract

Age: 6–8

Objective: Property of zero

Materials: Prepared page of problems

Instructions: Have the children look for patterns in the following set of problems. Ask them how they could tell what the products were even if they had never seen multiplication by zero before.

5 × 5 =	4 × 5 =	2 × 5 =
5 × 4 =	4 × 4 =	2 × 4 =
5 × 3 =	4 × 3 =	2 × 3 =
5 × 2 =	4 × 2 =	2 × 2 =
5 × 1 =	4 × 1 =	2 × 1 =
5 × 0 =	4 × 0 =	2 × 0 =

ACTIVITY 11

Type 1: Concrete

Age: 6–8

Objectives: Identity property of multiplication

Materials: A numberless multiplication table

Instructions: The children should investigate the results of using one as a factor for any number. They should examine the products of 1 × 2, 1 × 3, 1 × 4, 1 × 5, . . . , 1 × 9 and then examine the products of 2 × 1, 3 × 1, 4 × 1, 5 × 1, . . . , 9 × 1. Lead them in a discussion of how these arrays are different and how they are alike. They should discover that one as a factor gives a product that is the same as the other factor. This generalization is called the identity property of multiplication.

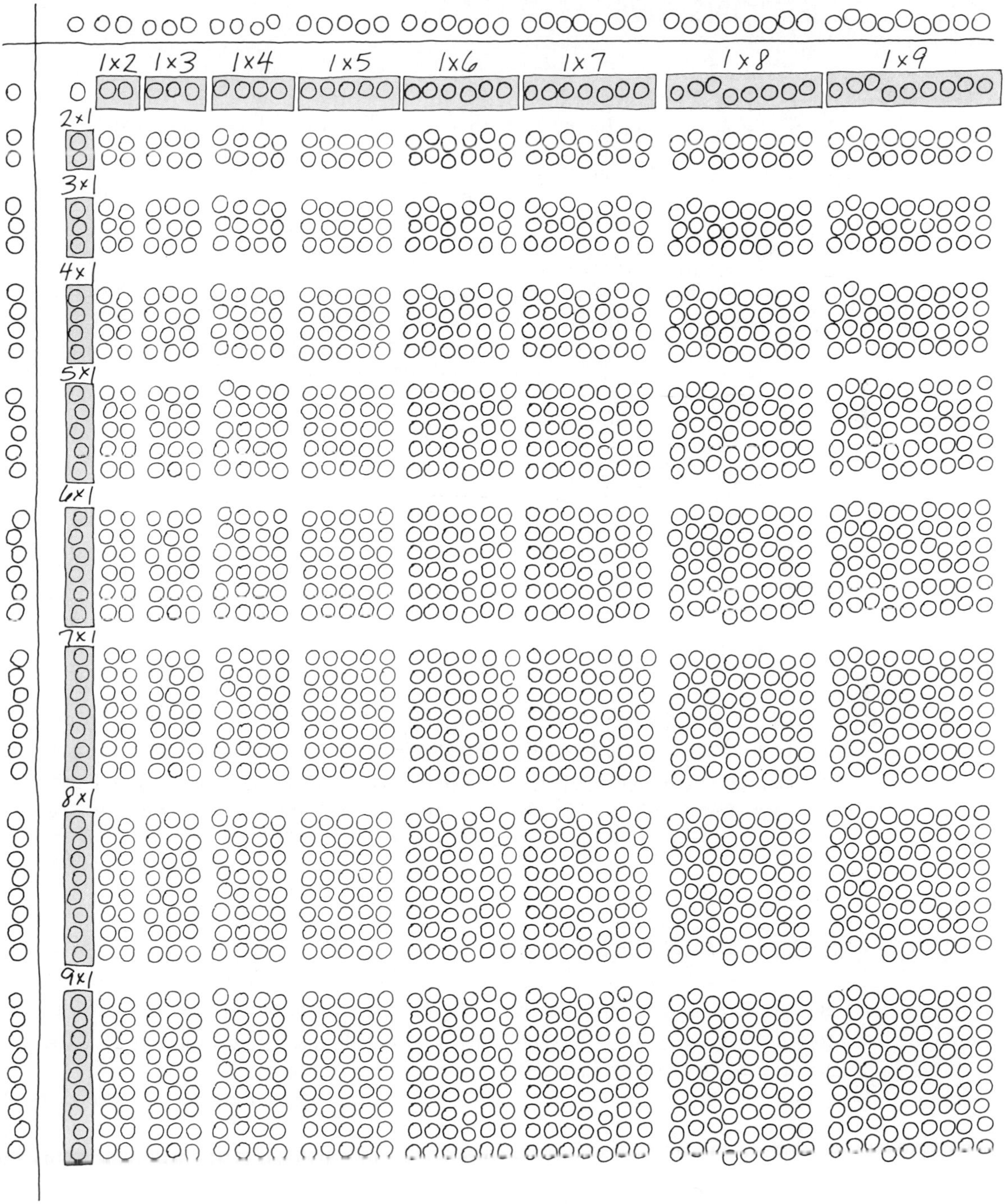
1×2
1×3
1×4
1×5
1×6
1×7
1×8
1×9
2×1
3×1
4×1
5×1
6×1
7×1
8×1
9×1

STUDY QUESTIONS AND ACTIVITIES

1. Without solving the following problems, tell all you can about the missing numbers. For example, in the first problem how many digits does the missing number have? Will the missing number be odd or even?

    a. $24\overline{)[\ ]}$ with 23 above

    b. $\begin{array}{r} [\ ] \\ \times\ \ 19 \\ \hline 380 \end{array}$

    c. $[\ ]\overline{)161}$ with 23 above

2. Write a Type 2 activity for the property of zero.

3. First, reflect on what you think children might think when listening to statements or questions such as the following. Then, rewrite the statements or questions to better guide the child's thinking.
    a. How many times does 5 go into 25?
    b. Write down the 5 and carry the 1.
    c. First you divide, then you multiply, subtract, and bring down.
    d. To multiply by 10, just add a 0.
    e. When you multiply by the second number, move over one space.
    f. When you divide nothing by a number, you just get nothing.

4. Describe how the students could use a calculator to help them with the following problems.

    $\begin{array}{r} 20[\ ] \\ \times\ \ \ \ 4 \\ \hline 8[\ ]2 \end{array}$

    $8\overline{)4[\ ]6}$ with $[\ ]2$ above

5. Write a division problem that has 5 as a quotient and 10 as a remainder. Is there more than one correct answer to this problem?

6. Select any Type 3 activity in this chapter. Make it into a Type 1 activity and then a Type 2 activity for the student who is having trouble understanding the concept at an abstract level.

REFERENCES AND RESOURCES

Baratta-Lorton, M. (1976). *Mathematics their way*. Reading, MA: Addison-Wesley.

Bates, T., & Rousseau, L. (1986). Will the real division algorithm please stand up? *Arithmetic Teacher, 33*(7), 42–46.

Bell, M. S., Fuson, K. C., & Lesh, R. A. (1976). *Algebraic and arithmetic structures: A concrete approach for elementary school teachers*. New York: The Free Press.

Broadbent, F. W. (1987). Lattice multiplication and division. *Arithmetic Teacher, 34*(5), 28–31.

Cheek, H. N., & Olson, M. (1986). A den of thieves investigates division. *Arithmetic Teacher, 33*(9), 34–35.

Folsom, M. (1975). Operations on whole numbers. In J. N. Payne (Ed.), *Mathematics learning in early childhood* (pp. 161–190). Reston, VA: NCTM.

Hendrickson, A. D. (1986). Verbal multiplication and division problems: Some difficulties and some solutions. *Arithmetic Teacher, 33*(8), 26–33.

Kamii, C., & DeVries, R. (1976). *Piaget, children and number*. Washington, DC: NAEYC

Katterns, B., & Carr, K. (1986). Talking with young children about multiplication. *Arithmetic Teacher, 33*(8), 18–21.

Labinowitz, E. (1985). *Learning from children: New beginnings for teaching numerical thinking*. Menlo Park, CA: Addison-Wesley.

Laing, R. A., & Meyer, R. A. (1982). Transitional division algorithms. *Arithmetic Teacher, 29*(9), 10–12.

Meyer, R. A., & Riley, J. E. (1986). Multiplication games. *Arithmetic Teacher, 33*(8), 22–25.

Nelson, R. S. (1979). Multiplication games that every child can play. *Arithmetic Teacher, 27*(2), 34–35.

Pea, R. D. (1987). Cognitive technologies for mathematics education. In A. H. Schoenfeld (Ed.), *Cognitive science and mathematics education* (pp. 89–122). Hillsdale, NJ: Lawrence Erlbaum Associates.

Robold, A. I. (1983). Grid arrays for multiplication. *Arithmetic Teacher, 30*(5), 14–17.

Weiland, L. (1985). Matching instruction to children's thinking about division. *Arithmetic Teacher, 33*(4), 34–35.

7

Rational Numbers

THE TOPICS IN this chapter are number theory, fractions, and decimals. Number theory is not only helpful for children during their study of rational numbers, it's also fun for them! Fractions and decimals are two ways of expressing rational numbers. This chapter emphasizes readiness for third, fourth, fifth, and sixth grade work. The foundation is laid for learning rational number concepts and algorithms in the primary grades.

VOCABULARY FOR TEACHERS

Terms teachers should know, which children will not have to learn formally at first, are *number theory, rational numbers, primes, prime factorization, composites,* and *multiplicative identity.* Children will be studying these concepts and teachers shouldn't equate knowing a term with knowing a concept. Readiness experiences will be emphasized for children younger than 8 years of age. The vocabulary can be introduced later, after the concepts have been well developed.

Number theory is the study of numbers—their relationships, ways to represent them, and patterns among them. Some number theory topics covered are odd and even numbers, factors and multiples, primes and composites, greatest common factors and least common multiples

Rational numbers can be expressed in the form $\frac{a}{b}$ where a is any integer (positive, negative, or zero) and b is any nonzero integer. The mathematical situations that require the use of an $\frac{a}{b}$ term are developed in this chapter. There are three ways to write rational numbers: as fractions (in the $\frac{a}{b}$ form), as decimal numerals, and as percents.

The **multiplicative identity** is the number 1. When any number is multiplied by 1, the result is that number. The number does not "lose" its identity.

Prime numbers are numbers greater than 1 that have only 1 and themselves as factors. Since 1 is the multiplicative identity, it is a special number and is not considered prime. Another definition of prime number is *any number greater than 0 that has exactly two different factors*. Children will have many experiences with prime numbers during the primary grades but they will probably not be able to identify them as such until the fourth or fifth grade. The list of prime numbers is 2, 3, 5, 7, 11, 13. . . . No pattern has ever been found.

Composite numbers are all the whole numbers greater than 1 that are not prime. Therefore, if any factors other than the number itself and 1 can be found for the number, it is composite. The list of composite numbers is 4, 6, 8, 9, 10, 12, 14, 15, . . . Again, there is no pattern!

The result of the procedure used to express a number as a product of prime numbers is called the **prime factorization** of that number. The Fundamental Theorem of Arithmetic states that any whole number can be expressed as a product of prime numbers in a unique way, differing only in arrangement. For example, $20 = 2 \times 2 \times 5$. The number 20 cannot be found by multiplying any other group of prime numbers.

VOCABULARY FOR STUDENTS

By age 2, children are experiencing the idea of part of an object. This idea is experienced very informally, intuitively, and naturally, without the accompanying rational number terminology. However, it isn't until second, third, or fourth grade that children learn certain number theory concepts, such as factors, multiples, or prime numbers.

The beginning stages of learning a new mathematical concept should be without formal terminology. First, children need to experience the concepts of number theory and rational numbers through embodiments and personal experiences, then terminology can be associated with these experiences. The most common number theory terms are *odd* and *even numbers, factors, multiples, primes, composites, least common multiples,* and *greatest common factors*. The most common rational number terms are *fractions, numerators, denominators, lowest terms, mixed numerals, improper fractions, decimals,* and *decimal points*.

Even numbers have 2 as a factor. That is, two equal-sized groups can be formed from the number. Outside of mathematics the term *even* has a different meaning. Consequently, it is a possible source of confusion for children.

Odd numbers are those numbers that do not have two as a factor. Any two groups formed by the number would be unequal. Just as the word *even* is used differently outside of mathematics, the word *odd* also has a meaning attached to it from nonmathematical usage.

Factors have been discussed in the chapter on multiplication and division. The definition presented there also applies in number theory.

Multiples of a number are the products that result from multiplying that number by some other whole number. Children will gain experience with the concept of multiples from studying multiplication and division. Since the term *multiple* is used in natural language with its mathematical meaning, there is less confusion between the mathematical context and the natural context. However, *multiple* is easily confused with the term *factor*. For 12 to be a multiple of 4, the number 4 must be a factor of 12. Teachers should help children distinguish between these two terms and use them correctly.

Prime numbers, discussed in the Vocabulary for Teachers section, are not emphasized until after grade 3, but the term may be introduced. Most certainly the concept can be introduced without using the term at all! Prime numbers can be informally discussed as numbers that have only the number 1 and themselves as factors. The distinction of the multiplicative identity as being a "special number," and therefore not a prime number, can be made. The word *prime* has another usage in natural language that may be slightly confusing for children, but it may not be prominent in their vocabulary.

Composites, also discussed under Vocabulary for Teachers, can be explained as any numbers that are not prime numbers. One of the confusing features about the definitions of primes and composites is that they are frequently defined as what they *are not* instead of what they *are*. For example, the number 7 is prime because no factors other than 7 and 1 can be found to yield the product 7. On the other hand, the number 6 is not prime, because the factors 2 and 3 give a product of 6. Since 6 is not prime, it must be composite. Children should be given ample opportunity to explore these concepts and use their terms.

The **least common multiple** (LCM) is the smallest number that is a common multiple of a set of given numbers. The least common denominator of two fractions is the LCM of the fraction denominators. The **greatest common factor** (GCF) is the largest common factor of a set of given numbers. The "given numbers" are usually the numerator and denominator of a fraction and the GCF is used to simplify (reduce) a fraction to lowest terms. As previously mentioned, confusion usually arises when children try to discriminate between the terms *factor and multiple*. Also, the combination of two sets of three unfamiliar terms—(a) "least," "common," and "multiple" and (b) "greatest," "common," and "factor"—requires children to have a command of each term individually as well as in combination. Furthermore, as mentioned earlier in this text, children don't usually think of numbers as being the "least" or "greatest," but rather they think of numbers as "small" or "big." If a teacher can anticipate how a child will perceive the terms used in mathematics, confusion can be avoided.

The term **fraction** is almost always used within a mathematical context. Informally, it means a part of some object. Fractions form the basis of the rational number system and have been defined previously under *rational numbers*. Children find working with fractions quite upsetting because they expect fractions to "behave" similarly to whole numbers. They often apply the same procedures and algorithms that work for whole numbers to fractions! This generalization is not correct, but there are enough similarities to make problems very confusing for children. As a result, frequently during the study of fractions students are inclined to just memorize procedures.

Numerator is not a word in common usage; it has a mathematical meaning. The a part of the fraction $\frac{a}{b}$ is called the **numerator.** The number of items out of a collection or the number of parts of a whole is indicated by the numerator. The word *denominator* does not have any other meaning to a young child other than the mathematical meaning. The **denominator** indicates how many items are in a collection or how many parts into which an object has been partitioned. A mnemonic device often helps children distinguish denominator from numerator such as "d" for *down* and *denominator*.

If a fraction is in **lowest terms,** it has no factors that are common to the numerator and denominator. The words *simplest terms, simplify, reduced terms,* or *reduce* are also used to describe a fraction in lowest terms. For example, we sometimes say a fraction is "reduced to lowest terms" or "reduced to simplest terms." Children must wonder what a simple term is or how a fraction can be lowered or reduced without making it a smaller number. Teachers need to help children with these concepts. Explain that these expressions have always been used to describe equivalent fractions having smaller terms.

A **mixed number** is part fraction and part whole number, such as the number $3\frac{1}{2}$. **Improper fractions** have numerators that are greater than or equal to their denominators. (Imagine what children think when they start hearing about the term *improper fractions*!) **Decimals** are a special notation for fractions whose denominators are powers of 10. Decimals are extensions of the place-value system. A **decimal point** is a punctuation mark used to separate the decimal fraction portion of a numeral from the whole number portion.

The significant vocabulary that children will need to know as they study number theory and rational numbers has been presented. Where possible, the ages and grades when the vocabulary would be needed have been noted. Beyond the concepts represented by this vocabulary, there are other concepts for which the associated formal vocabulary is not required in the early grades. However, the teacher must know this associated vocabulary. Teachers should make every effort to assist children in understanding the words—not just memorizing definitions. It is important for teachers to be sensitive to the potential confusions that arise when children learn new words while learning new concepts and procedures. The ideas involved in rational numbers are difficult enough!

NUMBER THEORY

There are certain concepts, such as factors and multiples, and certain algorithms, such as finding the greatest common factor and the least common multiple, that are needed for the study of rational numbers. Ordinarily, these number theory concepts are studied in isolation at first and later recalled and related to fractions. Number theory is enjoyable for children and lends itself to many nonroutine problems where the focus is looking for patterns. Although number theory ideas are sophisticated, they frequently require only simple mathematics and they greatly enhance an awareness of patterns and relationships among numbers.

Odd and Even Numbers

Odd and even numbers can be introduced as early as age 4 or 5 through such models as (a) using Cuisenaire rod trains to compare a train of white rods (ones) to a train of red rods (twos) as seen in Figure 7–1, (b) finding partners, or (c) arranging discrete objects in arrays such as eggs in an egg carton. Whether a number is even or odd is determined by whether it is divisible by two. When introducing the concepts of odd and even, discussion should be centered on the manipulation of objects and on natural situations where pairing or sorting into two groups occurs.

Only after children have had many such experiences, should the terms be introduced formally. This formal introduction usually occurs in grade 2.

Arrange discrete objects in pairs to test for odd and even numbers. Help children to associate the number 2 with even numbers. Also, explore what happens when two even amounts and two odd amounts of objects are added. Extend this exploration to multiplication. If children have not yet learned multiplication, use repeated addition. Explore what happens when an odd or an even amount of objects is multiplied by two or by three. Using these activities creates ample opportunities to focus on thinking. Depending on the

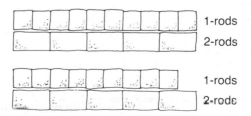

FIGURE 7–1
Odd and Even Numbers with Cuisenaire Rods

age and maturity of the learners, these ideas can be explored using Type 1, 2, or 3 behaviors.

Factors and Multiples

Learning about even numbers provides an intuitive exposure to two as a factor and to multiples of two. Furthermore, investigating adding two or more groups of numbers provides readiness for factors and multiples in general. In most cases, children are in the third or fourth grade when these concepts are formally taught. Informal learning can and should occur much earlier.

It is very tempting to immediately lecture with chalkboard examples. Remember, every new concept should first be introduced using a Type 1 experience, followed by a Type 2, and later by Type 3 experiences. Even if only a few minutes each day are devoted to Type 1 experiences, children will have a much better chance at understanding the concepts being addressed.

In Figure 7–2 the concepts of factors and multiples are illustrated. At the top of the figure, 5 red rods equal 1 orange rod, showing that 10 is a multiple of 5. Next, we see that 4 green rods equal a train of an orange rod and a red rod showing that 3 is a factor of 12. Fifteen crackers have been distributed among 5 plates (the same number are on each plate) showing that 5 is a factor of 15. The bottom portion of the figure illustrates 3 tables with 6 chairs at each table. There are 18 chairs in all. Therefore, the number 18 is a multiple of 6.

Readiness for Primes and Composites

By grade 3, children have explored different arrangements of groups of objects as readiness activities for the concepts of prime number and composite number. Any group of objects that can be placed in a two-dimensional array of rows and columns with no "leftovers" or "holes" represents a composite number. Except for the number 2, groups of objects that represent prime numbers cannot be arranged in a two-dimensional array such that all rows and columns are complete. Comparisons of trains of Cuisenaire rods can also be used to represent the concepts of prime and composite numbers. Given a train of rods or just a single rod, children can be asked to find a one-color train of rods that matches with the train they were given. If the *only* one-color train that can be found is a train of white rods (ones), then the number the given train represents is prime. If any other train can be found, then the number is composite. While pursuing such explorations, children can be encouraged to utilize good problem-solving techniques by organizing the trials and by recording them in such a way that patterns emerge. Whenever possible, create a problem-solving environment while covering the regular curriculum.

At the top of Figure 7–3, notice how discrete objects may be put into arrays to test whether there are a prime number of objects. Six buttons can be

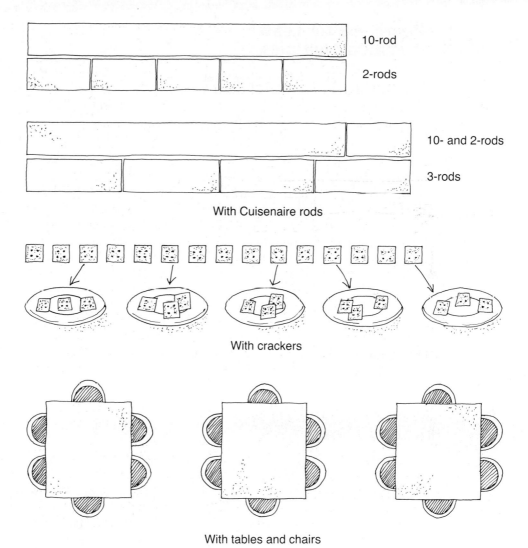

With Cuisenaire rods

With crackers

With tables and chairs

FIGURE 7–2
Factors and Multiples

arranged in a 2 × 3 array (or a 3 × 2 array), therefore, the number 6 cannot be prime. On the other hand, 7 buttons cannot be put in an array without "leftovers" or "holes," so 7 is a prime number. Continuous objects, such as individual Cuisenaire rods, may also be used to explore whether or not a number is prime. A blue (9) rod can be matched by a train of all green (3) rods, so 9 is not a prime number. However, a black (7) rod cannot be matched by trains of one color except white (1), so 7 is a prime number.

Readiness for Least Common Multiples

The concept of least common multiple uses at least two numbers. Readiness for this concept should involve Type 1 activities. Given two different types of Cuisenaire rods, children can be shown how to find the shortest equal trains of rods. (See Figure 7–4.) Have children make a train of yellow (5) rods and a train of red (2) rods. Ask children to find the shortest trains that are equal. Then have them make a train of purple (4) rods and a train of dark green (6) rods. Ask them to find the shortest equal train. The shortest train will represent the LCM of the two original rods. In the first case the LCM is 10 and in the second case it is 12.

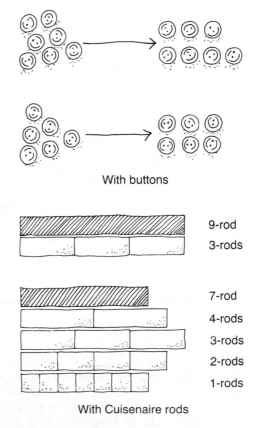

With buttons

9-rod

3-rods

7-rod

4-rods

3-rods

2-rods

1-rods

With Cuisenaire rods

FIGURE 7–3
Primes and Composites

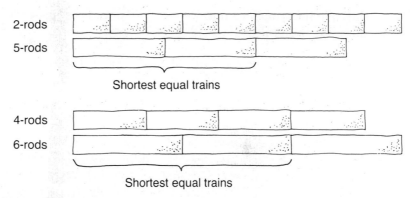

2-rods

5-rods

Shortest equal trains

4-rods

6-rods

Shortest equal trains

FIGURE 7–4
Least Common Multiple

Readiness for Greatest Common Factors

The concept of greatest common factor also uses at least two numbers. Readiness for this concept should also involve Type 1 activities. The following activity is appropriate for second and third grade. Given two trains of Cuisenaire rods, children can be shown how to make several trains of one color that will match the original trains. Then, the one-color trains that match each of the given trains can be compared. The longest one-color trains that are the same color and match up with each given train will be the GCF of the numbers represented by the original trains. For an illustration of how this activity works see Figure 7–5. The red (2) rods are the *largest* common rods.

In summary, number theory can be a lot of fun. Concepts, such as the concepts of odd and even numbers, can be explored and discovered without much sophistication on the part of the learner. Number theory is also a prerequisite for studying fractions. Teachers should not let too much time lapse between the time children learn a particular number theory concept and

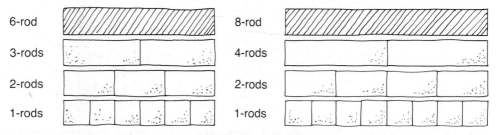

6-rod   8-rod

3-rods   4-rods

2-rods   2-rods

1-rods   1-rods

With Cuisenaire rods

FIGURE 7–5
Greatest Common Factor

the time they apply that concept to fractions. Working with fractions will help reinforce the usefulness of number theory.

FRACTIONS

Teachers need to consider two major aspects of teaching fractions. The first aspect to consider is the kinds of models that can be used to embody fractions. The second aspect is the types of thinking that generate the concept of fraction. The most common fraction models pictured in textbooks are regions, such as squares, circles, and triangles. Unfortunately, those models are not representative of the child's own world of reality! Since fractions are extremely difficult to learn as well as to teach, tremendous care should be taken to choose models that are the most suitable for children. Children should not have to struggle with an abstract model at the same time they are struggling with an abstract mathematical idea.

There are several suitable models from which to pick. These models can be classified as discrete or continuous. Discrete models are parts of sets of objects, whereas, continuous models are partitioned wholes. Figure 7–6 shows a kindergarten student separating a subset of blocks from a set of blocks. This is an example of parts of sets. Figure 7–7 shows a third grade student working with a whole circle partitioned into parts. This circle is an example of partitioned wholes. Although examples of "wholes" include one-, two-, and three-dimensional objects or shapes, also included are the attributes of time, distance, mass, and liquid capacity. However, for obvious reasons, the latter are too abstract for beginning studies in fractions and should probably be saved until the fourth or fifth grade. It is far wiser to use the one-, two-, and three-dimensional representations.

Three situations generate the concept of fractions: equal parts of a whole, ratio, and division. Examples of **equal parts of a whole** are liters of fruit juice to total liters of punch, equal slices of a pizza to all its slices, and number of miles driven to the total number of miles in a trip. The second situation, called **ratios,** compares different types of items. Examples are squeezed lemons to cups of water for lemonade, children to desks, playground equipment to children, and family members to family cars. The third thinking situation for fractions is **division.** When children are first introduced to the concept of division (informally in grades 3 and 4), the foundation for expressing division as a fraction can be laid. Eighteen divided by 6 can be expressed as $\frac{18}{6}$. This thinking situation, however, is not as useful for the development of fraction concepts as the previous two. It becomes more useful when children are introduced to methods of changing fractional numbers to decimal numbers and vice versa. Until then, simply mentioning that $\frac{24}{6}$ can be thought of as 24 divided by 6 will sufficiently develop the readiness children need for more advanced topics.

FIGURE 7–6
A kindergartner shows that one of her five blocks has been separated.

Either meaningful or indirectly meaningful models (these ideas are discussed in chapter 3) are best used when introducing the concept of fractions. Many of the models used in textbooks are based on continuous objects, such as regions that are partitioned into equal sections. One reason for this is that equivalency and addition and subtraction are very difficult to represent with discrete objects. For example, the fraction $\frac{2}{3}$ can be "added" to $\frac{1}{3}$ when using a region, but the same problem becomes more challenging when the fractions are subsets of sets; the concept is not so easily seen. Each type of model has its own advantages and disadvantages. Teachers are advised to choose models that offer the greatest flexibility. In Figures 7–6 and 7–7, two different models are illustrated. The question for Figure 7–6 is "What fraction of the blocks is moved over?" and for Figure 7–7 the question is "What fraction of the circle is red?"

Some children will become confused when learning the value of fractions. This confusion is related to their understanding of whole numbers. While 3 is greater than 2, the fraction $\frac{1}{3}$ is less than $\frac{1}{2}$. Therefore, it is important to provide a variety of Type 1 concrete learning experiences.

FIGURE 7–7
A third grader studies a circle partitioned into three parts.

Concept Formation

Children's concept formation is absolutely crucial to their success when working with fractions. If children fail to grasp the fundamental concept of fractions, in many cases they will be destined to memorize by rote a set of nearly meaningless procedures and rules for operating with fractions. Development of fraction concepts should be introduced early (even by preschool), should be carefully sequenced, and should be gradually introduced as the child's mathematical understanding matures. Numerous Type 1 experiences will help children become accustomed to the differences between the rational number and the whole number systems.

Activities at the end of this chapter labeled "Driving in Fraction City" will offer an indirectly meaningful experience with fractions as well as a scenic view! You can tell children that Fraction City is a very special place. When people are there, they really have to watch where they're going so as not to get lost. (There are already a lot of people lost in Fraction City!) That's why a map is recommended.

Therefore, as part of the concept formation process, a map of Fraction City is constructed. Strips of paper represent streets; all streets are the same length and aligned in parallel formation. Streets consist of blocks determined by folding the strips into equal parts. The name of a street is determined by the number of blocks in the street. For example, First Street has one block, Second Street has two equal blocks, Third Street has three equal blocks, and so forth. Figure 7–8 shows a first grader attempting the first few steps of constructing a Fraction City map. One *large* piece of construction paper and several uniform strips of construction paper are needed to begin. A vertical line is drawn down the left side of the large piece about 2 cm from the edge and the strips are folded into equal parts. Then, the strips are glued horizontally with the left edge of each strip at the folded vertical line on the large piece of paper.

Folding a strip into three equal parts for Third Street can be easily accomplished by making a loop with the strip and flattening the loop when the ends are an equal distance from each other as shown in Figure 7–9. Consider omitting Fifth, Seventh, Tenth, and Eleventh Streets because they are difficult to construct. Otherwise, use pre-marked strips of paper for ease in folding.

FIGURE 7–8
A first grader studies a folded strip for the Fraction City model.

FIGURE 7–9
Folding a Strip into an Odd Number of Parts

We recommend a map showing First, Second, Third, Fourth, Sixth, Eighth, Ninth, and Twelfth Streets. At first, not all of these streets should be attempted. Figure 7–10 shows the result of the efforts presented in Figure 7–8. This map has First, Second, Fourth, and Eighth Streets. The most important concepts of fractions, their equivalent forms, and addition and subtraction can all be learned from this arrangement. If children are ready to "drive" on Twenty-First Street, they probably don't need a map anymore. The teacher needs to carefully determine when the children are able to "drive" without a map!

As mentioned previously, the concept of fractions is introduced by the actual construction of the map. Then, the children can take a "drive" in their "cars" (small toy cars or markers) on the streets. Have them report where they are. To do this they count the number of blocks on the street where they have driven from left to right. For example, when the first grade girl in Figure 7–11 drove her car to the end of Fourth Street, she said, "I'm at the fourth block of Fourth Street."

It will become apparent to children that it is not easy to keep track of one's location on a street. Children should be encouraged to make "street signs" to label the blocks. For example, suggest that the signs for Second Street be

FIGURE 7–10
This completed map of Fraction City shows First, Second, Fourth, and Eighth Streets.

FIGURE 7–11
This first grader is ready to drive her cars in Fraction City.

written as $\frac{0}{2}$, $\frac{1}{2}$, and $\frac{2}{2}$. See Figure 7–12. For Third Street write $\frac{0}{3}$, $\frac{1}{3}$, $\frac{2}{3}$, and $\frac{3}{3}$. With these signs added, the use of the model now constitutes a Type 2 experience. If you are teaching kindergarten, first, or second grade children, you may wish to maintain all their fraction activities as Type 1. However, if you are teaching third or fourth graders, you may wish to move more quickly to a Type 2 use of the model.

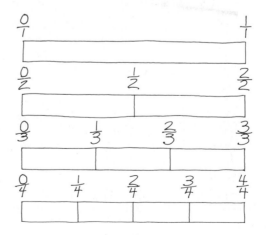

FIGURE 7–12
Putting Street Signs on the Fraction City Map

Equivalent Fractions

The concept of **equivalent fractions** may arise naturally when children notice that going one block on any street puts them at a different place for each street. Going two blocks on any street puts them at a different distance on each street. However, going two blocks on Third Street is the same distance as going four blocks on Sixth Street. See Figure 7–13.

In a Type 1 activity, children should be able to discuss the fact that in order to drive to the end of each street they have to drive one block on First Street, two blocks on Second Street, three blocks on Third Street, and so forth. This activity is readiness for learning that there are different names for *one*.

FIGURE 7–13
Showing Equivalent Fractions on the Fraction City Map

Continue by having them compare distances with two cars. Place the first car one block on Second Street and the other car two blocks on Fourth Street. In this way, children have the opportunity to change fractions to equivalent forms and to determine the relationships between fractions on an intuitive level. This activity provides excellent preparation for fractions and can be done as early as first grade.

Children should be encouraged to explore all the possible situations where they travel the same distance on different streets. A Type 2 activity would involve children in reading and writing the names of these equivalent locations in Fraction City. Students can show how one block on Second Street, two blocks on Fourth Street, three blocks on Sixth Street, four blocks on Eighth Street, and six blocks on Twelfth Street are the same distance.

In addition to driving in Fraction City, equivalent fractions can be explored using models such as regions, and set/subset models. The teacher should be especially careful to use correct language when speaking of equivalent fractions. When a region such as a pie is partitioned so that equivalent fractions can be found, the words *divided into* should not be used. Using these words creates confusion for children. Consider how difficult it is for a child to understand that for $\frac{3}{4}$ of a pie, the pie is divided into four equal parts, with three of them shaded. To show that $\frac{6}{8}$ is the same as $\frac{3}{4}$, each of the original parts is divided into two equal parts, thus obtaining twice as many parts and twice as many shaded parts.

In Figure 7–14, a circular region with 3 equal sections has been partitioned into 6 equal sections. The shaded regions show that $\frac{1}{3}$ is equivalent to $\frac{2}{6}$. Another circular region with 4 equal sections has had each section split into 3 sections showing that $\frac{2}{4}$ is equivalent to $\frac{6}{12}$. Similarly, one region has been partitioned from 4 to 8 sections and another region has been partitioned from 3 to 6 sections, showing that $\frac{1}{4}$ is equivalent to $\frac{2}{8}$ and that $\frac{2}{3}$ is equivalent to $\frac{4}{6}$, respectively.

You can imagine how confused children would be upon hearing that *dividing into 2* gives them *two times* as many parts! This unfortunate use of the phrase *divided into* should not be practiced by teachers who want their children to develop clear understanding. The teacher can use the words *split into two parts, sectioned into two parts*, or *partitioned into two parts*.

Addition and Subtraction of Fractions

Addition and subtraction of fractions with like denominators can be demonstrated using the same street in Fraction City. Drive a certain distance on the street, stop, and continue driving in the same direction for addition or go back in the opposite direction for subtraction. The sum or difference is found by reading the street sign at the last stop or counting to find the location on that street if street signs haven't been erected yet. Figure 7–15 shows that

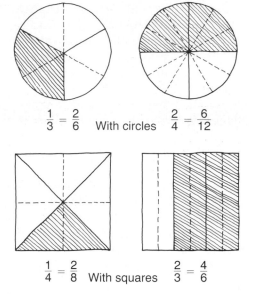

$$\frac{1}{3} = \frac{2}{6} \quad \text{With circles} \quad \frac{2}{4} = \frac{6}{12}$$

$$\frac{1}{4} = \frac{2}{8} \quad \text{With squares} \quad \frac{2}{3} = \frac{4}{6}$$

FIGURE 7–14
Equivalent Fractions

going two blocks on Sixth Street and driving one more block on Sixth Street positions the car at the third block of the street.

Addition and subtraction of fractions with like denominators can be represented by other models as well. One example is the regions or "pie" model where a number of regions are shaded initially and more regions are shaded later. Two of the 10 regions were shaded in Figure 7–16. Then, 3 more were shaded for a total of 5. The total number of shaded regions is noted and compared with the given number of regions.

Children should have many Type 1 experiences that require adding and subtracting like fractions and discussing problems with their results so the language and thinking models for addition and subtraction of fractions are well developed before continuing to Type 2 experiences. Type 2 experiences will eventually lead children to determine a general rule for writing the result of problems involving addition or subtraction of fractions. Children will notice that they can add or subtract the numerators and record or "bring down" the denominator. The term **common denominator** can be introduced about this time. Again, be careful not to indiscriminately use new words such as *common* or *bring down* without an explanation.

Addends used for practice are limited to the model used. For example, the Fraction City map children make probably won't have more than 12 streets, therefore, there won't be any denominators larger than 12 available to use. Also, problems including fractions with denominators of 5, 7, 10, and 11 should be omitted if the Fraction City map that was constructed does not include the

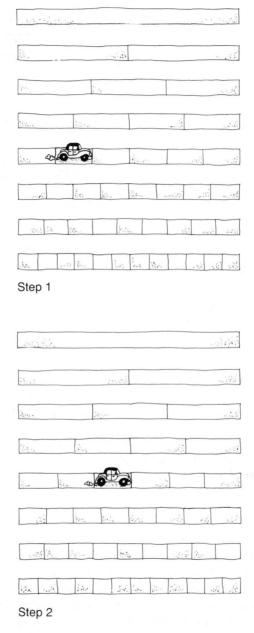

Step 1

Step 2

FIGURE 7–15
Adding Fractions with Like Denominators in Fraction City

Step 1 Shade $\frac{2}{10}$.

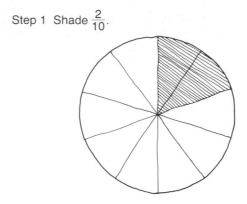

Step 2 Shade $\frac{3}{10}$ more.

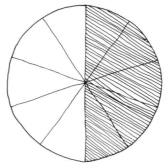

FIGURE 7–16
Adding Fractions with Like Denominators Using Circles

respective streets for those numbers. Finally, if children haven't studied improper fractions yet, addition problems resulting in improper fractions should be avoided.

On the other hand, offer children the problem-solving opportunity of thinking how they would obtain solutions to the problems mentioned previously when their maps do not provide the information. See if they can apply what they already know to these other situations. Have them provide a convincing argument to verify their solutions.

Addition and subtraction with unlike denominators begins with situations in which one denominator is a factor of the other, such as in the expressions $\frac{1}{4} + \frac{1}{2}$ or $\frac{5}{8} - \frac{3}{4}$. When children are driving in Fraction City, they may try to add $\frac{1}{4}$ and $\frac{1}{2}$ by driving on two streets at the same time. Remind them that no one drives that way! With careful questioning, however, they'll discover or remember that driving one block on Second Street is the same distance as driving two blocks on Fourth Street. When they discover that $\frac{1}{2}$ is the same distance as $\frac{2}{4}$, they'll be able to do all their driving on Fourth Street. Similar situations involving Third Street, Sixth Street, Ninth Street, and so on should be explored using Type 1 experiences. Type 2 experiences should not be omitted. Also, the teacher should not rush into Type 3 experiences. Often, children have insufficient Type 2 experiences for the algorithms related to rational numbers. As a result, these algorithms do not have any meaning to them; they are pushed too soon into Type 3 experiences where their only recourse is to "memorize what to do." When children resort to memorization without the underlying understanding, it may take years of remedial work to help them internalize why the rules really produce the "right answer." The need for careful pairing of experiences with notation, accompanied by discussion, cannot be overemphasized. Teachers should help children to develop the ability to think logically instead of pushing them too quickly into memorizing algorithms.

Models other than Fraction City can be used to represent addition and subtraction of fractions with unlike denominators. The pie or other region models are frequently found in textbooks. Suppose a region is partitioned to show a first fraction of $\frac{2}{4}$ as shown in Figure 7–17.

Then, a second fraction of $\frac{3}{8}$ is added to the region. However, in order to perform this addition, the region must be further partitioned into eighths instead of fourths. Each section must be split into two equal parts as shown in Step 2 of Figure 7–17. Then, the fraction $\frac{2}{4}$ is also called $\frac{4}{8}$.

Next, this area has three more eighths added to it as shown in Step 3 of Figure 7–17.

Adding or subtracting fractions in which the denominator of one fraction is not a factor of the other fraction's denominator requires several steps. The Fraction City model has fewer steps than the regional models. For example, consider the problem $\frac{1}{6} + \frac{3}{4}$. Help children to find a street that has the equivalent of $\frac{1}{6}$ and $\frac{3}{4}$ on it. Twelfth Street will be the solution as shown in Figure 7–18.

On the map of Fraction City show children how to drive the equivalent of $\frac{1}{6}$, which is $\frac{2}{12}$, then continue driving the equivalent of $\frac{3}{4}$, which is $\frac{9}{12}$, for a total drive of $\frac{11}{12}$. This problem is shown in Figure 7–19.

Using a regional model is more complicated. Consider the example of $\frac{1}{6} + \frac{3}{4}$. Step 1 in Figure 7–20 shows six equal parts of a circle with one part shaded. Step 2 shows another circle the same size as the first circle partitioned into fourths with three of its parts shaded.

Now, it must be determined how to partition these circles again so they have the same number of parts. In this case, the sixths must all be split into two equal parts, and the fourths must be split into three equal parts. This process is shown in Steps 3 and 4.

Next, the shaded portions of the second circle are joined to the shaded portions of the first circle. Then, the total number of shaded portions is determined and compared with the total number of parts in the circle as in Step 5 of Figure 7–20. Of course, if children have had sufficient experience with finding equivalent fractions using regional models, this procedure may be less cumbersome.

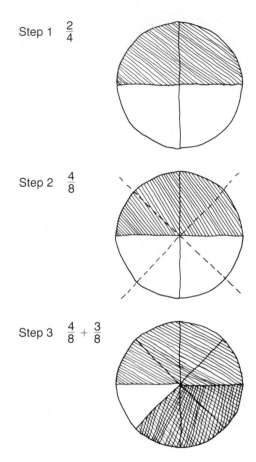

Step 1 $\frac{2}{4}$

Step 2 $\frac{4}{8}$

Step 3 $\frac{4}{8} + \frac{3}{8}$

FIGURE 7–17
Using Circles to Add Fractions When One Fraction Has the Common Denominator

Mixed Numbers

Mixed numbers will be a natural extension of whichever model children are using for fractions. A situation will occur in which the sum of two fractions will exceed one. At that point, the teacher can elicit ideas from children concerning how to represent numbers like these. Models such as Fraction City and regional models can be expanded to include fractions greater than one. There is no need to develop algorithms for dealing with mixed numbers until fourth grade or thereafter. Just let children explore this concept in a natural way as the need for its implementation develops in their work with fractions.

In summary, we have covered fractions from concept formation through mixed numbers using Fraction City as a model to teach these ideas. Fraction City puts the child in control of constructing concepts and procedures with

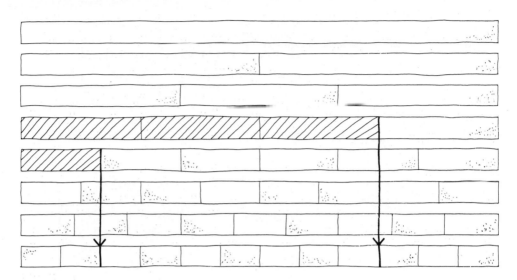

FIGURE 7–18
Finding Equivalent Distances in Fraction City

fractions—and it does so with language that is more familiar to children than fraction language. When children need to use fraction terms such as *equivalent* or *improper*, they will be able to relate the ideas associated with those terms with a model and experiences they understand. If Fraction City isn't used, the teacher needs to use another model throughout the study of fractions to facilitate children's understanding of the underlying ideas involved.

DECIMALS

Since children usually have their first exposure to decimal notation with money, it is recommended that formal instruction on decimals begin with money. By the time children are in kindergarten or first grade (or even earlier), they are cognizant of the price of things. At this stage, they are beginning to make the connection between price tags and the money they have to spend. They may still not be able to determine by themselves whether the money in their pocket is sufficient for a purchase, but they definitely connect the two concepts! By kindergarten or first grade, relationships between pieces of money are becoming established. A dime is perceived as being worth less than a dollar and a penny less than a dime. Decimal notation can be introduced through money, which provides a meaningful extension of the place-value system. Trading games, such as those used when introducing place-value concepts, can be applied to money to "extend" the place-value notation to $\frac{1}{10}$ and $\frac{1}{100}$ of a dollar.

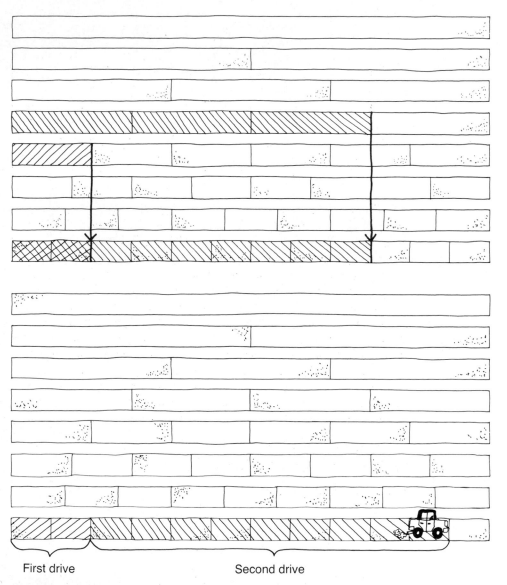

First drive   Second drive

FIGURE 7–19
Adding Fractions Where Neither Has the Common Denominator

Trading games with money can also be used to introduce another less cumbersome model for decimals. Dienes blocks or base 10 blocks can be used to represent decimals and decimal place values. If children are already familiar with the relationships among the centimeter cube, the long, the flat, and the decimeter cube, it will not take them much time to reverse the patterns they learned when working with whole-number numeration. A centimeter cube is

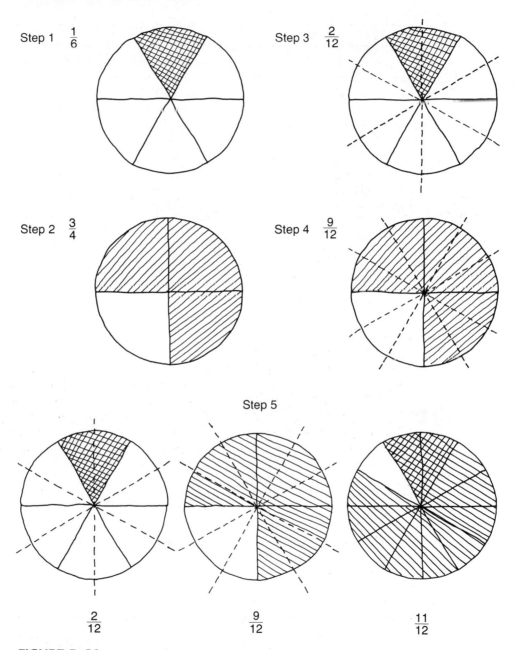

Step 1 $\frac{1}{6}$

Step 2 $\frac{3}{4}$

Step 3 $\frac{2}{12}$

Step 4 $\frac{9}{12}$

Step 5

$\frac{2}{12}$

$\frac{9}{12}$

$\frac{11}{12}$

FIGURE 7–20
Using Circles to Add Fractions Where Neither Has the Common Denominator

still $\frac{1}{1000}$ of a decimeter cube and a flat is still $\frac{1}{10}$ of a decimeter cube. These models can be quite useful in representing decimal numbers as in Figure 7–21.

An easier-to-handle model than the blocks is grid paper that shows the same relationships. Children may have used this grid-paper model when exploring whole-number notation as well. This model has the advantage of being inexpensive, portable, quiet, and easily replaceable. First, a book of 10 square pages (10 cm × 10 cm) that is stapled together is used. Each page is $\frac{1}{10}$ of a book, each strip (10 strips per page) is $\frac{1}{100}$ of a book, each square (10 squares per strip) is $\frac{1}{1000}$ of a book. See Figure 7–22. If you'd like to extend this model to greater whole-number place value, tens are represented by a volume of 10 books and hundreds are represented by a tome of 10 volumes fastened together.

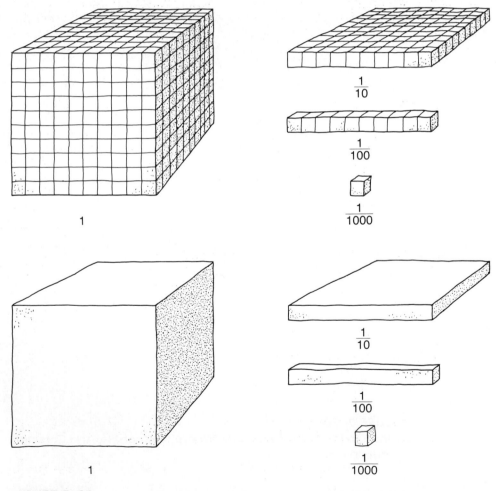

FIGURE 7–21
Dienes Blocks

Children who are functioning at a concrete cognitive level may become confused with the money model. When looking at the physical properties of money, children might compare size with value. However, a dime doesn't look like $\frac{1}{10}$ of one dollar, a nickel is only half the value of a dime but larger in size. Physical money is a nonproportional model, whereas the grid-paper model is a proportional model. For these children it might be best to start with a different model altogether, such as the grid-paper model, and then relate that model to money later.

Concept Formation

The most meaningful concept formation for decimal numbers comes from an extension of the place-value system, either through models such as the grid-paper model or through money relationships. The prerequisites for concept formation of decimals can be found in the concepts of fractions. Children must have a complete understanding of the concepts of $\frac{1}{10}$, $\frac{1}{100}$, and $\frac{1}{1000}$ for either model to be meaningful. Often, because the algorithms for computing with decimals are so similar to those of whole number algorithms, there is a tendency to teach decimals as just an extension of whole numbers. Of

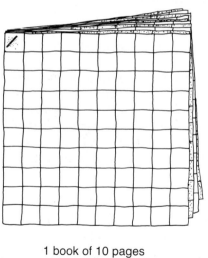

1 book of 10 pages

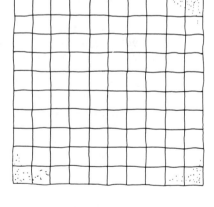

1 page is $\frac{1}{10}$ of a book

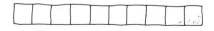

1 strip is $\frac{1}{100}$ of a book

1 square is $\frac{1}{1000}$ of a book

FIGURE 7–22
Grid-Paper Model

course, the similarities are great because decimal notation is an extension of whole-number notation. However, once you "cross the decimal point," the concepts are the concepts of fractions.

Children should have many Type 1 experiences with models, such as the grid-paper model, before progressing to Type 2 experiences. Decimal numbers should be talked about at length and shown with models before formal notation is introduced. The same place-value chart used to learn whole numbers can be used with a decimal point that is prominently displayed at the top of one of the left column markers.

When reading decimal numerals the only time the word *and* should occur is prior to the decimal point itself. For example, it is correct to say 204.3 as "two hundred four *and* three tenths," but not "two hundred *and* four *and* three tenths." Careful instruction in the concepts of decimals will prepare children for the complex algorithms of decimal computation that are introduced later. Extra time spent during concept formation will save on remedial time later! Activities 16 and 17 suggest ways of naming, reading, writing, and modeling decimal numerals.

Conversions Between Decimals and Fractions

Conversions between decimals and fractions should begin with the obvious ones, such as rewriting $\frac{1}{10}$ as 0.1 and $\frac{1}{100}$ as 0.01 and so forth. Then, a natural progression would be to rewrite $\frac{3}{10}$ and $\frac{8}{100}$ as 0.3 and 0.08, respectively. Place-value charts and many Type 1 experiences will have paved the way for understanding that numbers such as $\frac{34}{100}$ can be rewritten as 0.34 and $\frac{109}{1000}$ can be rewritten as 0.109. Rewriting the fraction $\frac{6}{10}$ as 0.6, 0.60, or 0.600 can be confusing to children. See Activities 18 and 19 for ideas on how to help children understand these different ways of expressing the same fraction. If children are having difficulty understanding the different ways of writing the same fraction, expansion of fractions should be retaught. The fractional form of $\frac{6}{10}$ can be written in expanded form as $\frac{60}{100}$ or $\frac{600}{1000}$, which all have the same value. Thus, the different decimal forms will also have the same value.

As early as third grade, teachers can reasonably expect children to change fractional numbers such as $\frac{1}{2}$, $\frac{1}{4}$, and $\frac{3}{4}$ to fractions with tenths or hundredths as denominators by using models. This activity should help children to rewrite these fractions in decimal forms. More than this type of activity should not be expected at this age. If children appear ready for more, have them explore ways to solve problems requiring more sophisticated work with fractions and decimals.

To rewrite a decimal numeral as a fraction, children must be able to say the numeral aloud in order to know its meaning in fraction form. Thus, being able to read decimal numerals is important. See Activity 17 for some ideas on teaching approaches. For example, the decimal 0.7 is said "seven tenths," which tells the child how to write the fraction. Similarly, 0.65 is read "sixty-five hundredths" and is written $\frac{65}{100}$. Then, children can be encouraged to rename the fractions in simplest terms—if they have previously learned that concept.

Addition and Subtraction of Decimals

Addition and subtraction of decimals can be introduced as a concept by using the money model again. Adding pennies, dimes, and dollars with and without grouping is a good readiness activity. Type 2 activities using money for addition and subtraction of decimals will reinforce the concept of place value—a vital concept for this type of computation. Of course, the money model has the limitation that thousandths and smaller decimals cannot be represented with it.

From the money model it is best to work with a model similar to the grid-paper model. As children show addition and subtraction of decimal numbers using the grid-paper model, they will experience the similarities that these processes have with whole-number computation. When Type 2 activities are introduced, it is important to talk about where the numbers are being positioned on the place-value chart and why. When children have had many experiences with adding numbers such as 0.03 and 0.16 using a place-value chart, they will not need to "memorize" the rule that "the decimal places must be lined up above each other." See Figure 7–23. This rule will become obvious to children when they are questioned as to where the decimal point is located with respect to the numbers. Encourage them to verbalize their reasons for working in a particular fashion rather than presenting these concepts in lecture form.

The regrouping and renaming procedures for decimals follow the procedures used for whole numbers. Grid paper or other models using place-value charts should be used. Figure 7–24 shows how to set up 0.716 − 0.234 by showing 0.716 on the chart. In the second step taking 4 thousandths from 6 thousandths leaves 2 thousandths, but in order to subtract 3 hundredths from the next column some regrouping is needed. After this regrouping and subtraction, 2 tenths are taken away from the tenths column. The result of 0.482 is shown in Step 3. Regrouping from right to left would be performed for addition of decimal numbers when regrouping is required.

In summary, remember that Type 1 experiences should not be neglected with decimals, even though it is tempting to just tell children how to do the problems. Don't give in to this temptation! Give your students opportunities to construct mathematics. Listen carefully to their understandings and help them to internalize decimal ideas.

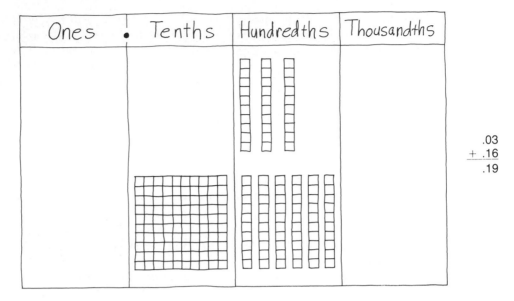

FIGURE 7–23
Decimal Place-Value Chart

USING THE CALCULATOR TO LEARN ABOUT RATIONAL NUMBERS

Using the calculator to explore rational numbers and number theory can be of great benefit to children. They will be able to make guesses and explore avenues of thought that would be far too cumbersome otherwise. For example, the calculator can be used to count by tenths or hundredths greater than or less than a given number. The relationship between rational numbers written in fractional form and decimal form can be made clearer by using a calculator. At this age, because children have not yet been taught how to divide to obtain the decimal form of a fraction, the calculator is quite valuable for showing that $\frac{7}{8}$ can be expressed as a decimal. Of course, not all fractions have terminating decimal forms, so an appropriate explanation of the meaning of the other digits is necessary. For example, $\frac{1}{6}$ does not make a "nice" decimal numeral. It shows up as 0.1666666 on the calculator. It is not clear to children this age that the sixes continue, so the best solution is to teach rounding of decimals as a means of approximating the fraction. Rounding to hundredths will probably be sufficient. (See Estimation and Problem Solving in this chapter.) By using the calculator, children will also be able to order rational numbers whether these numbers appear in fractional or decimal form. See Activities 18 and 19 for ideas on using grid paper to order rational numbers.

The calculator can also be used to reinforce the concepts of place value that are needed for adding and subtracting decimals. Not all decimal addition

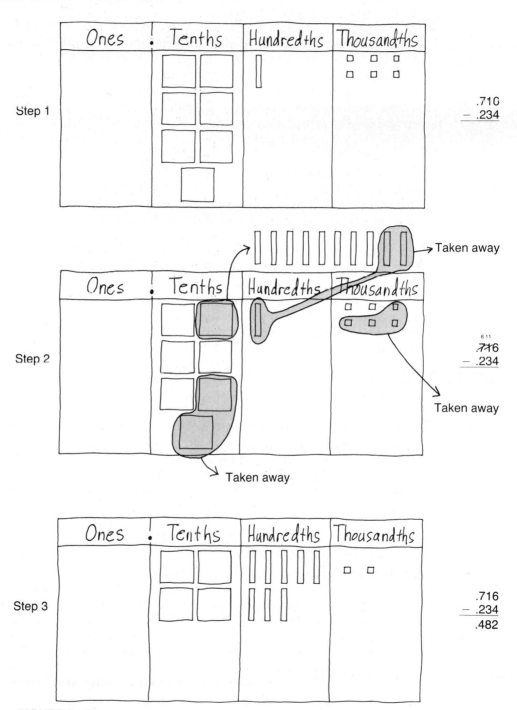

FIGURE 7–24
Subtracting with Decimals on a Decimal Place-Value Chart

problems given should use vertical notation with the decimals already aligned. Children should be able to change the problem to vertical notation to perform the addition. If they are allowed to check their work with a calculator, some of them will discover that they forgot to align the decimal places correctly in a particular problem. Most children will accept the calculator answer as correct rather than their own, so they will realize they have made some error and will probably try to track it down. The practice that children get in estimating will be very important in helping them understand what may have gone wrong in their problem.

The calculator is ideal for exploring the concepts of number theory. It saves a great deal of wear and tear on the teacher and on the children. Also, it encourages children to freely explore concepts without the limitations of paper and pencil computation. Once children have grasped the concept of least common multiple (LCM), they can use the calculator to investigate problems such as finding the LCM of 81 and 126—a problem that would ordinarily be beyond the reach of a child this age. Finding the greatest common factor of the numbers 600 and 420 would usually be more than a third grade child could be expected to do, but the calculator also makes this problem possible.

In many instances, using the calculator to introduce concepts of number theory is practical. Asking children to determine whether 321 is a prime number is not unreasonable if they can use a calculator to divide 321 by different numbers to see which, if any, divide exactly. Problem-solving strategies—making organized lists is an example—can enhance calculator explorations, such as finding the LCM of 45 and 36. Children can use the calculator to find multiples of 45 by repeated addition and keep a record of these multiples. Following the same process with 36 will reveal that the least number that is a multiple of both 45 and 36 is 180. Similar examples can be explored for the GCF. The different procedures used on the calculator to find multiples and to find factors will help the children make the distinction between the two concepts. See Activities 5 and 6.

USING THE COMPUTER TO LEARN ABOUT RATIONAL NUMBERS

The computer can be used in several ways to help children learn about rational numbers and number theory. One of the most obvious ways is to use the many commercially prepared programs that "teach" rational number concepts. In addition to the usual considerations for selecting software, keep in mind the types of models this software presents to students. The most recently developed software will have some type of model presented to the student via screen graphics. The lessons will seldom be exclusively Type 3 lessons, but there are some software packages that are limited to Type 3 experiences. The chances of finding software accompanied by some hands-on model are slim! Teachers may consider selecting software that uses similar models as those used in their initial instruction, or they may want to deliberately select software that presents different models than those used in the classroom. Either way, a conscious, deliberate choice should be made.

Most classroom teachers do not have time to create programs for students to use. Another obstacle is that comprehensive programs dealing with rational numbers can be extremely complex. The teacher may decide to limit teacher-made programs to those that deal with number theory. Often, number theory programs do not need to be as sophisticated as those programs dealing with rational numbers. Some simple programs that can be modified by children are included in the activities for this chapter. (These programs were written for the Apple family of computers. If your computer is not an Apple, some changes may be necessary.)

ESTIMATION AND PROBLEM SOLVING

Experiences with estimation and problem solving can be very beneficial to children. Estimation practice can help children make a clear distinction between two concepts that are frequently confused: the least common multiple of two numbers and the greatest common factor of two numbers. A guess and check strategy can be used to emphasize the differences between factors and multiples. Given two numbers, such as 36 and 48, children can be asked to guess the largest number that is a factor of both of them. Then, by using a calculator they can check which of their guesses will divide both numbers evenly and determine the largest factor. By having children do this type of problem together as a class, the teacher can help children recognize that any factor can be only as large as the number itself. A similar process can be used for exploring least common multiples. In this case, the children can be helped to realize that the smallest number that is a multiple of a given number is the number itself. All other multiples must be larger.

The concept of fraction can also be further developed by using estimating and problem-solving skills. When presented with regional models whose portions are colored or shaded, children can be asked to classify which models are close to 1, $\frac{1}{2}$, and 0. The children can also order the fractions represented and be prepared to defend the order selected by explaining how they know which fraction is more or less than another. The relationship between the whole unit and the portion used for the numerator of the fraction can be emphasized by estimation. An example of this relationship can be shown with a group of white buttons and green buttons. Some of the buttons are covered up and children are asked to predict what fraction of the buttons is green. Then, the estimates can be evaluated by revealing the whole collection of buttons and letting children see what fraction of the buttons is green. See Figure 7–25. In this example, four out of eight buttons were green when all of the buttons were shown. Children can try to determine who had the closest guesses. A similar activity can be done with shaded regions or fraction strips where the whole item is not revealed to children until they have had an opportunity to guess.

For addition and subtraction of fractions, estimation can be helpful. This strategy may keep children from obtaining totally unrealistic answers without realizing that they have made mistakes. When a child has added $\frac{2}{5}$ and $\frac{1}{4}$ and gets $\frac{3}{9}$, which is reduced to $\frac{1}{3}$, this result should indicate to the child that this

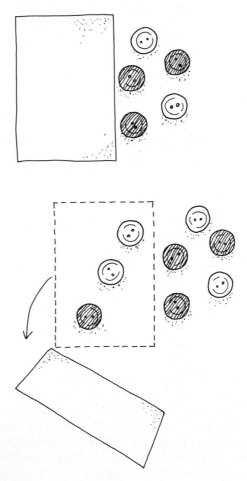

There are buttons under the card.
Predict the fraction of green buttons
in all.

FIGURE 7–25
Estimating Fractional Parts with Buttons

answer is not reasonable. The fraction $\frac{2}{5}$ is already greater than $\frac{1}{3}$. The reasonableness of results for operations with fractions can be built up gradually using several simple techniques. For example, children can be asked to examine pairs of fractions to classify them by which pairs have sums close to 1, $\frac{1}{2}$, and 0. Then, the pairs could be added using regional models or fraction strips to verify the results. A numerator for a fraction can be written on the board and children can be asked to give denominators that will make the fraction close to 1. The same exercise can be done by asking for denominators that will make the fraction close to 0 or to $\frac{1}{2}$ instead. A similar activity can be done with the denominator being given and children being asked to find numerators that would make the fraction close to 1, $\frac{1}{2}$, or 0.

Rounding and truncating strategies can be very useful for estimating the results of addition and subtraction problems with decimals. Children can be shown that rounding for decimals is quite similar to rounding for whole numbers. In fact, the procedures are the same except for the names of the places in the place-value chart. As with fractions, children can be asked to classify decimal numbers as close to 1, $\frac{1}{2}$, or 0 and then to discuss the reasons for their classification. Estimation of decimal sums and differences can be taught using either truncation or rounding. Truncation is done by simply "lopping off" the digits to the right of a specified decimal place. For example, the decimals 0.345, 0.781, and 0.277 could be truncated to 0.3, 0.7, and 0.2, respectively.

Rounding is done in the usual fashion. Sums or differences of decimals can be estimated using either method. For example, the sum of the three decimals given previously would be estimated as 1.2 using truncation (0.3 + 0.7 + 0.2) and as 1.4 using rounding (0.3 + 0.8 + 0.3). These estimation techniques, if incorporated into regular classroom activities, can greatly increase the children's success by giving them a means to evaluate the reasonableness of results. Specifically, for a problem such as 0.3 + 4.56 + 0.92 the children would realize that 1.676 would be as unlikely an answer as 16.76 would be. Since the largest number is close to 4, the smallest number is close to 0.5, and the "middle" number is close to 1, the answer would not be far from 5.5. Teachers should present many decimal problems in horizontal form to emphasize the concept of estimation and the concept of place value in the computational algorithm.

Many children start having difficulty for the first time in mathematics when they encounter fractional forms of rational numbers. One reason children have difficulty is that the algorithms they have learned for working with whole numbers no longer serve them for operations with fractional forms. These whole-number algorithms become useful again when dealing with decimal forms. Consequently, children often resort to memorizing fraction rules in order to bluff their way through until the teacher presents a new topic. Teachers need to exercise care to ensure that solid understanding and conceptual development are established.

SUMMARY

In this chapter, rational number concepts were connected with number theory. Models to guide the formation of the concepts of fractions and decimals were examined in detail. Representations that may aid children's understanding of addition and subtraction of rationals were discussed. Multiplication and division of rationals are usually not approached until after third grade. Therefore, these topics were not included in this chapter. At the end of the chapter, suggestions were given for incorporating calculators and computers as well as for incorporating estimation and problem solving.

PLANNING FOR INSTRUCTION

In the Instructional Planner for this chapter, nearly all the activities are at the Type 2 level. The reason is that the concepts and procedures covered in this chapter are developmental. The drill and practice stage is not reached. The activities emphasize helping the child to develop an understanding of rational numbers. Any of these Type 2 activities can be redesigned into Type 1 activities. The teacher should seriously consider redesigning the activities if children are unable to function symbolically.

INSTRUCTIONAL PLANNER
Rational Numbers

Age	Types of Learning	Mathematical Objectives	Types of Behavior and Experiences			
			Type 1 Concrete	Type 1 Pictorial	Type 2 Transitional	Type 3 Abstract
	Concept Formation	**Number Theory**				
3–7		Odd and Even Numbers	1			
5–8		Multiples and Factors	2			
6–9		Primes and Composites	3		4	
7–9		Least Common Multiples	5			32
7–9		Greatest Common Factor	6			33

INSTRUCTIONAL PLANNER (continued)
Rational Numbers

Age	Types of Learning	Mathematical Objectives	Types of Behavior and Experiences			
			Type 1 Concrete	Type 1 Pictorial	Type 2 Transitional	Type 3 Abstract
		Fractions				
5–6		Part/Whole	7		7	
6–9		Ratio	8		8	
6–9		Division			9	
6–9		Reading/Writing Fractions			10, 11, 12	
6–9		Reading/Writing Mixed Numbers			13	
6–9		Comparing Fractions			14, 15	
		Decimals				
7–9		Decimals			16	16
7–9		Reading/Writing Decimals			17	
7–9		Comparing Decimals			18, 19	
	Algorithms	**Fractions**				
7–9		Adding Fractions with Like Denominators			20	
7–9		Subtracting Fractions with Like Denominators			21	
7–9		Adding Fractions with Unlike Denominators			22	
7–9		Subtracting Fractions with Unlike Denominators			23	
7–9		Adding Mixed Numbers			29, 31	
7–9		Subtracting Mixed Numbers	30		30, 31	

INSTRUCTIONAL PLANNER (continued)
Rational Numbers

			Types of Behavior and Experiences			
Age	Types of Learning	Mathematical Objectives	Type 1 Concrete	Type 1 Pictorial	Type 2 Transitional	Type 3 Abstract
		Decimals				
7–9		Adding Decimals with Tenths	24		24, 26	
7–9		Subtracting Decimals with Tenths	25		25, 26	
7–9		Adding Decimals with Hundredths			27, 28	
7–9		Subtracting Decimals with Hundredths			27, 28	
7–9		Adding Decimals with Tenths			26	
7–9		Subtracting Decimals with Tenths			26	
7–9		Adding Decimals with Hundredths			28	
7–9		Subtracting Decimals with Hundredths			28	

ACTIVITY 1

Type 1: Concrete

Age: 4–7

Objective: Odd and even numbers

Materials: Groups of small objects, soufflé cups

Instructions: Let children take a group of 6 to 12 objects and count the number of objects in the group. Then, ask them to distribute the objects between two soufflé cups. Ask them to count how many objects are in each cup. Ask whether they have the same number in each cup. Then, ask them to line up the objects two by two. Discuss with them that sometimes each object will be matched and sometimes there is one object "left over." Let children have several experiences of this nature before you introduce the words *odd* or *even*.

ACTIVITY 2

Type 1: Concrete

Age: 4–8

Objective: Multiples and factors

Materials: Chips and index cards

Instructions: Give the children a group of 6 to 24 chips and ask each child to count the number of chips in the group. Ask the children to take two index cards and distribute their chips between the two cards. Ask them if they had any chips left over. Then, ask them to perform the same activity using three cards. They should continue until they have used six cards, and each time they should determine whether there were any chips left over. Encourage them to explore. Show the class a number of chips and ask them to predict whether there will be any chips left over if they are distributed between two cards, among three cards, among four cards, etc. It is not necessary to use the terms *factor* and *multiple* until children are in the second or third grade.

ACTIVITY 3

Type 1: Concrete

Age: 6–9

Objective: Primes and composites

Material: Chips or other objects

Instructions: Have the children select a random group of chips. Ask them to count the chips in the group. Have them try to position their chips in two rows, then three rows, four rows, etc., with each row having the same number of chips. At each stage, ask the children if the rows were all alike, or if there were any chips left over. Let children explore many different groups of chips in this way.

ACTIVITY 4

Type 2: Transitional

Age/Grade:	6–9
Objective:	Primes and composites
Materials:	Chips, index cards, and pencils

Instructions: The children should each take 6 chips. Show a 2 by 3 array on an index card. They should explore how many other ways an array can be formed with these chips. (They will arrange either a 3 by 2, a 6 by 1, or a 1 by 6 array.) Ask children to record how many arrays they formed with the 6 chips. Then, use 4 chips. Help them find the 2 by 2 array. Continue using up to 20 chips. Discuss which numbers of chips had only 2 possible arrays (these are prime numbers), and which numbers of chips had more than 2 possible arrays (these are composite numbers). Use of the terms *prime* and *composite* at this level is not important.

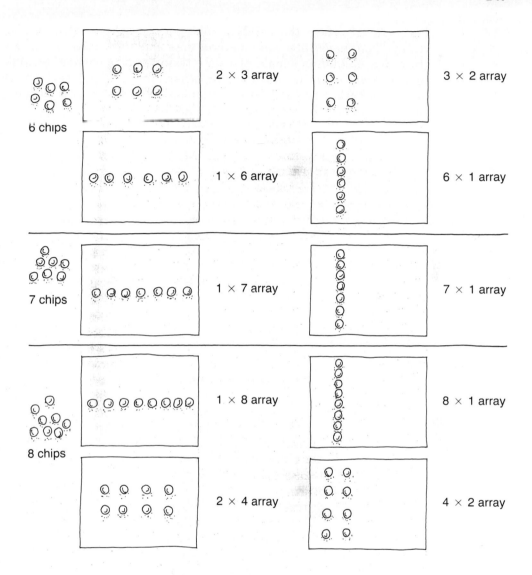

6 chips	2 × 3 array	3 × 2 array
	1 × 6 array	6 × 1 array
7 chips	1 × 7 array	7 × 1 array
8 chips	1 × 8 array	8 × 1 array
	2 × 4 array	4 × 2 array

ACTIVITY 5

Type 1: Concrete

Age: 7–9

Objective: Least common multiple

Materials: Cuisenaire rods

Instructions: Have the children take several purple (4) rods and make a train. Then, have them take several dark green (6) rods and make another train. Next, children should place the trains next to each other. Ask them to find where the trains match each other. They should perform this same activity for other sets of one-color trains. Encourage them to explore whether there will always be a place to match any two trains.

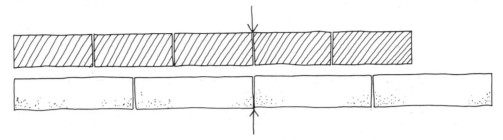

Three purple rods match two dark green rods.

ACTIVITY 6

Type 1: Concrete

Age: 7–9

Objective: Greatest common factor

Materials: Cuisenaire rods

Instructions: a. Have the children take a dark green (6) rod and a blue (9) rod. Ask them to make trains of one-color rods to match each of these rods. Talk about which color train matched both the dark green (6) rod and the blue (9) rod exactly.

b. Have children make a train of orange (10) + yellow (5) and another train of orange (10) + brown (8). Ask them to find one-color trains that match both these given trains exactly. Discuss which trains besides white rod trains match. Children should perform this activity with many different kinds of trains.

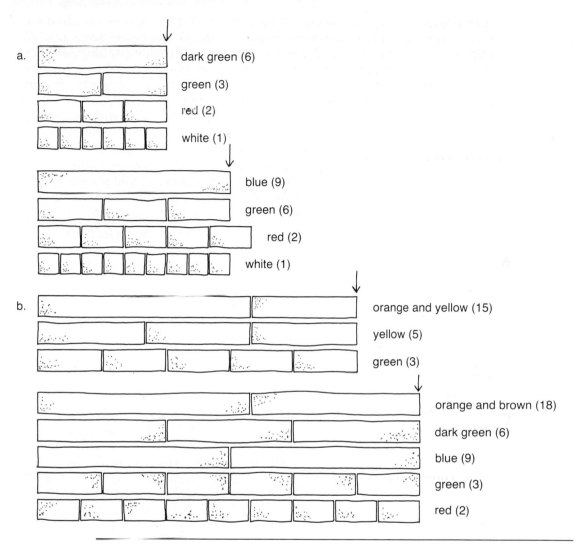

a.
dark green (6)
green (3)
red (2)
white (1)
blue (9)
green (6)
red (2)
white (1)

b.
orange and yellow (15)
yellow (5)
green (3)
orange and brown (18)
dark green (6)
blue (9)
green (3)
red (2)

ACTIVITY 7

Type 1: Concrete

Age: 5–7

Objective: Fraction (part/whole)

Materials: Two-inch wide paper strips (cut from sheets or from adding machine tape)

Instructions: Have each child take one strip and fold it into two equal parts. Ask them how many folds were made. Then, ask how many parts were made by folding. Have children fold carefully to ensure that the parts are the same size (as close to the same size as possible considering the ages of the children). Next, have the children cover one part and discuss how many parts are still showing as well as how many parts they started with. This discussion will get them to think about one part out of two. Have each child take another strip and fold it into four equal parts. Discuss the number of parts and, uncovering one part at a time, discuss the number of parts that are showing in comparison to the number of parts in the whole strip. Continue this process with other folds. (Folding into three equal parts is difficult for children, but first graders can get close to equal parts if the strip is pre-marked by the teacher. Fifths and sevenths can also be handled in this fashion.) An extension of this activity would be for you to name the parts and have the children fold a strip to show what you name. It is important for children to have an opportunity to "create" the fraction as well as recognize it.

Type 2: Transitional   Have children label the sections with fractions: $\frac{1}{2}$ and $\frac{2}{2}$; $\frac{1}{3}$, $\frac{2}{3}$, and $\frac{3}{3}$; etc.

ACTIVITY 8

Type 1: Concrete

Age:	5–9
Objective:	Fraction (ratio)
Materials:	Two colors of chips or beans and paper plates

Instructions: Have the children put one red bean on a paper plate. Then, have them put two white beans on the same plate. Ask the children to make another plate like the first one. Next, ask how many red beans there are altogether and how many white beans there are altogether. Have the children make a third plate like the first two. Ask them how many red beans there are now, and how many white beans there are now. Continue this process with more plates. Change the ratio of red to white beans and go through the process again. Continue this activity until children understand the process. After they perform this activity for some time, children might be able to predict the outcome. Encourage them to predict how many red beans altogether and white beans altogether there would be on three plates if the ratio is two red beans to four white beans.

Type 2: Transitional   Have the children record the number of red beans and the number of white beans as they go through the activity. They can make a chart for the number of beans on each plate and the number of beans of each color at each stage.

Red beans	2	4	6	8	10 . . .
White beans	4	8	12	16	20 . . .

A further development would be to hold up a card with a fraction written on it and have the children prepare a plate or plates with that ratio of red to white beans. Use different ratios, some of them improper fractions such as $\frac{5}{2}$. Be sure to let children talk about what they are doing and encourage them to ask questions.

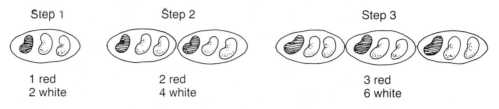

Step 1	Step 2	Step 3
1 red 2 white	2 red 4 white	3 red 6 white

ACTIVITY 9

Type 2: Transitional

Age: 6–9

Objective: Fraction (division)

Materials: Chips or other objects, index cards, and pencils

Instructions: Give each child 24 chips and 2 index cards. Ask the children to distribute the chips between the 2 cards. Ask them how many chips are on each card. Then, have them record $\frac{24}{2} = 12$. Now, ask children to distribute the 24 chips among 3 index cards. They should determine how many chips are on each card and record $\frac{24}{3} = 8$. Continue this activity for 4 through 12 cards. Discuss the significance of chips that are left over, such as in the case of using 5 index cards. Ask them to explore ways of dealing with the chips that are left. Some of the children may suggest splitting the chips and using pieces of chips to distribute to the cards. Other children may suggest throwing out the extra chips. The teacher should not limit the discussion unnecessarily or tell children what to do—creativity should be encouraged throughout the learning of mathematics.

ACTIVITY 10

Type 2: Transitional

Age: 6–9

Objective: Fractions (part/whole)

Materials: Paper strips, $8\frac{1}{2} \times 11$ sheets of paper

$$\frac{24}{2} = 12$$

$$\frac{24}{3} = 8$$

$$\frac{24}{4} = 6$$

$$\frac{24}{5} = 4 \text{ with 4 left over}$$

24 chips

Instructions: Have each child take a paper strip and fold it in the center. Ask children how many parts there are in the paper strip now. Then, ask them to color one part. On the board write "1 colored part to 2 parts." Follow this same process for several fractions, such as 1 colored part to 3 parts, 2 colored parts to 3 parts, 2 colored parts to 4 parts, 1 colored part to 4 parts, and so forth. Then, use the chalkboard to demonstrate writing fractions in vertical form like $\frac{1}{3}$.

A similar exercise should be done with sheets of paper so children will be familiar with the area model as well as the linear model.

After children have a full understanding of how to write fractions, the teacher should show them fractions written on cards and ask them to fold and color paper strips to show the fractions. (The teacher should choose examples carefully since students will have difficulty folding odd denominator fractions.)

A further extension of this activity is to ask children to match fractions written on cards with folded and colored strips.

An important addition to this activity is to have children fold some strips and/or sheets of paper into unequal parts and shade some of the parts. It is important for children to recognize that 1 part out of 3 shaded parts does not necessarily mean $\frac{1}{3}$, unless the parts are of equal size. Ask children how these strips are similar to and also different from the strips they have previously been using. They should be led to discover that the regions or lengths are not equal, and that equality is a fundamental requisite for this type of representation of fractions.

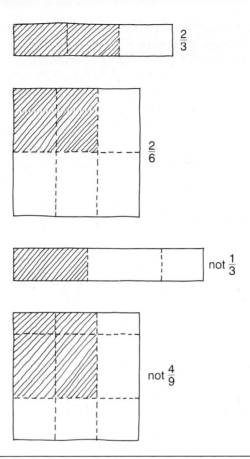

ACTIVITY 11

Type 2: Transitional

Age: 6–9

Objective: Fractions (ratio)

Materials: Chips (or beans) in two colors

Instructions: Demonstrate the ratio model of fractions by showing one blue chip next to two white chips. Write on the board "1 blue to 2 white." Have the children show different ratios of blue and white chips and record them in a similar manner. (This activity can be used for odd denominators more easily than paper folding.) After children have recorded the ratios of 2 blue to 7 white, 3 blue to 5 white, etc., show them how to write the ratios in vertical form.

$$\frac{1\text{ blue}}{2\text{ white}} \qquad \frac{2\text{ blue}}{7\text{ white}} \qquad \frac{3\text{ blue}}{5\text{ white}}$$

Retaining the labels of blue and white will be beneficial for preparing children for equivalent fractions. For this reason, keep the labels for awhile as children are becoming familiar with this notation.

Help children to show the chip representation of a ratio, such as 3 blue to 5 white, that is written on the board. Show different ratios written on cards and ask children to show these ratios with the chips.

This activity can be further extended by having cards depicting different ratios of colored chips or beans and by asking children to match these cards to numerical ratios written on another set of cards.

ACTIVITY 12

Type 2: Transitional

Age:	6–9
Objective:	Reading/writing fractions
Materials:	Large sheets of construction paper (12″ × 18″), strips of construction paper (13″ × 1″) in a different color from the large sheet, glue, pencils, game markers or tiny toy cars

Instructions: Tell children they are going to make maps of Fraction City.

a. Have children practice folding paper strips into equal parts (thirds, sixths, ninths, etc., are more difficult for children to fold). Discuss how many parts and folds are in each strip. Mark the large piece of construction paper with a vertical line about 2 cm from the left margin. Glue one unfolded strip lengthwise on the sheet—place it flush against the vertical line.

b. Show children how to fold a strip into two equal parts, by working with the fold until the strip lies flat, and how to darken the crease with a pencil. Place this strip below the first one, leaving 2–3 cm between the strips. (Do not glue the strips at this point.)

c. Work with children to fold another strip in half and then in half again. Open the strip and fold it back and forth so it will stay flat. Darken the folds and place this strip about 2–3 cm below the second strip. Continue the same process for eighths.

d. Help children to fold another strip in thirds. Take the time needed to make the folds as accurate as possible. If necessary, you may want to pre-mark the strips in thirds for the children. Prepare this strip as before and place it next in order on the large sheet, leaving about 2–3 cm space between all the strips.

e. Fold the next strip in thirds and then fold those sections in half to get sixths. Prepare and position the strip in the same manner as previously described. Discuss how the same result can be obtained by folding a strip in half and then by folding those sections into thirds. Have the children try it. Continue for ninths and twelfths.

f. Throughout this process, ask children to look for patterns. How many folds does a strip have? How many parts does it have? This discussion should lead to rearranging the strips so that the strip with 2 parts is followed by the strips with 3 parts, 4 parts, 6 parts, 8 parts, 9 parts, and then 12 parts. Glue the strips to the construction paper.

g. Each strip of paper is a street and all streets are the same length. Each part of a street is a block, and all the blocks on one street are the same length. So First Street has 1 block; Second Street has 2 blocks; Third Street has 3 blocks; Fourth Street has 4 blocks; Sixth Street has 6 blocks; and so forth.

h. Have children "drive" their cars on some street and help them discuss on which street they are located and how many blocks they have driven. Help them to become aware that there is a different name for the total distance on each street because each street has a different number of blocks. At some point in this general discussion, point out how hard it is to figure out where their cars are located. Try to get children to devise a scheme to keep track of where they are. Lead them into identifying their location by street signs in which the bottom number tells how many blocks a street has, and the top number tells how many blocks on that street their car has driven.

$$\frac{1}{2}$$ The number of blocks driven
The number of blocks on the street

i. Now, children can put street signs at all the blocks on their map of Fraction City.

ACTIVITY 13

Type 2: Transitional

Age: 7–9

Objective: Mixed numbers

Materials: Paper strips of uniform length

Instructions: Take two paper strips and fold them in half. Hold up one strip and ask children how many parts are shown. Then color one of the parts. Ask children what fraction of the strip is colored. Then, color the rest of the strip and ask what fraction is colored. They should say two halves. Color half of the second strip and ask what fraction is colored. Then, go back to the first strip. Ask how many halves are colored on it (two). Next, put the half-colored strip with the first strip and ask how many halves are colored (three).

Show a similar progression of $\frac{1}{3}$, $\frac{2}{3}$, $\frac{3}{3}$, $\frac{4}{3}$, $\frac{5}{3}$, followed by a progression of fourths.

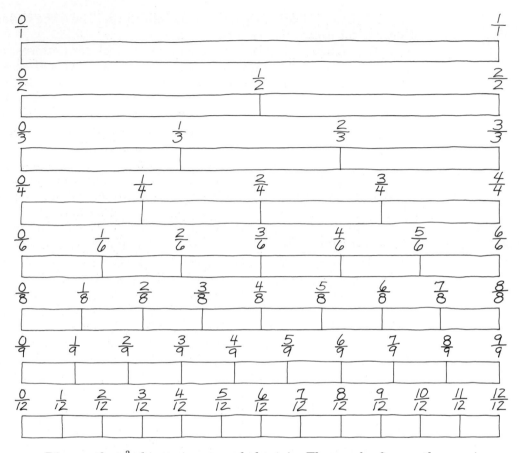

Discuss that $\frac{3}{3}$ also means one whole strip. Then go back over the previous examples to express them as combinations of whole numbers and fractions. For example, $\frac{5}{3}$ becomes $1\frac{2}{3}$.

show: record:

$\frac{1}{3}$

$\frac{2}{3}$

$\frac{3}{3}$

$\frac{4}{3}$

ACTIVITY 14

Type 2: Transitional

Age: 6–9

Objective: Comparing fractions

Materials: Fraction City maps (see Activity 12 for directions on how to construct the map with street signs) and cars for driving in Fraction City

Instructions: Have children use several game markers or toy cars to drive in Fraction City. Ask them to drive two blocks on Third Street and park. Ask them to drive another car two blocks on Fourth Street and park. Encourage them to discuss how far the two cars are from the beginning of each street. (If each child has cars of the same two colors, discussing the relationship between the distances the cars have traveled is easier.) Encourage them to explore the fact that even though each car traveled two blocks, the cars did not travel the same distance. Children must read the street signs to determine where they are parked. Help them explore why this is true. After this discussion, have children drive the same number of blocks on other streets, park, and then compare distances. Encourage exploration and discussion.

As an extension of this activity have children drive pairs of cars in Fraction City and record where they park their cars. Then, they can compare their positions using the symbols for less than, greater than, or equal to. The fraction pairs $\frac{2}{3}$, $\frac{2}{4}$ and $\frac{2}{3}$, $\frac{9}{12}$ are representative examples.

ACTIVITY 15

Type 2: Transitional

Age: 6–9

Objective: Equivalent fractions

Materials: Fraction City maps with street signs and cars

Instructions: Have children drive one car to the first block on Second Street and park it. Ask them to find as many streets as possible where they can park a car the same distance as the first one. Encourage them to discuss choices: Three blocks on Sixth Street works, but two blocks on Fifth Street does not. After all the possibilities are explored, change to a distance such as $\frac{2}{3}$ and find all the parking positions that are the same distance. Continue to explore fractions. Later, challenge children by asking them to find parking positions that are not the same distance as any others in Fraction City.

Let children record other parking positions that *are* the same distance. Ask them to name a distance the same as $\frac{1}{2}$ that is not found in Fraction City. For example, how could they write the parking position for Eighteenth Street that is the same distance as $\frac{1}{2}$?

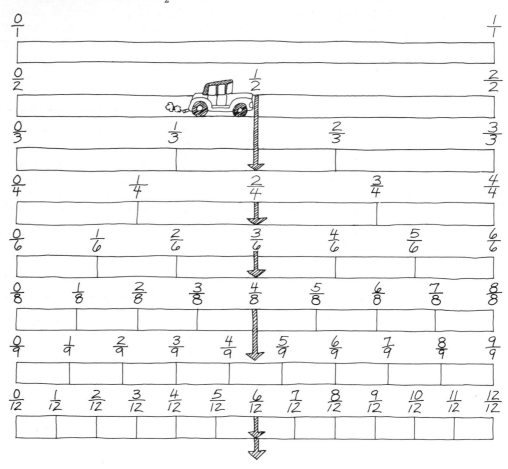

same distance as $\frac{1}{2}$

ACTIVITY 16

Type 2: Transitional

Age: 7–9

Objective: Concept of decimals

Materials: 10 × 10 grid paper, colored markers

Instructions: Have children shade 50 of the 100 squares. Ask them how they would write this relationship as a fraction. Next, have them shade 20 of 100 squares on another grid. Then, ask them how they would write this relationship as a fraction. Ask them how they could show $\frac{4}{10}$ on the grid. Help them explore the idea that 10 of the small squares together form $\frac{1}{10}$ of the large 100 square grid. Next, ask them how they could show $\frac{7}{10}$. Have them color these grids. After they have become accustomed to this concept, write some fractions on the board and ask the children to color these amounts on the grids.

Type 3: Abstract Show children another way of writing the previous amounts. Show that the fraction $\frac{4}{10}$ can also be written as 0.4, the fraction $\frac{1}{10}$ as 0.1, the fraction $\frac{7}{10}$ as 0.7, and so on. If children are ready, tell them that $\frac{20}{100}$ can be written as 0.20, that $\frac{50}{100}$ can be written as 0.50, and that $\frac{90}{100}$ can be written as 0.90. Also, show them that $\frac{5}{100}$ is 0.05 and $\frac{9}{100}$ is 0.09. Have them look for patterns and practice writing the two forms.

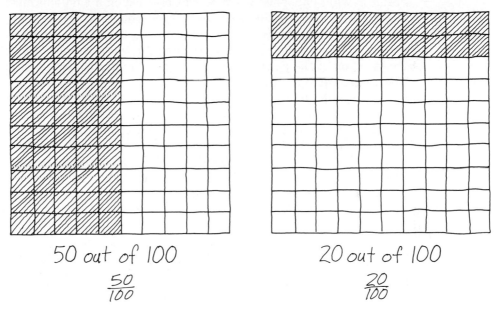

50 out of 100

$\frac{50}{100}$

20 out of 100

$\frac{20}{100}$

ACTIVITY 17

Type 2: Transitional

Age: 7–9

Objective: Decimals to thousandths

Materials: Centimeter grid paper and decimal place-value charts (both as shown previously in chapter)

Instructions: Have each child make a set of decimal grids and store these grids in a small plastic bag. Show children how to make a set of decimal grids, by cutting out at least twenty 10 cm × 10 cm squares. Staple 10 of these squares together to form a booklet. Then, cut at least twenty strips that are 10 cm × 1 cm. Finally, cut out at least thirty small 1 cm × 1 cm squares.

Help children to explore the relationships among the decimal grids. Let the book of ten 10 cm × 10 cm squares be one unit. Ask them what fraction a single 10 cm × 10 cm square is of the book, what fraction one 10 cm × 1 cm strip is of the book, and what fraction the single 1 cm × 1 cm square is of the book.

Have children make a place-value chart with a movable decimal point and label the columns from left to right as "ones, tenths, hundredths, thousandths."

Help children to read and write decimals by starting with the 1 cm × 1 cm squares in the $\frac{1}{1000}$ place and counting on by ones until $\frac{10}{1000}$ is reached. Remind children what happened when 10 was reached on a whole number place-value chart. Then, regroup for a 10 cm × 1 cm strip and place it in the $\frac{1}{100}$ place. Count 10 of these strips and show regrouping to the $\frac{1}{10}$ place with a 10 cm × 10 cm square. Continue this procedure until the whole number 1 is reached. After this portion of the activity, explore the decimal place-value chart further by discussing various numbers shown on it.

Show children how to write the decimals being displayed on the chart, such as 0.123 in the following figure. Be sure to introduce the writing portion of this activity only after several days of working with and talking about the decimal place-value chart. Children should practice writing decimals shown on the chart. They should be asked to show numbers that are written on the board on their charts. Be sure not to rush this process. This activity works best if it is done very slowly and over a period of time.

Ones .	Tenths	Hundredths	Thousandths

ACTIVITY 18

Type 2: Transitional

Age: 7–9

Objective: Comparing decimals

Materials: Index cards with decimal numbers (to thousandths) written on them, decimal grid paper, decimal place-value chart

Instructions: Give each child three cards with numbers. Have the children represent each of the three numbers on the decimal place-value chart. Then, have them arrange the cards in order from largest to smallest using the information from the decimal place-value chart. Discuss the relative sizes of two- and three-digit decimals. (Point out that with whole numbers more digits means the number is larger, but this is not true for decimals.) Help children explore these relationships. Encourage them to compare numbers such as 0.6, 0.57, 0.562, 0.5, 0.52, 0.513, etc.

A further extension of this activity is to give children three decimal cards each and ask them to estimate the order of the cards from largest to smallest. Then, have them verify their prediction by using the decimal grids and decimal place-value chart.

ACTIVITY 19

Type 2: Transitional

Age: 6–9

Objective: Equivalent decimals

Materials: Index cards with equivalent decimals written on them, decimal grid paper that is 10 cm × 10 cm, and strips of grid paper that are 10 cm × 1 cm

Instructions: Each child should have several decimal pages, several strips, and a set of two cards with equivalent decimals written on them—such as 0.40 and 0.4 or 0.60 and 0.6. Initiate a discussion about how many small squares are on their decimal pages. Help them find a way to determine how many there are before proceeding. Talk with them about what fraction of a page is shown by an individual strip. Children should then be directed to use the decimal grid paper to shade in the two-digit decimals in their set, and to use the strips to represent the one-digit decimals in their set. The child with 0.40 and 0.4 will shade 40 of the small squares on one grid sheet, and 4 of the strips, respectively. Similarly, the child will represent 0.60 by shading 60 squares on the grid and 0.6 by shading 6 strips. After the children are finished shading, have them compare the amount shaded on their grid with the strips that are shaded.

A further extension is to have children use the same number cards but instead have them place the grid paper on the decimal place-value chart. Encourage discussion of how these numbers mean the same amount, even though one "looks" larger than the other in numerical form. This discussion will help reinforce and more clearly establish the concept that the place of a digit determines how much it represents—whether that amount is 40 hundredths or 4 tenths. While children are using the decimal place-value charts, ask them to show decimals such as 0.670 compared with 0.67, or 0.040 compared with 0.04.

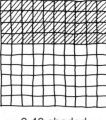 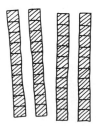

0.40 shaded   .4 shaded

ACTIVITY 20

Type 2: Transitional

Age: 7–9

Objective: Adding fractions with like denominators (sums less than or equal to one)

Materials: Fraction City maps with street signs, cars, and index cards with fractions from Fraction City

Instructions: Ask children to drive one block on Fourth Street and then one more block on Fourth Street. Ask them where they are. Have them drive one block on Third Street and then ask them to drive one more block on Third Street. Again, ask them where they are. Have them compare the distances they have just driven. Now, ask them to drive four blocks on Ninth Street and then three more blocks. Discuss with them where they are. At this point, you might want to let children select on which street they want to drive, how many blocks to drive the first time, and how many blocks to drive the second time. They will discover naturally that some drives will take them beyond the edge of Fraction City. Discuss why this happens and ask for suggestions on how to deal with the situation. Children may decide that they should extend Fraction City by lengthening the streets. Another possibility would be to determine the maximum number of blocks that can be driven for the second move, and limit that move to fewer blocks. Either way, this experience will be beneficial to students as they explore improper fractions. Have children show the distance to be driven using index card fractions.

ACTIVITY 21

Type 2: Transitional

Age: 7–9

Objective: Subtracting fractions with like denominators (sums less than or equal to one)

Materials: Fraction City maps (with street signs as shown previously in this chapter), cars, and index cards with fractions from Fraction City

Instructions: Have children drive their cars four blocks on Sixth Street (or tell them to "drive a distance of four-sixths"). Then, have them turn around and drive back two blocks. This may be the first time children have been asked to drive any direction besides left-to-right, so allow time for some confusion and uncertainty. Ask them where they are located on Sixth Street. If their Fraction City maps have numbers on them, you can let them read the street signs to determine their location. Now, ask them to drive five blocks on Eighth

Street and then go back left three blocks and discuss where the drive ended. Repeat this procedure using other streets. After the children are comfortable with this subtracting situation, you might ask them what would happen if they drove forward seven blocks on Twelfth Street and then drove back nine blocks. Let them explore this idea. Try to resist the urge to tell them that it "can't be done." By letting them think about this dilemma, you are setting the stage for introducing signed numbers.

Also, use the index cards with fractions written on them to indicate where the children should drive. Another possibility is to have children record their locations during each part of each drive.

ACTIVITY 22

Type 2: Transitional

Age: 6–9

Objective: Adding fractions with unlike denominators (sums less than or equal to one)

Materials: Fraction City maps with street signs, cars, and index cards with fractions from Fraction City.

Instructions: Before beginning this activity, the children should have had extensive experience with equivalent fractions by driving in Fraction City. (See Activity 15.) For example, they should be able to recognize almost instantly that one block on Second Street is the same distance as two blocks on Fourth Street. Have the children drive one block on Third Street and ask them to drive the same distance as one block on Second Street next. They will find that this activity is not easily accomplished. Thus, they are "forced" to consider how they can accomplish it. Encourage them to remember what they know about equivalent fractions. Lead them into finding that one block on Third Street is the same as two blocks on Sixth Street and that one block on Second Street is the same as three blocks on Sixth Street. Using this information, they can move their cars to Sixth Street and complete the task. Have them perform this activity again with another pair of fractions. The fractions need to be carefully chosen so that they have equivalents in Fraction City. This activity can be further extended by using fractions written on cards (or on the board) for children to use. Children can also keep a written record of their steps in completing the problem.

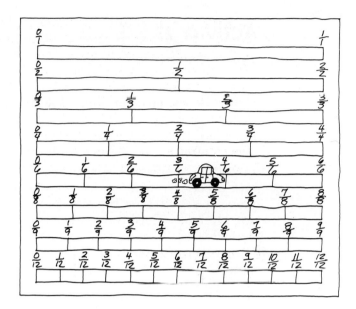

Step 1
Drive 4 blocks
on Sixth Street

Step 2
Drive back
2 blocks on
Sixth Street

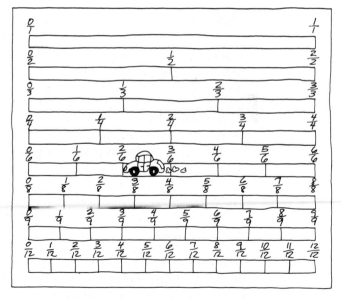

ACTIVITY 23

Type 2: Transitional

Age:	7–9
Objective:	Subtracting fractions with unlike denominators (sums less than or equal to one)
Materials:	Maps of Fraction City with street signs, cars, and index cards with fractions from Fraction City.

Instructions: Before beginning this activity, children should have had extensive experience with equivalent fractions by driving in Fraction City. (See previous activities on Fraction City.) Ask the children how they would drive two blocks on Third Street and then turn around and go back one block on Second Street. They will not be able to do this directly because it is not possible to drive on two streets with the same car! Discuss what can be done in this case. They should recognize that driving two blocks on Third Street is the same as driving four blocks on Sixth Street, and that driving one block on Second Street is the same as driving three blocks on Sixth Street. Now, they can solve the problem on Sixth Street where they will drive four blocks forward and three blocks back, finishing at $\frac{1}{6}$. Do several problems of this type before using numerals with the problems. Select some problems that will go beyond the edge of Fraction City and have children discuss where their cars might end up. They may decide that there are some numbers that "come before" the beginning of Fraction City. On the other hand, they may not be able to reach a definite conclusion, which is fine at this point.

This activity can be further extended by using fractions written on cards (or on the board) for children to use. They can also keep a written record of their steps in completing the problem.

ACTIVITY 24

Type 1: Concrete

Age:	7–9
Objective:	Adding decimals with tenths (with addends less than one)
Materials:	Decimal place-value charts, decimal grids as shown previously in this chapter, and decimals on index cards (tenths only)

Instructions: Have children show $\frac{4}{10}$ on the place-value chart with the decimal grids. Then, have them show $\frac{3}{10}$ more and ask them what the result would be if they joined these two quantities. They should get $\frac{7}{10}$. Ask them if the steps they just followed were similar to steps they had followed in the past. Let them solve several more problems. Be sure to include some problems that require regrouping to the ones place. Help children remember how to regroup by asking them questions rather than telling them what to do.

Type 2: Transitional   Use decimal numbers written on cards to extend this to a Type 2 activity. Children can also keep a written record of their problems.

Chips or beans can be used to make the activity more abstract than the decimal grids, but the more abstract form should follow only after children have had a great deal of practice with the grids.

ACTIVITY 25

Type 1: Concrete

Age: 7–9

Objective: Subtracting decimals with tenths (with addends less than one)

Materials: Decimal place-value charts, decimal grid pieces as shown previously in this chapter, and decimals on index cards (tenths only)

Instructions: Have children show $\frac{8}{10}$ on their charts. Then, take away $\frac{5}{10}$. Encourage them to discuss what they already know about subtraction that will be useful in this situation. Try to help them see the relationship between whole-number subtraction and what they are doing now. Also help them relate this new procedure to decimal addition. Have them do several of these problems.

Type 2: Transitional   To make this a Type 2 activity, let children record their steps as they do the problems. Later, have children use beans or chips on the place-value chart rather than the grid pieces.

Ones	.	Tenths	Hundredths	Thousandths
	.	□ □ □ □ □ □ □ □		

Step 1
Show 0.8.

Ones	.	Tenths	Hundredths	Thousandths
	.	□ □ □ ▨ ▨ ▨ ▨ ▨		

Step 2
Take away 0.5.

Ones	.	Tenths	Hundredths	Thousandths
	.	□ □ □		

Step 3
Show result.

ACTIVITY 26

Type 2: Transitional

Age: 7–9

Objective: Adding and subtracting decimals with tenths

Materials: Decimal place-value charts, decimal grid pieces, prepared worksheet with addition and subtraction problems

Instructions: Have children use the decimal grid pieces to demonstrate the problems on the worksheet. Have them record the results. Remind children of how they decide where the grid pieces go on the place-value chart. Do not let them rewrite these problems in vertical form until they have solved them using the grid pieces. Ask children to estimate what their answers will be before they set up problems on the place-value chart. Discuss how to handle problems such as problem 5, which requires regrouping to tens as well as ones.

Suggested problems for worksheet:

1.	3.4 + 0.5	6.	8.5 − 0.3
2.	2.7 + 1.2	7.	7.2 − 0.6
3.	0.5 + 3.7	8.	2.8 − 1.6
4.	4.3 + 2.9	9.	4.3 − 0.9
5.	6.7 + 3.8	10.	5.4 − 2.8

ACTIVITY 27

Type 2: Transitional

Age: 7–9

Objective: Adding and subtracting decimals with hundredths (addends less than one)

Materials: Decimal place-value charts, decimal grid pieces, decimals on index cards (tenths and hundredths)

Instructions: Show students a card with 0.34 on it and ask them to show this amount on the place-value chart. Then, show them 0.62 and ask them to add this number to their first number. They can perform subtraction in a similar manner. Be sure that they try problems such as 0.73 + 0.4 and 0.82 − 0.09. These types of problems need to be discussed with children as they are working on them. Help them to remember regrouping.

ACTIVITY 28

Type 2: Transitional

Age: 7–9

Objective: Adding and subtracting decimals with hundredths

Materials: Decimal place-value charts, decimal grid pieces, prepared worksheet

Instructions: Have children demonstrate the problems on the place-value chart and record their results on the worksheet. Do not allow them to rewrite the problems in vertical form until they have solved the problems with the decimal grid pieces and place-value chart first, and have estimated their answers to each problem. Discuss with them how to handle problems that require regrouping more than once. You might need to remind them how they dealt with such situations for whole numbers.

Suggested problems for worksheet:

1.	$0.72 + 0.16$	6.	$1.59 - 0.43$
2.	$5.18 + 0.63$	7.	$3.05 - 2.03$
3.	$6.03 + 2.58$	8.	$6.40 - 0.25$
4.	$1.76 + 3.65$	9.	$3.00 - 0.06$
5.	$5.49 + 4.78$	10.	$5.00 - 0.73$

ACTIVITY 29

Type 2: Transitional

Age: 7–9

Objective: Adding mixed numbers with like denominators (addends greater than or equal to one)

Materials: Three or four maps of Fraction City with street signs lined up side by side so that the ends of the streets match and adjoin each other, cars, and index cards with mixed numbers formed by fractions from Fraction City

Instructions: Small groups of children will need three or four maps of Fraction City lined up side by side so that the streets match with each other. Ask the children how they would take a drive on Fourth Street a total distance of 1 and $\frac{3}{4}$ (or say "one street and three blocks on Fourth Street," if you are still using that language). They should decide to drive four blocks on Fourth Street to represent the distance 1, and then drive three blocks on Fourth Street by moving to the next map. Since the maps are placed side by side, this process should be relatively easy for them to see. After children have decided how they can travel more than a distance of 1, ask them how they would show the addition of another 1 and $\frac{1}{4}$. They will probably need help in thinking this procedure through. Children can be encouraged to explore how they could show even larger mixed numbers, although the examples they use initially will be limited to those that can be shown on three or four maps. Sometimes it is not necessary to actually demonstrate an extension of a process, if it can be discussed by the group. Select other pairs of small mixed numbers to have the children add, such as $\frac{2}{8} + 1\frac{3}{8}$.

This activity can be extended by showing the mixed numbers to be added written on index cards and/or by having the children keep a written record of their processes in solving these problems.

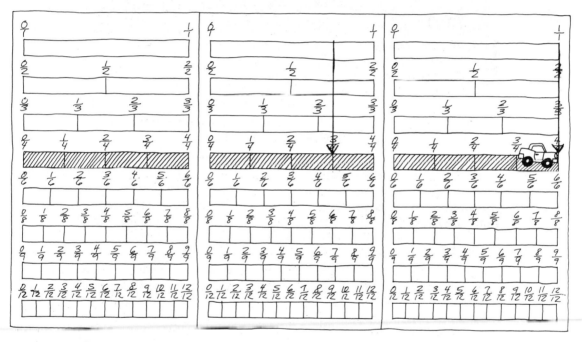

A drive of $1\frac{3}{4}$ and $1\frac{1}{4}$ more ends at 3.

ACTIVITY 30

Type 1: Concrete

Age: 7–9

Objective: Subtracting mixed numbers with like denominators (addends greater than or equal to one)

Materials: Fraction City maps, cars, and mixed numbers from Fraction City on index cards

Instructions: Ask the children to subtract $\frac{1}{4}$ from $1\frac{3}{4}$. They will need to be reminded of how they performed subtraction of fractions in Fraction City. They will probably want to place two maps side by side in order to drive the $1\frac{3}{4}$ to start the problem. Then, they will need to drive back one block on Fourth Street to complete the problem. Have children explore more mixed number and fraction combinations.

Type 2: Transitional   To make this a Type 2 activity, you may use the mixed numbers on index cards and/or have children keep a written record of their processes in solving these problems.

ACTIVITY 31

Type 2: Transitional

Age:	7–9
Objective:	Adding or subtracting mixed numbers with unlike denominators (addends greater than or equal to one)
Materials:	Fraction City maps, cars, and mixed numbers from Fraction City on index cards

Instructions: Have children place three maps of Fraction City side by side and have them use their cars to drive a distance equal to $1\frac{1}{3}$. (See Activities 10, 11, 12, 13, 29, and 30 for further details.) Then, have them drive $\frac{1}{2}$ street more from the first distance. They will need to recognize that since they cannot drive on two streets at the same time, they need to find one street that has equivalent distances to those in the problem. Lead them into a discussion about how they would find this street. Remind them of how they have dealt with this problem before (see Activities 29 and 30). They will discover that Sixth Street will help them solve the given problem. Continue this activity with subtraction problems such as $1\frac{7}{8} - \frac{3}{4}$. The children should keep records of the steps used in solving these problems.

ACTIVITY 32

Type 3: Abstract

Age:	7–9
Objective:	Least common multiple
Materials:	Computer

Instructions: Enter this program into the computer and show the children how to run it. Feel free to modify it as needed to obtain multiples that are useful to your class. If more than 40 multiples are needed you could have the computer print the list of multiples.

```
 10 HOME
 20 PRINT "THIS PROGRAM WILL HELP YOU"
 30 PRINT "FIND MULTIPLES FOR TWO NUMBERS."
 40 PRINT
 50 PRINT "WHAT IS THE FIRST NUMBER";
 60 INPUT A
 70 PRINT
 80 PRINT "WHAT IS THE SECOND NUMBER";
 90 INPUT B
100 HOME
110 FOR I=1 TO 40
120 PRINT "MULTIPLES OF ";A;" :"
130 PRINT I*A;", ";
140 NEXT I
150 FOR I=1 TO 40
160 PRINT
170 PRINT
180 PRINT "MULTIPLES OF ";B;" :"
190 PRINT I*B;", ";
200 NEXT I
210 PRINT
220 PRINT
230 PRINT "WHICH ONES ARE ALIKE?"
240 END
```

ACTIVITY 33

Type 3: Abstract

Age: 7–9

Objective: Greatest common factor

Materials: Computer

Instructions: Enter the program in the computer. The program can be modified to find factors of three numbers instead of just two. The children might want to get a printout of the factors.

```
 10 HOME
 20 PRINT "THIS PROGRAM WILL HELP YOU"
 30 PRINT "FIND FACTORS OF TWO NUMBERS."
 40 PRINT
 50 PRINT "WHAT IS THE FIRST NUMBER";
 60 INPUT A
 70 PRINT
 80 PRINT "WHAT IS THE SECOND NUMBER";
 90 INPUT B
100 PRINT
110 PRINT "FACTORS OF ";A;" ARE:"
120 FOR I=1 TO A
130 IF A/I=INT(A/I) THEN PRINT I;" ";
```

```
140 NEXT I
150 PRINT
160 PRINT
170 FOR J=1 TO B
180 IF B/J=INT(B*J) THEN PRINT J;" ";
190 NEXT J
200 PRINT
210 PRINT
220 PRINT "WHICH ONES ARE ALIKE?"
230 END
```

STUDY QUESTIONS AND ACTIVITIES

1. Describe a Type 1 activity for adding odds to odds, evens to evens, and odds to evens.

2. First, reflect on what you think children might think when they hear or read statements or questions such as the following. Then, rewrite each to suggest better ways to think about the mathematics involved.
   a. Reduce the following fractions to lowest terms.
   b. To add fractions with the same denominator, add the numerators and bring down the denominator.
   c. To simplify $\frac{3}{9}$, we say 3 goes into 3 one time and 3 goes into 9 three times.
   d. Add a 0 to 0.1 to get 0.10.
   e. 0.1 and 0.10 mean the same thing.

3. Describe Type 1, 2, and 3 activities that would help children understand why a fraction decreases in value when its denominator increases.

4. Tell all you can about the numbers missing below. Do not solve.

   a. $0.57 + [\ ] =$

   b. $\frac{15}{100} + \frac{95}{100} = [\ ]$

   c. $5.5 - \frac{[\ ]}{10} = 4$

5. Find two fractions, reduced to simplest terms, whose denominators are different and whose difference is

   a. $\frac{1}{2}$ b. $\frac{1}{3}$

6. Take any Type 3 activity and make it into a Type 1 and Type 2 for the student who is having trouble understanding a concept in abstract form.

REFERENCES AND RESOURCES

Beattie, I. D. (1986). Building understanding with blocks. *Arithmetic Teacher, 34*(2), 5–11.

Bell, M. S., Fuson, K. C., & Lesh, R. A. (1976). *Algebraic and arithmetic structures: A concrete approach for elementary school teachers.* New York: Free Press.

California State Department of Education. (1985). *Mathematics framework for California public schools: Kindergarten through grade twelve.* Sacramento: Bureau of Publications, California State Department of Education.

Coxford, A. F. (1975). Fractional numbers. In J. N. Payne (Ed.), *Mathematics learning in early childhood* (pp. 192–203). Reston, VA: NCTM.

Edge, D. (1987). Fractions and panes. *Arithmetic Teacher, 34*(8), 13–17.

Quintero, A. H. (1987). Helping children understand ratios. *Arithmetic Teacher, 34*(9), 17–21.

8

Geometry

GEOMETRY IS far more important at the early childhood level than most people realize. For example, geometric models are used to teach and learn arithmetic concepts and knowledge of informal geometry is needed to teach and learn reading and writing. For children with special needs, geometry offers rich opportunities to strengthen perceptual and motor skills as well as visual discrimination abilities.

The concept of triangle can be studied without using the term *triangle* until around age 3, although some children as young as age 2 can already name a circle and a square. After age 3, the term becomes part of the child's vocabulary. Other concepts, such as transformations, are studied without ever applying terms to them until the middle school level. It is not possible to classify each type of term easily, because of different curricula and student abilities. Also, it is not possible to separate teacher vocabulary from student vocabulary because so many geometry terms are considered intuitive or informal content. Therefore, the following section is called Vocabulary for Teachers and Students. In the discussion, terms will be identified as those most likely *not* to occur in curriculum materials before the middle school level and those that probably *will* occur before that time.

This section also includes terms that are not limited to Euclidean geometry. It is no longer considered appropriate to limit the early study of geometry to only Euclidean concepts. In some geometries straightness and length are not important. Topology is one of those geometries. Even projective geometry can be studied before children are ready for Euclidean concepts. All three geometries are included in this chapter.

VOCABULARY FOR TEACHERS AND STUDENTS

Let's start with the term *model*. This term is a teacher's term; it shouldn't have to enter the vocabulary of the young student until perhaps grade 2. A **model** is a physical or graphical representation of a geometric figure of any dimension. For example, a model of a prism can be a real object such as a shoe box or it can be specially constructed or drawn. Just as numbers are not real objects, but instead are ideas embodied by objects or events, geometric ideas are ideas embodied in models.

Often the terms *figure* and *shape* are used interchangeably with *model*. Teachers should be aware that when preschoolers are asked to name a *shape* or to label a *figure,* they are as unfamiliar with these terms as they are with the terms *triangle* or *square*. Consider asking questions such as "Can you name this picture?" *Picture* is a much more frequently heard term and one that children learn to use early in their lives. Perhaps by age 4 or 5 the terms *shape* and *figure* will not interfere with learning the terms *triangle* and *square,* although it could be later for some children. The issue just described is classification and language development. It is more important for the child to understand the concepts of dimensions, properties, and transformations than to know and use the labels for these concepts. In other words, a child's ability to recognize straightness or order in objects is more important than his or her ability to know that these concepts are classified under *property*.

Models have *dimensions*. Dimensions of a figure generally refer to the number of horizontal/vertical measures possible. For example, a string has one possible measure of length, a window pane has two measures—length and width, and a cereal box has three—length, width, and height. Children can be led to recognize the concept of dimension, but shouldn't be expected to master the term itself.

Geometric models as well as physical objects have *properties*. Some geometric properties are enclosure, separation, order, proximity, number of dimensions, straightness or curvature, size, shape (number of segments, sides, faces, points), position, and orientation (right/left, up/down).

Four of these properties need some description. *Enclosure* describes the position of an item between two others on a line, within a region, or within a figure in space. *Separation* describes the place where one object breaks from another. *Order* describes an arrangement of objects by pattern or classification. *Proximity* describes the nearness of one object to another.

When models are changed or altered in some way, mathematically we say they are transformed. There are several types of *transformations,* but we will only consider three: topological, projective, and Euclidean. Properties are characteristics or features of a figure that are conserved (not changed) under transformations. Under topological transformations (sometimes called "stretches and shrinks"), shape or size can change, but proximity, order, enclosure, and separation cannot change. Projective transformations, which occur from changes in visual perspective, can change the shape and/or size of a figure but not its straightness. Euclidean transformations of slides, flips, or turns may change location and/or orientation of figures but not their shape or size. The following lists give a more inclusive look at these ideas. The lists are followed by some examples in Figure 8 1. In the first part of the figure, a balloon is inflated as a demonstration of a topological transformation. Shape and size are altered but enclosure, proximity, order, and separation are not. In the figure, the second example shows the changing perspective of the viewer as a projective transformation. Shape and size are not altered but straightness is. The last example shows that changing the position of an object is a Euclidean transformation. Position is altered but not size and shape.

Transformation	What Does Not Change	What May Change
Topological	Proximity	Shape
	Order	Size
	Enclosure	Straightness
	Separation	Orientation
		Location
Projective	Proximity	Shape
	Order	Size
	Enclosure	Orientation
	Separation	Location
	Straightness	
Euclidean	Proximity	Orientation
	Order	Location (position)
	Enclosure	
	Separation	
	Straightness	
	Size	
	Shape	

At the middle school and high school levels, slides are also called *translations,* flips are also called *reflections,* and turns are also called *rotations.* Most of the terms in the following discussion represent concepts for children to learn but not to name until at least the middle grades. Some exceptions are the terms *order, separation, slide, flip, turn, shape, and size.* Teachers should be sensitive to children's readiness to use these terms meaningfully.

a. Topological

An uninflated
balloon.

The same
balloon inflated.

b. Projective

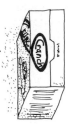

A cereal box
viewed from
above.

The same cereal
box viewed from
the right corner.

c. Euclidean

A magazine
faceup on
the corner
of a table.

The same magazine
moved diagonally and
turned on the table.

FIGURE 8–1
Examples of Transformations

Geometric models and real objects have other properties associated with shape and size that are illustrated in Figure 8–2. *Similarity* refers to figures that have the same shape and also have respective measures that are in proportion to each other. *Congruent* figures have the same shape and the same size. Two kinds of *symmetry* are *reflective symmetry* and *rotational symmetry*.

Reflective symmetry means that the two parts of a figure, when folded, match each other exactly. Rotational symmetry means that a shape can be turned (less than 360 degrees) about a point so the figure, when turned, coincides with the original. Two more important terms are *parallel* and *perpendicular*. Two lines or planes that are parallel never meet. Two lines or planes that meet at a right angle are perpendicular. In most curricula, children should learn all these terms at least by the fourth grade. However, children can obtain informal understanding of these concepts earlier.

The early study of Euclidean geometry includes polyhedra, polygons, lines, and points. The concepts that these terms represent and other related concepts can also be learned at the preschool level. Introduction of terminology follows concept learning. By the end of fourth grade, children will have had opportunities to master all the terms presented here.

Let's start with three-dimensional shapes. Two special classes of *polyhedra* are *prisms* and *pyramids*. Prisms shown in Figure 8–3 have two straight-sided figures (polygons) that are parallel to each other. The shapes that "connect" the two polygon bases are four-sided and have parallel opposite edges (parallelograms). If the bases are rectangles, the prism is called a *rectangular prism*. If the bases are squares, it is called a *square prism*. In addition, if the height is the same distance as the edge of the square base, it is called a *cube*. If the bases are triangles, it is called a *triangular prism*. Figure 8–3 also shows *pyramids*, which like prisms, can have any straight-sided figure (polygon) as a base, but, unlike prisms, they have only one base instead of two. The sides other than the base are triangles. A pyramid with a triangular base is called a triangular pyramid, one with a square base is called a square pyramid, and so forth. Another classification of three-dimensional models includes those models associated with the circle such as *spheres, cylinders,* and *cones*. A ball is a model of a sphere. By definition a sphere is a three-dimensional surface that has all its points the same distance from a given interior point. Cylinders and cones are the circular counterparts to prisms and pyramids, respectively. A can is a model of a cylinder. By definition, a cylinder has two parallel circular bases of the same size with a side surface connecting one circle to the other. The familiar pastry shell used to hold a scoop of ice cream is a model of a cone. A cone has a circle base and a side surface that slopes to a point. Models associated with the circle are also shown in Figure 8–3.

In a plane, *polygons* are simple closed figures composed of three or more straight line segments. They can be classified according to the number of sides they have, the measures of their sides, the measures of their angles, or the number of lines of symmetry they have. For example, a three-sided polygon is a triangle, a four-sided polygon is a quadrilateral, and a five-sided polygon is a pentagon. Polygons with all sides equal and all angles equal have special names. For triangles, quadrilaterals, and pentagons the special cases are called *equilateral triangles, squares,* and *regular polygons,* respectively. Triangles with no two sides equal are called *scalene*; those with at least two sides equal are called *isosceles*. A triangle can also be named according to the sizes

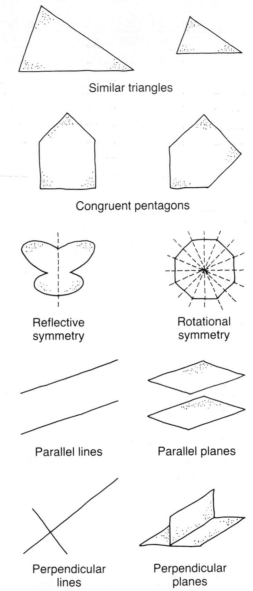

Similar triangles

Congruent pentagons

Reflective
symmetry

Rotational
symmetry

Parallel lines

Parallel planes

Perpendicular
lines

Perpendicular
planes

FIGURE 8–2
Other Properties Associated with Shape and Size

of its angles. A triangle with a 90° angle is called a *right triangle,* one with an angle greater than 90° is called an *obtuse triangle,* and one with no angles equal to or greater than 90° is called an *acute triangle.* Some examples are shown in Figure 8–4.

A *line* is a one-dimensional shape that consists of a set of points extending infinitely in a straight path. The set of points between two given points on a

a. Prisms

b. Pyramids

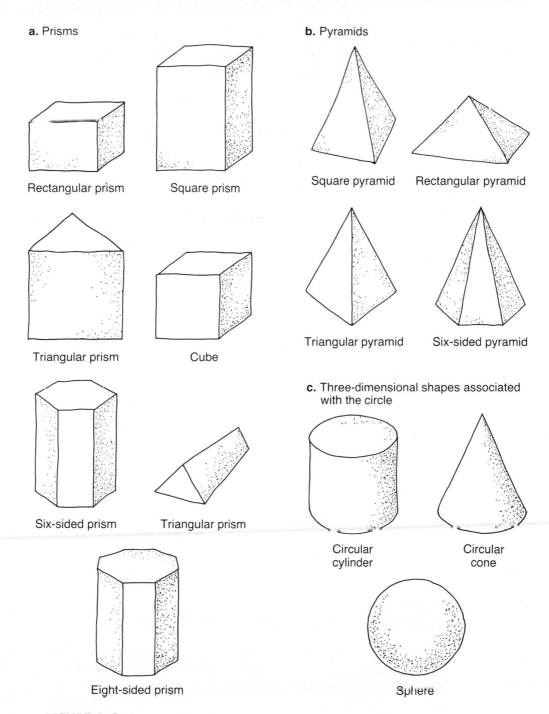

Rectangular prism   Square prism

Square pyramid   Rectangular pyramid

Triangular prism   Cube

Triangular pyramid   Six-sided pyramid

c. Three-dimensional shapes associated with the circle

Six-sided prism   Triangular prism

Circular cylinder   Circular cone

Eight-sided prism

Sphere

FIGURE 8–3
Classifications and Examples of Three-dimensional Figures

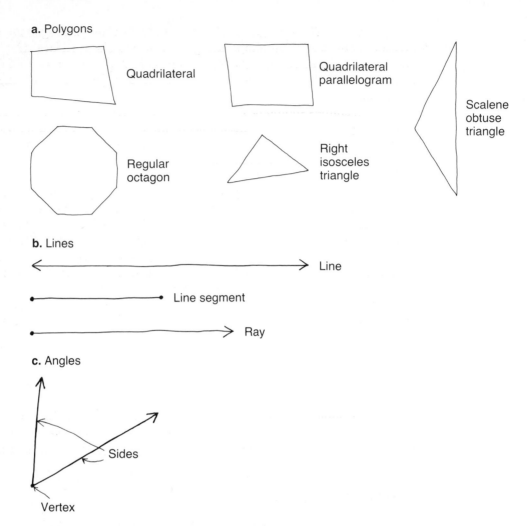

a. Polygons

Quadrilateral

Quadrilateral parallelogram

Scalene obtuse triangle

Regular octagon

Right isosceles triangle

b. Lines

Line

Line segment

Ray

c. Angles

Sides

Vertex

FIGURE 8–4
Polygons, Lines, and Angles

line is called a *line segment*. A *ray* is a point on a line and all points on one side of that point. An *angle* is the union of two rays having the same endpoint. This endpoint is called the *vertex* and the rays are called the *sides* of the angle. Finally, a *point* is defined as a location that has no dimensions. Pictures of points are usually shown with dots.

Teachers should avoid using some of the terms just presented, such as *triangle, rectangle, square,* and *circle,* until children are able to pronounce and use them meaningfully. Teachers can listen to the labels children give for different shapes and use those labels to define the formal terms. For example, a square or a rectangle might be called a box, a line might be called a stick, and so on. Teachers can include those terms in an activity, by saying, "Your red box is a square" or "The straight stick you drew is a line." It might be advisable to avoid using the term *shape* altogether when children are first learning other terms such as circle, square, etc. For children at ages 3 and 4, knowing the meaning of a circle or square is more important than knowing what a "shape" is.

At first, shapes should be called what they are, such as blocks, cups, rubber bands, and pencils. Parts of these objects should also be named with language available to the child. Some examples are corner for *angle,* point for *vertex,* line for *edge,* bottom for *base,* and so on.

Teachers should be aware of the idiosyncratic uses of some terms. For example, although mathematically the term *area* is applied to two-dimensions, it often implies three-dimensions in everyday language. Some examples are "reading area" or "art area" in a classroom, which includes a spatial section of a room. Ironically, the reverse often occurs with the term *space.* When children color a coloring book page with a crayon, they often refer to the two-dimensional shape they are coloring as a space. Another term that can cause confusion is *region,* because it can refer to either a surface or space.

The word *edge* is used in the same context as in everyday language. Other words, like *face,* are familiar words used in a new context. Then, there are words like *base,* that fall in neither category.

DIMENSIONS

The illustrations in Figure 8–6 should help you visualize the examples discussed for three-, two-, one-, and zero-dimensional shapes. Try to think of other examples that would apply—examples that children might identify in their own environments.

Three Dimensions

The first geometric experiences children have are primarily with three-dimensional space and solid figures. Some examples are baby bottles, drinking cups, stuffed animals, balls, blocks, balloons, and sand buckets. All of these objects have length, width, and depth. Hollow objects are models of space figures, and those that are not hollow are models of solids. Many of these objects can be traced with pencil to make two-dimensional shapes. See Activity 1 at the end of the chapter for directions.

Two Dimensions

Two-dimensional shapes are those regions that have length and width. Technically, a sheet of paper, a piece of cardboard, a plastic chip, or a plastic attribute or tangram piece not only have length and width, they have thickness as well. However, for instructional purposes they are used as two-dimensional models. Thus, some examples of two-dimensional models are paper valentines, puzzle pieces, and pictures in a book. In some cases, it is not clear how to determine whether a model is two- or three-dimensional, such as the model the 3-year-old is playing with in Figure 8–5. This model is actually a three-dimensional plastic wheel that has the shape of a circle. However, this child can correctly respond "circle" when asked what she is playing with. As with three-dimensional figures, two-dimensional figures that are small enough can be traced to make lines, curves, and angles as shown in Activity 15 at the end of the chapter.

One Dimension

Models of line segments are generally noticed in situations where they are important, such as the skyline in a coloring book page; kite string of a flying kite; pick-up sticks; cracks on a sidewalk; and certain parts of letters such as *T, L, P,* and *W.* As with two-dimensional models, lines can be generated by tracing the edges of three-dimensional shapes. Some one-dimensional models are pictured in Figure 8–6.

Zero Dimensions

Some models for points are the vertices of polyhedra, polygons, and angles. Marks are used to identify points on a surface or in space. Children generally become aware of points when they engage in connect-the-dot activities,

FIGURE 8–5
A 3-year-old plays with a model of a circle.

practice dotting their i's and j's, and recognize punctuation marks such as periods or the dots that are part of exclamation or question marks.

In conclusion, remember that there are exceptions to these simplified classifications of different dimensions. Many examples cannot be classified easily. For example, a page of a book is two-dimensional. However, when the book is closed, the page contributes to the three dimensions of the book. Recall the plastic three-dimensional circular wheel in Figure 8–5. Finally, consider an illustration in a book. A picture of a telephone pole is a one-dimensional representation of a three-dimensional object. The illustrations in this chapter, including those of all three-dimensional objects, are illustrated in just two dimensions. Therefore, this fact makes a strong case for using objects during instruction in geometry.

TRANSFORMATIONS AND PROPERTIES

The following discussion will give you some ideas on the integral part that transformations play in children's everyday experiences. Making transformations a part of geometry instruction will facilitate children's ability to observe what changes and what doesn't change in the environment. It will also facilitate children's flexibility of thinking and language development. Figures 8–7, 8–8, and 8–10, respectively, illustrate topological, projective, and Euclidean transformations. Also, see the activities after the Instructional Planner for Geometry at the end of this chapter.

Topological

Topology is also called *rubber sheet geometry,* because, in general, children's first geometric ideas are related to stretching and shrinking instead of size, shape, direction, or angle. The topological properties of proximity, order, enclosure, and separation remain unchanged under irregular stretchings and shrinkings that create distortions. For example, when observing his or her mother's smile, a baby notices that the smile transforms the mother's facial features from her nonsmiling face. The smile stretches some parts of her face and shrinks other parts. Despite this transformation, the young child grows to accept some things as unchanging or conserved, such as the order of the mother's eyes, nose, and mouth; the separation of her eyes from each other; the proximity of her eyes to each other; and the enclosure of all her features within the boundary of her face.

Even though most of the development of topological understanding in children occurs through observations of human facial features and body movements, there are many observations that occur elsewhere such as with food. Examples are melting ice cream or baking a cake or cookies.

Before a child has become topologically aware, certain interesting observations can be made to indicate varying degrees of development. For example,

a. Three-dimensional objects

Sand bucket

Drinking cup

Building block

Cereal box

Shoe

Playground ball

b. Two-dimensional objects

Paper valentine   Tangram pieces   Puzzle piece   Picture in a book

c. One-dimensional objects

Kite string   Pick-up sticks   Alphabet letter parts

d. Zero-dimensional "objects"

Dots on Dot-to-dot picture   Vertex of polyhedron   Dots on i's and j's   Vertex of an angle

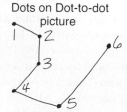

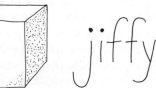

FIGURE 8–6
Examples of Geometry in the Child's World

when Douglas, age 3, drew a picture of his father, there was a disregard for separation because he did not draw the body between his father's head and his arms and legs. However, his father's beard was drawn prominently, connected to his chin. Douglas had an awareness of the boundary of the face where the facial features are enclosed. He also had an awareness of order since his father's eyes, nose, and mouth were placed in the proper vertical order. The same understanding of order was shown for the major body parts. Notice that the picture is constructed with simple curves and line segments that are aligned properly with respect to horizontal and vertical references. However, Douglas did disregard size. Notice the size of his father's eyes relative to the size of his head!

To demonstrate the phenomenon of irregular stretches and shrinks, use small sheets of rubber (cut-up balloons) or stretchable material (jersey or cut-up rubber gloves) with pictures or shapes sketched on them. Then, pull from the edges and watch the shapes stretch and shrink. Inflating balloons is another way to show stretching. Also, the shape of a ball of clay can be changed by flattening it, rolling it, and so on.

Observations of irregular stretches and shrinks do not require that children connect unconnected parts nor does it require them to disconnect connected parts of a figure. Therefore, when demonstrating these same transformations in the classroom with the materials suggested, there should be no breaking, tearing, cutting, or folding needed.

As various stretches and shrinkings occur, ask children what stays the same and what changes in the picture. For example, Activity 6 at the end of this chapter directs children to observe a smiley face drawn on a balloon while the balloon is slowly inflated and deflated. Ask questions such as, "Are the eyes still closer to each other than to the smile?" (proximity); "Is the nose touching the smile?" (separation); "Is the nose still between the eyes and smile?" (order); "Is the smile still inside the face?" (enclosure).

Understanding proximity and separation are prerequisite to understanding order. Children need to be able to identify the relative closeness of objects and at the same time they need to be able to distinguish one object from another.

Projective

A tree right in front of you appears larger than it did when you stood a block away. When a vehicle is close to you it appears to be large and when it is at a distance it appears to be small. Airplanes are large enough for hundreds of people, yet when they are flying they appear very tiny in the sky! Each of these examples shows how objects seem to uniformly stretch and shrink before our eyes!

Consider the following situations. The angle of the corner of a table looks like a right angle if you are viewing it from above and looking straight down. However, when the corner is viewed from one side or the other, the angle looks

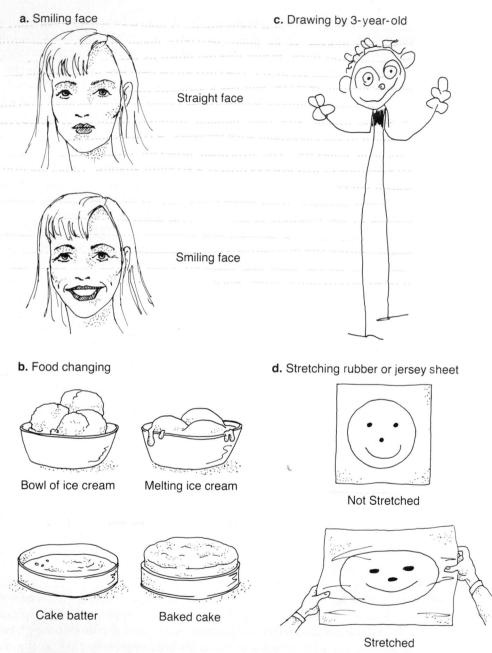

a. Smiling face

Straight face

Smiling face

c. Drawing by 3-year-old

b. Food changing

Bowl of ice cream   Melting ice cream

Cake batter   Baked cake

d. Stretching rubber or jersey sheet

Not Stretched

Stretched

FIGURE 8–7
Topological Transformations

smaller or larger than a right angle. A doorway with a door that is partially open can appear to be open, partially open, or closed depending on what viewpoint you have. When looking down at the rim of a cup, you can see the curve of the rim. However, the cup can be held eye level so that the curve is no longer visible. Instead, you see a straight line!

Projective geometry is sometimes called *shadow geometry* because changes of shape and/or size that happen through changes of perspective can be modeled in the classroom with shadows. A convenient light source to use is the overhead projector. The overhead projector creates fine transformations. A straight object will always project a straight shadow. Experimentation reveals that a curve can also project a straight line! (Consider the cup rim that was discussed earlier.) With projections, size is not necessarily constant as evidenced by the example of the tree from different viewpoints.

When projecting images, ask children what stays the same and what changes from the original object. For example, project an overhead transparency of a clown, then ask children what stayed the same (characteristics related to proximity, order, enclosure, separation, and straightness) and what changed (characteristics related to size). Now, project an object like a pencil. Hold the pencil over the light of the overhead projector. Have children observe the shadow on the screen while the pencil's orientation to the light is altered. Ask if the pencil shadow can be moved to look shorter. Try other objects such as pipe cleaners that are bent into open or closed curves or angles. Project the pipe cleaners by holding them one at a time. Ask children if the angle can be moved to make it look smaller or larger, ask them if the closed curve can be moved to make it look open, or if the open curve can be moved to make it look closed. All of these activities are designed to encourage children's visual discrimination skills as well as language skills needed to communicate observed differences and likenesses.

Euclidean

Puzzle pieces are slid, flipped, and rotated until the proper orientation and location have been found (see Figure 8–9). During this process the shape and size of each piece do not change. The actions of turning book pages, opening and closing doors, or sliding chairs in and out from under a table do not change the shape or size of these objects. These types of changes are sometimes called the geometry of *slides, flips,* and *turns;* shape and size are conserved.

Have children focus their attention on what changes and what stays the same after certain motions. For example, use an overhead transparency with a shape on it, such as a sailboat with a star on one sail. Slide, flip, and turn the transparency. In each case, ask children what stayed the same and what changed. An example of each transformation is illustrated in Figure 8–10.

To perform a slide transformation requires a direction and a length. The direction and length are shown with an arrow called a vector. Direction is given by the direction of the arrow and length is given by its length.

a. Changing point of view

Tabletop
looking straight
down

Tabletop
looking from
the right

(notice the emphasized angle)

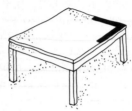

Tabletop looking
from the front at
eye level

Tabletop looking
from the left

b. Inflating balloon

Face on
uninflated
balloon

Face on inflated
balloon

c. Projecting image

Projected image
of clown

Transparency
slide of clown

FIGURE 8–8
Projective Transformations

FIGURE 8–9
Putting a puzzle together involves sliding, flipping, and turning pieces.

The flip transformation needs a direction and a length, too. Direction is shown by the placement of the line about which the flip is made (sometimes called the *line of symmetry* or the *line of reflection*), and length is shown by the distance between the line and the picture being flipped.

The turn transformation needs direction, length, and the center of the turn. Direction is indicated by an arrow, length is indicated by the length of that arrow, and the center of the turn (also called the *center of rotation*) is given by a point.

After each transformation, ask children the following questions:

Concepts to Introduce	Questions to Ask
Nearness of one sail to the other	"Are the sails closer now? The same?"
Enclosure of star on sail	"Is the star on the sail?"
Connectedness of sails to boat	"Are the sails still on the boat?"
Straightness of parts	"Are the pieces still straight?"
Shape of parts	"Are the sails still triangles?"
Sizes of parts	"Are the parts bigger? The same?"

All these properties should be conserved. Topological and projective properties are said to be subsumed in Euclidean geometry—the geometry of shape and size.

In summary, the informal study of topological, projective, and Euclidean transformations is rich with the potential to help children visually and cognitively perceive shapes and changes on those shapes in the environment. There are hundreds of opportunities every day for children to observe, interact with, and discuss these changes. These opportunities may happen automatically, such as in a smiling face, in shadows made by the sun or in the rotation of the hands of a clock, or they may happen deliberately in the laboratory of the classroom. Seeing is believing—that is what geometry is all about!

CONSTRUCTIONS

Give children many opportunities to construct figures of different dimensions. The activities in this chapter include using many of the construction tools, media, or techniques in the following list. Teachers and children should be encouraged to add to this list.

straws, pipe cleaners, popsicle sticks
straws or toothpicks with miniature marshmallows
the Mira — LIKE A MIRROR, REFLECTS.
Cuisenaire rods, Legos
geoboard
dot paper, square grid paper
clay, Play Doh, cookie dough
paper folding, paper ripping
paper, pencil, straightedge
tracing two-dimensional shapes to make one-dimensional shapes
tracing three-dimensional shapes to make two-dimensional shapes

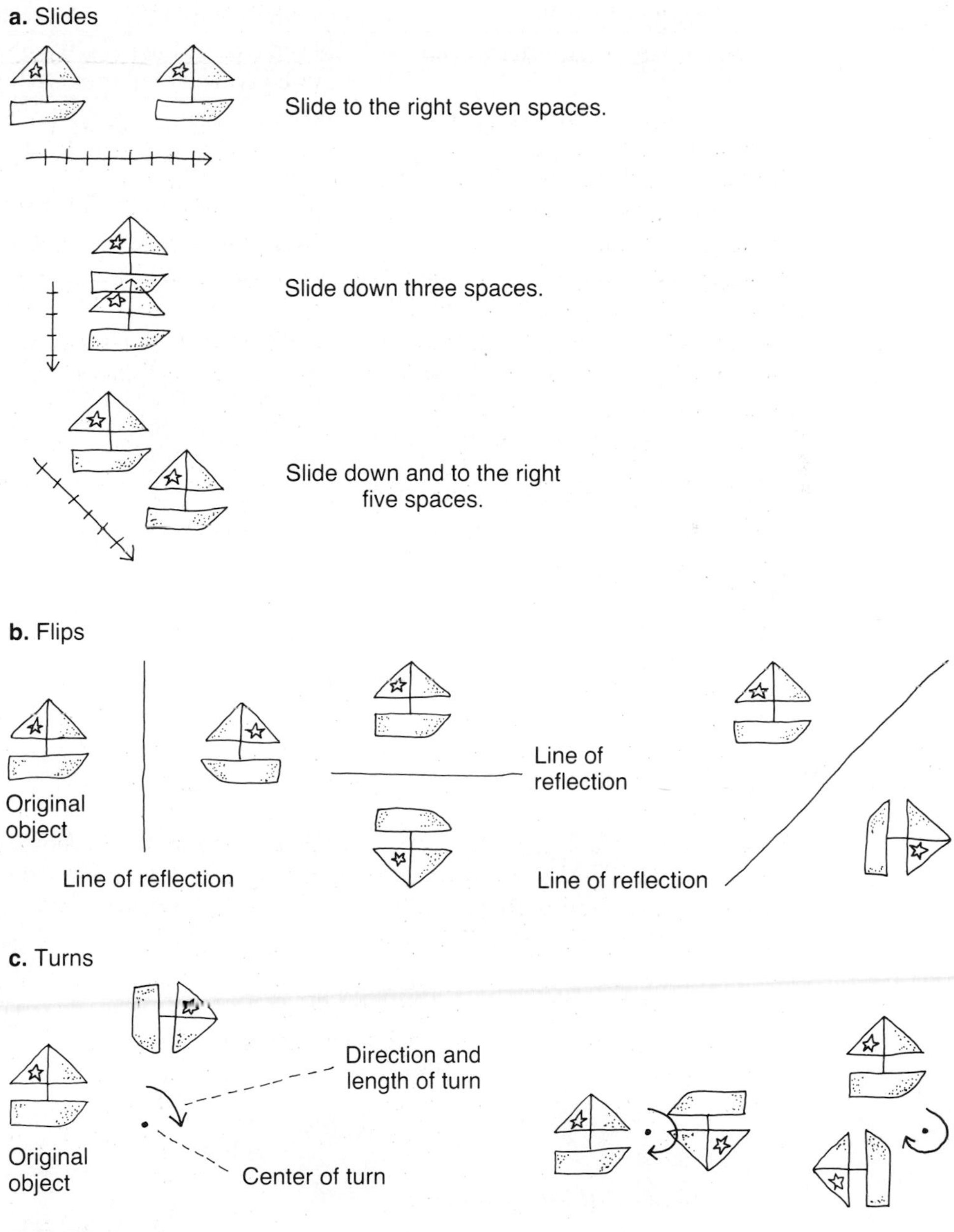

a. Slides

Slide to the right seven spaces.

Slide down three spaces.

Slide down and to the right
five spaces.

b. Flips

Original
object

Line of reflection

Line of
reflection

Line of reflection

c. Turns

Direction and
length of turn

Original
object

Center of turn

FIGURE 8–10
Euclidean Transformations

Of the items listed, two may not be familiar. The Mira, being used by a third grader in Figure 8–11, is a commercially produced red plexiglas shape that can serve in many ways in teaching and learning geometry. (See the

Appendix for the listing of school supply companies.) The Mira reflects in much the same way as a mirror, but with the additional capability of allowing the user to look through it so that images can be traced on paper with a pencil. The Mira allows students to construct a shape congruent to a given shape, find the midpoint of a line segment, construct a line perpendicular to a given line, and construct a symmetric shape. The Mira can be used for many other creative geometric constructions invented by children. Three last significant features of the Mira are that its reflections are flips of given images, which in turn can be slid or turned to new locations. Therefore, the Mira is an excellent tool to use to construct the shapes that result from Euclidean transformations.

The geoboard is usually a square or otherwise rectangular piece of wood or plastic in which pegs are positioned in rows and columns or circular arrangements. Geoboards are also commercially produced, though it is possible to make wooden versions. Rubber bands in different colors stretched across the pegs are used to make shapes and to show relationships. Some of the constructions possible on the geoboard are lines, angles, triangles, squares, parallel and perpendicular line segments, and shapes that are symmetric. Children can record their constructions on dot paper. In chapter 9, we will discuss using the geoboard for finding the perimeter and area of triangles and quadrilaterals. Children should be challenged to discover other activities they can perform with the geoboard.

Play and creativity should be the theme of geometry construction activities (if not all geometry activities!). Consider having a permanent "construction site" learning center located in the classroom. Two or three play construction safety hats could be supplied at the site to be worn by children as a signal that

FIGURE 8–11
This third grader is using a Mira.

they are engaged in building some special shape to share with the class at a later designated time. Have different materials set out each week for children to use. One example is to supply different colored sheets of paper for paper folding. Students can fold a sheet of paper in several ways and then darken the folds with a crayon to highlight the two-dimensional shapes they have constructed. Adding glue or tape offers the children other possibilities with their constructions. Another example is to distribute miniature marshmallows and toothpicks (flat, round-ended ones are safer) to encourage children to make three-dimensional constructions. Children, especially preschoolers, enjoy this activity. All these activities encourage hand-eye coordination. Figure 8–12 shows a symmetric construction at a Cuisenaire rod construction site.

FIGURE 8–12
A kindergartner constructs a symmetric figure by using Cuisenaire rods.

TEACHING AND LEARNING GEOMETRY

Knowing the order that children experience shapes in the environment as well as transformations on those shapes gives teachers guidance on which topics to teach in geometry and the general order in which these topics should be taught. The teacher should start by providing experiences with three-dimensional shapes, moving gradually to two-, one-, and zero-dimensional shapes. Remember that children learn topological properties before projective and Euclidean properties. This fact suggests that experiences with topological transformations should be offered to children first, then experiences with projective transformations, and finally Euclidean. Now, it's time to consider *how* to teach the geometry content. Let's examine the works of two Dutch educators, Dina van Hiele-Goldof and Pierre van Hiele (Crowley, 1987; Hoffer, 1983) who are renowned for their collaborative research in this area. The van Hiele model of geometric thought explains children's levels of geometric understanding and the phases of learning within each level.

Levels of Geometric Understanding

An abbreviated description of the van Hiele levels of geometric understanding follows. According to the van Hieles, primary grade children function mainly at Level 0, which is visualization. Some primary grade students may be functional at Level 1—analysis, depending on the type of classroom instruction they are given. Levels 2 through 4 are not included since they apply only to middle grade and secondary student learning.

Level 0: Visualization (Primary Grade Level)

Students recognize figures by their overall appearance. They can say *triangle, square, cube,* and so forth, but they do not explicitly identify properties of figures.

Level 1: Analysis (Primary Grade Level)

Students analyze properties of figures. They may be able to explain that squares have all equal sides and that the sides across from each other in a rectangle are equal but they can't interrelate figures or properties. That is, they do not understand that a square is a special case of a rectangle.

Phases of Learning

Progress through each level of geometric understanding is a function of the phases of learning. These phases move from direct instruction by the teacher to the students' independence from the teacher. A description follows.

Phase 1: Inquiry Information

The teacher involves students in two-way conversations and activities concerning the topic to be studied. Observations are made and questions asked. In this way, the teacher learns what prior knowledge students have and students receive a preview of the direction their study will take. This phase aligns with the constructivist perspective that was previously discussed.

Phase 2: Directed Orientation

With less prompting by the teacher, students explore a topic through carefully prepared and sequenced materials. During this phase, students become more aware of the geometric structures under study. Most directed orientation work consists of small tasks designed to elicit specific responses.

Phase 3: Explication

With even less prompting by the teacher than in Phase 2, students continue to build from their previous experiences, to refine their vocabulary and to express their understanding of the geometric structures being studied. Students begin to see relationships between structures.

Phase 4: Free Orientation

Students undertake tasks that have several steps and several paths to complete, and that are open-ended. Students work independently to complete these tasks.

Phase 5: Integration

Students review the structures they have encountered and form an overview of them. During this phase, students complete a level of learning and are ready to use this overview to move into the next level of learning.

Properties of the van Hiele Model

Some important generalities about the levels of learning provide guidance for instruction and, therefore, are particularly significant to teachers. These generalities are referred to as *properties* of the model. The first property is **sequencing.** A child must proceed through the levels in order. The second property, **advancement,** indicates that progress or failure to progress to a succeeding level depends more on content (Instructional Planner) and instructional methods (Phases of Learning) than on age. Third, the **intrinsic/ extrinsic** property means that the concepts that are inherent in the experiences at one level become the object of study in the next level. For example, tracing three-dimensional shapes to obtain and name two-dimensional shapes is the inherent object of a Level 0 learning experience on visualization. To analyze the shapes from which the two-dimensional objects came is the object of study at Level 1 analysis. The fourth property of **linguistics** means that each level of learning has its own language and its own way of relating with the language. For example, at Level 0 students might understand square and rectangle, but it isn't until Level 1 that they understand the relationship between square and rectangle. Finally, there is the fifth property, called **mismatch.** This property means that if the student is operating at one level and instruction is at another level, learning will not occur!

USING THE COMPUTER TO LEARN ABOUT GEOMETRY

Some of the most interesting and stimulating experiences that the computer offers for learning about geometry are provided by the Logo language. Logo promotes learning through discovery, develops problem-solving ability, and supports the teaching of geometry. This easy-to-use and simple-to-understand computer language enables even children as young as kindergarten age to explore many aspects of plane geometry. Logo features a *turtle*—a small triangle, actually—that appears on the computer screen and can be directed to move around the screen through the use of simple commands. Children can learn about turning and lengths and can construct triangles, squares, and other polygons by using this language. Logo also has commands that enable a child to repeat a figure many times for successive iterations of procedures.

Unlike drill and practice programs that do not encourage much, if any, flexibility of thinking, Logo programs give children the means to express their own creativity. They can even develop their own drill and practice programs! Turtle geometry makes it possible for children to study a wide range of mathematical concepts. Many quality Logo software packages are currently available.

There are many ways to learn about Logo. The best way might be to attend a Logo workshop at your nearest NCTM regional or national meeting. In this environment, you will have hands-on experience with the language, and begin to see its potential for teaching geometry to children in an enjoyable and informal way. This type of workshop will help you to select books about Logo that will be most useful to you and your students from the large variety of books publishers offer.

ESTIMATION AND PROBLEM SOLVING

One of the natural ways nonnumerical estimation occurs is during the exploration of transformations. This type of nonnumerical estimation is referred to as *anticipatory imagery* (Piaget, 1971). Even 4-year-olds can guess what will be the same and what will be different as they anticipate various transformations. Children should be encouraged to verify their guesses by observing or by performing the transformations themselves.

Children can also be encouraged to test the validity of geometric propositions by experimentation. An example would be to have them guess what kind of angle can be formed from the three angles of a triangle. They could verify their guesses by cutting out a triangle (carefully drawn), tearing off the three corners, and placing the points together to form an angle. Challenge 4- and 5-year-olds to find out if the same type of angle is formed by the angles of different triangles.

Another exploration activity would involve asking children whether three given straws can be used to form a triangle. Children should explore the situations in which the straws will not work and the situations in which they will. Help children look for similarities and differences in these situations. Even though preschoolers can perform many of these activities, the activities are still very useful through grade 3 and beyond.

SUMMARY

The study of geometry can be summarized in a similar way as the study of arithmetic. Recall that the study of arithmetic was viewed as a study of number systems, operations on those number systems, and properties of number systems under certain operations. Likewise, the study of geometry can be viewed as the study of shapes of different dimensions, transformations of those shapes, and properties of shapes under certain transformations. In addition, the study of geometry includes constructions of shapes. The Instructional Planner for Geometry uses the chart shown in chapter 3. (See Table 3–2.) When planning for geometry instruction, you should include activities and discussions that attend to all five aspects of learning geometry.

PLANNING FOR INSTRUCTION

The Instructional Planner for Geometry has 17 activities listed according to the dimensions, transformations, and properties involved. As in the Instructional Planners for the arithmetic chapters, one activity number can be in more than one place on the chart. Some of the activities can be modified for placement in other categories. For example, Activity 9 can be modified for

Euclidean transformation of a zero-dimensional shape. Depending on the activity, some categories won't apply conveniently, such as a topological transformation of a zero-dimensional shape for Activity 9.

The activities following the Instructional Planner for Geometry are designed primarily at the van Hiele Levels 0 and 1. When using these activities in your classroom, notice the potential for advancing a Level 0 activity into a Level 1 activity. Notice also that the students' experiences progress through the Phases of Learning from inquiry and information gathering (Phase 1), such as Activity 1 on tracing, to directed orientation (Phase 2), such as Activity 2 where students are directed to analyze the relationship between the tracings and the objects being traced.

INSTRUCTIONAL PLANNER
Geometry

Dimensions	Transformations			Properties			Construc-tions
	Topological	*Projective*	*Euclidean*	*Topological*	*Projective*	*Euclidean*	
three		1, 2, 4, 5, 15	3		4, 5	2, 3, 15	1, 2
two	6, 7	7, 8, 9, 10, 11, 14, 15	3, 16	6, 7, 10	5, 7, 8, 9, 10, 11, 15	9, 12, 13, 14, 15, 16, 17	9, 12, 14, 15, 16, 17
one		8, 9	16		5, 8, 9	9, 16, 17	9, 16, 17
zero		9	16		9	9, 17	9, 16, 17

ACTIVITY 1

Age: 3–8

Objective: Three-dimensional figures, projective transformations, and constructions

Materials: Three-dimensional objects such as blocks, cereal boxes, footballs, shoes, cups, toys, etc.; construction paper; and pencils or crayons

Instructions: Have children place the object of their choice on their sheet of construction paper and show them how to trace around it. Talk with the children about how easy or how difficult it is to trace their objects. Ask them why some objects might be easier to trace than others. Ask them if they can find a different way to trace their object. (If necessary, suggest turning the object on its side, or turning it upside down, etc.)

Extension: On a sunny day, let the children take their objects outside and put them on a large piece of clear, rigid plastic. The piece of plastic should be supported about two feet off the ground, perhaps suspended between two chairs. (Most hardware and lumber stores carry plastic storm door replacement panes; these will work very nicely.) Let a few children at a time place their objects on the plastic sheet, put their construction paper or newsprint on the ground, and trace the shadow of the object. Encourage children to make two different tracings of the object by repositioning it on the plastic to get a different shadow. Help them discuss the differences in the two types of tracings: the tracings using the object itself and the tracings using the shadow of the object.

ACTIVITY 2

Age: 3–8

Objective: Three-dimensional figures, projective transformations, Euclidean properties, and constructions

Materials: Simple three-dimensional objects such as blocks, books, cups, etc.; construction paper; pencils or crayons; and scissors

Instructions: Ask the children to trace their object on the construction paper, then have them cut out the pattern they traced. Ask them to place the pattern on the object so the object fits the pattern. Then, have them trace the same object from a different "side" and cut out that tracing also. Ask them to fit the tracing and the object as before. Then, have them compare the tracings to each other. Get them to talk about how the tracings are alike and how they are different.

Extension: For an individual activity, place several objects on a table along with the two tracings of each of those objects which have been pasted onto a large sheet of construction paper. Let the children try to match the two objects with their corresponding tracings. After every child who wants to do this task has completed it, get the whole group involved in a discussion to decide which tracings match which objects. Have the children explain how they are making their choices.

ACTIVITY 3

Age: 3–8

Objective: Two- and three-dimensional figures, Euclidean transformations, and Euclidean properties

Materials: Overhead projector, transparency with a sailboat

Instructions: Project the sailboat. Slide it to the right. Ask the children what is different and what is the same. Perform the same action again, if necessary. Next, return the boat to its original position and slide it down. Ask the children what has changed now. Ask the children if the boat is still going the same direction, if it is still right-side-up, etc. Wait for the children to respond in each case. Return the boat to its original position and slide it diagonally. Keep asking questions until the children are sure what has changed and what has not. Ask them how they could make the boat point in the other direction. It may take awhile for them to realize that the boat needs to be flipped over. Show them the flip and then ask them, in the same way as before, what has changed and what has not. Flip the boat in several ways, including upside down and diagonally. Each time, return to the original position. When each move is made, encourage children to talk about what is different and what is the same. Then, show them a rotation or turn. Be sure to ask questions as you have been throughout this activity. Show several turns in different directions and through different angles.

Extension: Ask the children what would be needed to get the boat in position 1 to be in position 2.

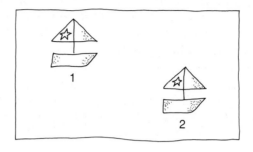

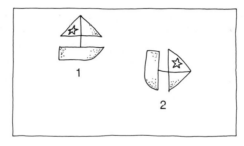

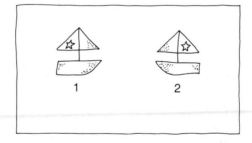

ACTIVITY 4

Age: 4–7

Objective: Three-dimensional figures, projective transformations, and projective properties

Materials: Half-sheets of construction paper with windows cut out

Instructions: Take the children into the hallway or out to the playground. Have each of them select an object, stand close to it, and look at it through the larger window in the construction paper. Ask them if they can see the whole object. If they can, ask them to hold the window away from their faces so they can't see the whole object through it. Then, tell them to walk backwards, holding the window steady, until they can barely see the whole object through it. Have them take note of how far they are from the object before they switch to the smaller window. At this point, they will need to back up again until they can see the whole object through the smaller window. Have them compare how far away from the object they are now with how far away they were when looking through the larger window. Discuss with them what they noticed, such as whether the whole object or only part of it seemed to get smaller and whether they could make the object look larger again.

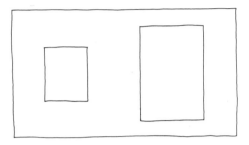

ACTIVITY 5

Age: 5–8

Objective: Three-dimensional figures, projective transformations, and projective properties

Materials: Construction paper circles and strips, drinking cups, cereal boxes, an overhead projector, and overhead transparencies prepared from the given pattern

Instructions: Give each of the children a paper circle, a drinking cup, and a cereal box. Show the transparency of the paper circle with the first figure on the slide showing and the others covered. Ask the children to position their paper circles to match the shape on the screen. Then, uncover the second picture and ask them to position their circles so their outlines match the second silhouette. Continue in a similar fashion with the other pictures of the circle. Discuss with children what they did to the circles to change the outlines. Follow this same process with the other objects, one shape at a time.

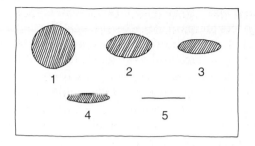

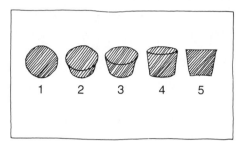

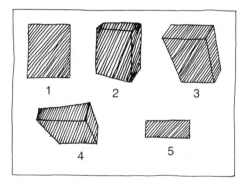

ACTIVITY 6

Age: 3–9

Objective: Two-dimensional figures, topological transformations, and topological properties

Materials: Pieces cut from rubber gloves, balloons, or similar stretchy materials and permanent markers

Instructions: Draw simple pictures, such as a smiling face, a fish, a house, etc., on the pieces of stretchy material by using markers. Give one piece to each child. Let the children explore stretching the pictures for a short time. Then, take your picture and ask the children to explain what you can do with it. If your picture is a smiling face, ask them if you could, by stretching, move the mouth outside of the face, if you could place the mouth between the eyes and the nose, if you could position the eyes farther away from the nose, etc. Let them try to accomplish these changes with their own pieces.

ACTIVITY 7

Age: 3–8

Objective: Two-dimensional figures, topological transformations, projective transformations, topological properties, and projective properties

Materials: Overhead projector, transparency with a smiling face, a balloon with a smiling face drawn on it

Instructions: Project the smiling face on the screen. Ask the children how the face on the screen is similar to and how it is different from the one on the uninflated balloon. Move the projector away from the screen to make the image larger (adjust the focus accordingly). Ask the children what the difference is between the face on the screen becoming larger and the face on the balloon becoming larger. (Reinflate the balloon as you discuss the difference.) The distinction between these two situations may be very subtle, so be prepared to help the children to see it.

ACTIVITY 8

Age: 2–9

Objective: One- and two-dimensional figures, projective transformations, and projective properties

Materials: Overhead projector, simple drawings on transparencies

Instructions: Place a transparency with a simple drawing, such as a smiling face, on the projector and tape it down. Move the image of the drawing by tilting and/or moving the projector. After each move, ask the children to tell you what is different about the picture and what is the same. Help the children to see that the eyes, nose and mouth of the smiling face have not gone outside the face or shifted around inside the face, even though their size and shape may have changed somewhat. Follow this process with other drawings. Ask children questions about the straightness of lines, such as "Can a curved line be made to look straight?"

ACTIVITY 9

Age: 2–8

Objective: Two-, one-, and zero-dimensional figures, projective trans-
              formations, Euclidean properties, and constructions

Materials: Wooden blocks of any shape that are designated for this activity
              (after one use, they cannot be used for anything else), ink pad of
              washable ink or tempera paint, construction paper (consider
              using aprons to protect clothes)

Instructions: Demonstrate how to touch the pad with corner (vertex) of the
block to make dots (points) on the paper. Next, show how to touch an edge of
the block to the pad to make lines, and finally, show how to touch the side of
the block to make shapes (squares, rectangles, or triangles depending on which
types of blocks are being used). Have children follow the same process by
making whatever shapes they wish to make. Compare and discuss their
finished pictures using language available.

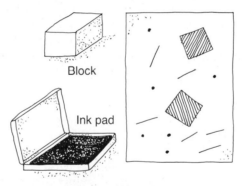

Block

Ink pad

ACTIVITY 10

Age: 5–8

Objective: Two-dimensional figures, projective transformations, topological properties, and projective properties

Materials: Overhead projector, straws, pipe cleaners

Instructions: Insert a pipe cleaner into the end of a straw. Insert the other end of the pipe cleaner into another straw. Push the straws together so they meet. Bend to form an angle. Use a third straw and another pipe cleaner to make various open and closed figures. Experiment with cutting the straws into various lengths. Use the overhead projector to project these shapes one at a time. Turn them and angle them so they project different images. In each case, ask the children what has changed, and what has stayed the same. Ask them if straight-sided objects can ever look curved and vice versa. Ask them if open curves can be made to appear closed and vice versa.

Extension: Let children take the objects formed by straws and pipe cleaners with a piece of tan construction paper (white could be too bright) to project shadows outside in the sunshine. Have them work in teams of two. One child should hold the object and the other should trace its shadow, then they can trade places. Be sure to discuss what they discovered. In particular, be sure to discuss how the sun shadows are different from the overhead shadows.

ACTIVITY 11

Age: 4–9

Objective: Two-dimensional figures, projective transformations, and projective properties

Materials: Slide projector, screen, slides of pictures of simple objects

Instructions: Start with a slide of a simple picture and with the projector positioned very close to the screen. As you slowly move the projector away from the screen, adjust the focus as needed. Let the children explain what is happening. Ask them why the image is changing. Move the projector until the image fills the whole screen.

Ask them how projected images are different from real objects. (With a projector, the size of the image increases when the distance from the screen increases, but in real life the further away an object is the smaller it appears.)

ACTIVITY 12

Age: 7–9

Objective: Two-dimensional figures and Euclidean properties

Materials: Masking tape, meter stick

Instructions: Place two 2-foot long strips of masking tape on the floor to form an angle. One at a time, let the children stand at the vertex of the angle, facing one ray. From that position, have the child turn to face the other ray by turning his or her body. Encourage each child to move this way a couple of times to get the feel of how much turning is needed. Then, ask each child to extend his or her arms in front with palms together. Have the child turn as before. Ask if the amount of turning was the same or different. Next, let the child hold a meter stick between his or her hands and (with arms extended) turn from one ray to the other as before. The meter stick should line up with the rays of the angle at the beginning and the end of the turn. Ask the child to compare the amount of turning done this time with the other times. Try to get the child to guess how much turning would be needed if the meter stick were much longer. (The turning should be the same, regardless of the length of the stick.)

ACTIVITY 13

Age: 2–9

Objective: Two-dimensional figures and Euclidean properties

Materials: Tangram pieces, attribute blocks®, and/or cardboard cutouts of geometric figures

Instructions: Give each child seven or eight dissimilar figures. Ask the children to sort their figures into groups. Allow some time for this task and let the children sort any way they wish. Then, have each child explain to the rest of the children why the pieces of each group belong together. Children may have sorted according to color, number of sides, roundness, type of material, and so forth. Select another piece (perhaps borrowed from another child) that was not in the original collection and ask the child in which group it should be placed and why.

After this part of the activity has been thoroughly explored, collect all the pieces that the children have been using and redistribute them. Then, ask "Who has a shape with three sides?" Let them put all the shapes with three sides in one large group. Ask other questions such as "Who has a round shape?" or "Who has a four-sided shape?" For this part of the activity make sure that the groups are described in terms of geometric properties rather than by color or material. After all the shapes have been placed in large groups, ask the children to tell you what words describe each group.

Extension: Repeat the second part of this activity, but after the large groups have been formed, talk to children about the names for three-sided shapes, four-sided shapes, round shapes and so on. (Give them an opportunity to tell you what they already know; you could be surprised!) Then, place cards with the appropriate classification word near each of the groups and talk about how these words are spelled and what they mean.

After this discussion, redistribute all the pieces again. This time, put the labeling cards on the floor or on a table and have the children place their pieces on the appropriate card.

ACTIVITY 14

Age: 3–9

Objective: Two-dimensional figures, projective transformations, Euclidean properties, and constructions

Materials: Objects in the classroom such as erasers, pencils, attribute blocks, cans, books, etc., construction paper, and scissors.

Instructions: Have the children begin by tracing the shape of an object on construction paper. Then, have them use different objects and the same objects in different positions for variety. Help them cut their tracings out. Use the cutouts to talk about the shapes they made from the objects. Ask questions such as:

How many sides does this shape have?

Does it have all straight sides?

How many corners are in this shape?

ACTIVITY 15

Age: 5–8

Objective: Three- and two-dimensional figures, projective transformations, Euclidean properties, and constructions

Materials: Cardboard shapes, attribute blocks, pattern blocks, tangram pieces, construction paper, pencils, and rulers

Instructions: Give each of the children a variety of objects to trace. Ask them to trace along one side, around the corner, and along another side to form an angle. Encourage them to trace several angles this way. Talk about the sizes of the angles they traced. Discuss how many sides the original shape had and how big the angles in the traced shape were.

Then, let them select objects, trace any two sides of those objects, and use a ruler to extend the traced sides. Discuss what happens to the extended lines. Have them extend lines in different ways with different objects. Ask children if they can get different results from the same object and similar results from different objects. Let them discuss the possibilities without telling them the "right answer" at this point.

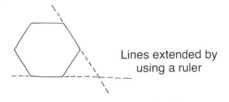

Lines extended by using a ruler

ACTIVITY 16

Age: 4–9

Objective: Two-, one-, zero-dimensional figures, Euclidean transformations, Euclidean properties, and constructions

Materials: Wax paper, color markers, and an overhead projector

Instructions: Demonstrate how to fold a sheet of wax paper two or three times until lines intersect and polygons are formed. The folds can be highlighted using color markers. Project the wax paper to show the children what you did. Discuss the polygons formed using available language. Next, have the children fold their sheets of wax paper in a similar manner, color the creases, project on the screen, and discuss. Depending on the age and experience of the children, consider extending the discussion to finding angles, perpendicular lines, parallel lines, the midpoint of a segment, and half an angle.

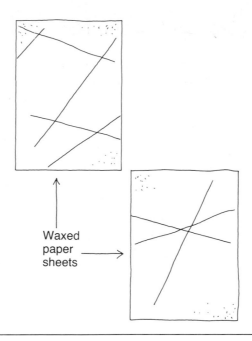

Waxed
paper
sheets

ACTIVITY 17

Age: 3–6

Objective: Two-, one-, zero-dimensional figures, Euclidean properties, and constructions

Materials: Paper, pencil, crayons

Instructions: Give each child a piece of paper and a pencil. Using the overhead projector, demonstrate how to scatter 10 to 15 dots on the paper. Then, connect the dots in a random manner. For older children, you can demonstrate using a straightedge. Color in the polygons. Have children try this activity themselves. Encourge them to share and discuss their results— triangles or any other polygons they found. Display their final pictures.

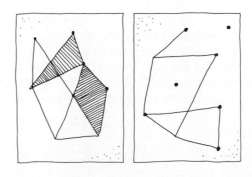

STUDY QUESTIONS AND ACTIVITIES

1. First, reflect on what you think children might misunderstand in response to the following items. Then, rewrite and/or redraw each item to suggest a better way to think about the mathematics involved.
    a. Show a cube from at least two different perspectives. Say "All the angles in this shape are right angles."
    b. Show the following illustration. Say "Here are some pictures of triangles."

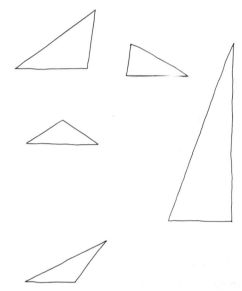

    c. Point to an airplane in the sky. Say "Look at the *big* airplane in the sky!"

2. For each of the materials listed under the heading Constructions in this chapter, list as many three-dimensional shapes as possible that could be constructed, then do the same for two-dimensional shapes, one-dimensional shapes, and the zero-dimensional shape.

3. Explain what you see in the following illustration.

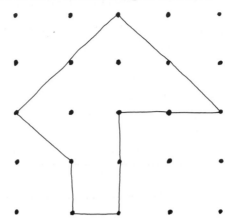

4. Observe some preschool children playing with Cuisenaire rods or building blocks of different sizes and shapes. Make note of the informal knowledge about shape and size they use as they're constructing.

REFERENCES AND RESOURCES

Baust, J. A. (1981). Spatial relationships and young children. *Arithmetic Teacher, 29*(1), 13–14.

Bazik, E. F., & Tucker, B. J. (1983). Ideas. *Arithmetic Teacher, 30*(5), 27-32.

Bearden, D., & Martin, K. (1984). *Primarily Logo*. Reston, VA: Reston Publishing.

Cangelosi, J. S. (1985). A "fair" way to discover circles. *Arithmetic Teacher, 33*(3), 11–13.

Crowley, M. L. (1987). The van Hiele model of the development of geometric thought. In M. M. Lindquist (Ed.), *Learning and teaching geometry, K-12, 1987 yearbook* (pp. 1–16). Reston, VA: NCTM.

Damarin, S. K. (1981). What makes a triangle? *Arithmetic Teacher, 29*(1), 39–41.

Del Grande, J. J. (1987). Spatial perception and primary geometry. In M. M. Lindquist (Ed.), *Learning and teaching geometry, K-12, 1987 yearbook* (pp. 126–135). Reston, VA: NCTM.

Hoffer, A. (1983). Van Hiele-based research. In R. Lesh & M. Landau (Eds.), *Acquisition of mathematics concepts and processes* (pp. 205–227). New York: Academic Press.

Jensen, R., & O'Neil, D. R. (1983). Let's do it: Informal geometry through geometric blocks. *Arithmetic Teacher, 30*(8), 4–5.

Lindquist, M. M. (Ed.). (1987). *Learning and teaching geometry, K-12, 1987 yearbook*. Reston, VA: NCTM.

Mason, M. (1985). Computer corner. *Arithmetic Teacher, 33*(2), 46–47.

Papert, S. A. (1980). *Mindstorms: Children, computers and powerful ideas.* New York: Basic Books.

Piaget, J., & Barbel, I. (1971). *Mental imagery in the child.* New York: Basic Books.

Piaget, J., & Inhelder, B. (1967). *The child's conception of space.* New York: W. W. Norton & Co.

Piaget, J., Inhelder, B., & Szeminska, A. (1960). *The child's conception of geometry.* London: Routledge and Paul.

Reisman, F. K. (1981). *Teaching mathematics: Methods and content* (2nd ed.). Boston: Houghton Mifflin.

Robinson, G. E. (1975). Geometry. In J. Payne (Ed.), *Mathematics learning in early childhood* (pp. 205–225). Reston, VA: NCTM.

Schultz, K. (1978). Variables influencing the difficulty of rigid transformations during the transition between the concrete and formal operational stages of cognitive development. In R. Lesh & D. Mierkiewicz (Eds.), *Recent research concerning the development of spatial and geometric concepts* (pp. 195–212). Columbus, OH: ERIC/SMEAC.

Torgerson, S., Kriley, M. K., & Stone, J. (1984). *Logo in the classroom.* Eugene, OR: International Council for Computers in Education/University of Oregon.

Troutman, A. P., & Lichtenberg, B. K. (1982). *Mathematics a good beginning: Strategies for teaching children* (3rd ed.). Monterey, CA: Brooks/Cole.

Woodward, E., & Buckner, P. G. (1987). Reflections and symmetry—a second-grade miniunit. *Arithmetic Teacher, 35*(2), 8–11.

9

Measurement

CHILDREN ARE frequently exposed to measuring devices, such as clocks, watches, measuring spoons, measuring cups, scales, thermometers, and rulers. As early as preschool age, children have an interest in how much more one amount is than another or how big something is, so they often make comparisons. By kindergarten, words like *inch* and *liter* have been introduced to children at home and at school. Although they may be familiar with these terms, children don't yet realize they are living in a dual system. Today, using both inches and liters is just as natural for children as using the customary system was for those who grew up with just inches, pounds, and quarts.

In the last 25 years, much research has been done concerning how children learn to think about measurement. This research has come primarily from the works of Piaget (Copeland, 1984; Piaget, 1965; Piaget & Inhelder, 1964). One of the findings of this research is that children progress through stages when they learn measurement. This fact has been useful for curriculum developers, textbook authors, and teachers. As a result, children are having more success learning measurement.

The stages of learning measurement and the attributes of length, area, volume, capacity, mass, temperature, time, and money are the major focus of this chapter. As in previous chapters, consideration is given to vocabulary, calculators, computers, estimation, and problem solving.

VOCABULARY FOR TEACHERS

Some terms related to measurement should be part of the teacher's measurement background, but not the student's. Other terms are clearly intended to become part of the child's measurement vocabulary. Key terms that are useful to consider for each group are identified in the following discussion. In some cases, a student term will have a different meaning that the teacher should know.

The difference between *discrete* and *continuous* objects is important for teachers to know and to demonstrate when teaching early number and measurement concepts. Discrete objects are counted, whereas continuous objects are measured. Another term only teachers need to know is *attribute*. This term refers to a characteristic of an object. Important attributes in the study of measurement are length, area, volume, capacity, mass, temperature, time, and money (where time and money are actually measures of change and value, respectively). *Conservation* is another term teachers should know. For a specific object, conservation refers to an attribute that has not changed despite the change of certain other attributes. For example, the amount of a liquid does not change when its shape changes as a result of its container being altered. One container might be short and wide and the other might be tall and narrow.

By the third or fourth grade, children still aren't sophisticated enough to appreciate the relationships among the *cubic decimeter, liter,* and *kilogram,* but the teacher should. These units of measure represent *volume, capacity,* and *mass,* respectively. By definition, the kilogram is the mass of a liter of pure water (at 4° Celsius at sea level). A liter is, by definition, the amount of liquid contained in a cubic decimeter. These units are discussed more fully later in this chapter.

The teacher should know the difference between weight and mass even though children at the early childhood level are not expected to understand the distinction. *Weight* refers to the pull of the earth on an object. The weight of an object decreases as it is moved away from the earth. *Mass,* on the other hand, refers to the measure of a body's resistance to movement or the measure of the material in an object. The mass of an object is the same whether the object is near the earth or anywhere else in space. Technically, mass is the correct term for the study of measurement, but the familiar terms of *weight* and *weigh* will dominate.

VOCABULARY FOR STUDENTS

In addition to the terms *mass* and *weight,* there are other terms that shouldn't be introduced at the early childhood level but should eventually be learned by children. Remember that the earlier stages of learning do not need to include the use of formal terminology. However, by grades 3 and 4 most of the language presented here will be familiar.

The terms *line, area,* and *volume* are discussed in nonmetric geometry as well as in measurement, thereby giving double exposure to the concepts and language. Two terms that have unusual connotations and uses are *volume* and *capacity. Volume* describes the amount of space an object occupies and *capacity* describes the amount of space inside a container (Reisman, 1981), assuming, of course, that the container is hollow! People usually use measures of capacity when referring to liquid. At the earliest stages of measurement—before formal language has been introduced—there is no need for children to be able to discriminate between these two concepts.

The vocabulary that children use for *temperature, time,* and *money* comes from very early learning. A toddler learns the meaning of the word *hot* when approaching a hot oven door, when curious about the flames in a fireplace, or when blowing out the candles on a birthday cake. The meaning of *cold* comes from the children's experiences with popsicles, ice cream, cold winter days, or snowfalls. Children first understand the words related to time from many familiar expressions such as, "Just a minute!" or "Wait a second!" To children, the reality of the concepts of minute and second don't correspond to timepieces, however. Children may have an intuitive social understanding of what *minute* means in the expression, "Just a minute!" However, formal education has to undo this intuitive understanding and replace it with the actual measurement terms for time. Toddler and preschool experiences also encompass early exposure to certain denominations of money. Usually, pennies are introduced first. Adult friends and relatives are generous with pennies for the piggy bank. By the end of first grade, children have an operational understanding of most of the everyday vocabulary associated with temperature, time, and money.

In summary, the major terms that children should learn are the names given to the *attributes* of measure. However, children also need to understand the term *measure* itself. Robinson, Mahaffey, and Nelson (1975) describe how informative it is to tell children to take a ruler and measure the length of an object.

> This might be as informative as telling them a "plark is used to whiffle a thintch." Thus both the behavior of the instrument as a means to an end as well as the mysteries of its calibration may present difficulties for children. (p. 239)

Teachers should make every attempt to prepare students for the vocabulary that they will use in measurement.

THE LEARNING OF MEASUREMENT

Children go through several stages of learning before they learn how to measure (Copeland, 1974; Sohns & Buffington, 1977). Since these stages have been shown to occur naturally, they should be considered when planning for instruction. The Instructional Planner for measurement at the end of the chapter presents sample activities for the different attributes according to stage. Many other activities can be derived from those presented in this chapter.

Attribute Recognition

It is important for children to recognize the attribute they are going to measure before they are asked to measure it. They need to play with objects in the environment so that they develop an intuitive understanding of the various attributes. The teacher needs to guide this play, otherwise attributes such as color, noise, or enjoyment might be what a child recognizes first about an object, not the mass, length, or any of the attributes that the teacher keeps talking about! It is important for the teacher to make sure the child is "seeing" the same attribute that he or she is "seeing." Making sure the child is recognizing the same attribute is particularly important for the attributes of length, area, volume, capacity, and mass. Even though the attributes of temperature, change, and value are learned early in both social and home environments, these attributes should receive some special attention in the preschool and early grades before moving to the other stages.

The kindergarten children in Figure 9–1 made a path with coffee stir sticks—an activity that focused on recognizing length. During their play, the teacher interacted enough with them to ensure that their efforts did not result in large spaces between sticks or in overlapping sticks. In this activity, the teacher could also lead children to place sticks along the path of an existing line, such as between floor tiles or a design on a carpet. The children were not asked to count how many sticks they had used to make their path. Although if they did count the sticks, those comments were considered. The activities following the Instructional Planner give suggestions for how to help children to recognize specific attributes.

Conservation

Children's understanding of measurement concepts develops in relationship to their understanding of conservation. Children who understand how a particular attribute is conserved know that the amount of that attribute has not changed even if other characteristics have. For example, the length of the two identical pencils shown in Figure 9–2 doesn't change even when their location changes. It is very important that children understand how the attribute they are measuring is conserved. Otherwise, they may perform the operation of measuring mostly by rote. Although it's been argued that conservation cannot be taught, teachers can provide opportunities where the development of conservation is nurtured. When teaching measurement, teachers should consider the conservation of each attribute, except for the attributes

FIGURE 9–1
These kindergartners are studying length informally by making a path with coffee stir sticks.

of time, money, and temperature. There are, however, conservation activities for these exceptions as well as the other attributes in the Instructional Planner for measurement.

Comparison

Comparison is the association of one attribute with two or more objects. One example of comparison is when two people match their heights to see who is taller. This comparison can be done directly by observing whose head is higher before measuring each height and comparing the measurements. The two- and three-year-olds in Figure 9–3 are building towers. The teacher asked the children to tell her about their towers. Using the same language that the children used in their responses (which included references to color as well as references to which tower was made by whom), the teacher then asked which tower was *bigger* and which was *smaller* and why. She substituted the measurement terms *taller* and *shorter* in subsequent discussions.

Likewise, to compare the capacity of one container to a second container, one container can be filled with a liquid, then that liquid can be transferred

Pencils aligned

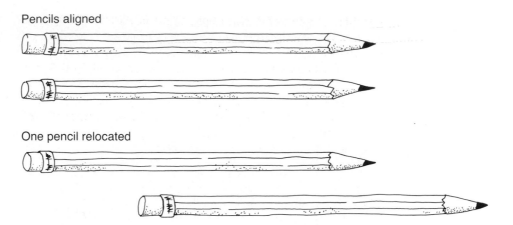

One pencil relocated

FIGURE 9–2
Conservation of Length

into the other container. The amounts of liquid each container can hold can then be compared. Children should be encouraged to play with capacity cups to help them develop an intuitive understanding of volume and capacity.

To order objects according to a particular attribute, children should be guided to compare two items at a time. A series of such comparisons will result in a set of ordered objects. At this point, children have not been asked to give any measures.

FIGURE 9–3
Preschoolers enjoy learning how to compare the heights of towers through play.

In addition to *direct comparison*, there is *indirect comparison.* In indirect comparison, a third object is used to compare to each of two other objects that are intended for comparison. For example, suppose someone wants to know if the length of a bookshelf is wider than the distance between two doors in a classroom. It would be useful to know if there is room for the bookshelf *before* it is moved to the new location. A piece of string could be cut off that equals the length of the bookshelf. Then, the string could be compared with the distance between the two doors to determine if the bookshelf would fit. A similar procedure would be followed for other attributes.

Application of Nonstandard Units

The idea of *iteration, or repetition*, is important when children start to use units of any kind. *Iteration* as applied to measurement means to compare an attribute of an object with a repetition of a given unit of measurement. Iteration is essential for understanding measurement and determining the measure of a given attribute. Teachers can encourage children to develop an understanding of iteration by varying the units of measure before applying a standard unit (where the iterative process is already done).

To further prepare for teaching nonstandard units, it is useful to consider direct and indirect measurement. *Direct measurement* means that the object whose attribute is being measured is in direct contact with the attribute unit. On the other hand, *indirect measurement* means that the object whose attribute is being measured is *not* in direct contact with the attribute unit. Table 9–1 lists attributes and accounts for their direct and indirect measurement. This table should provide better insight into measurement itself and into the teaching and learning of measurement. The focus of the following discussion concerns the representations in Table 9–1.

TABLE 9–1
Direct and Indirect Measurement of Attributes

Attribute	Direct Measurement	Indirect Measurement
length	×	× (computational)
area	×	× (computational)
volume	×	× (computational)
capacity	×	× (mechanical)
mass/weight	×	× (mechanical or electronic)
temperature		× (physical or electronic)
time	×	× (mechanical or electronic)

Length is directly compared by physically aligning a unit, such as a paper clip, along an object to be measured and by counting how many units long the object is. Figure 9–4 shows another example of direct measurement of length—a three-year-old measuring how tall he is by using large cardboard bricks. He is only mimicking the counting strategy and he has an unstable concept of what "how many blocks tall" means. Nevertheless, this experience is preparing him for measuring length with nonstandard units. Indirect measure of length is not learned until middle school or high school where computational procedures are applied to measurement—such as the Pythagorean theorem.

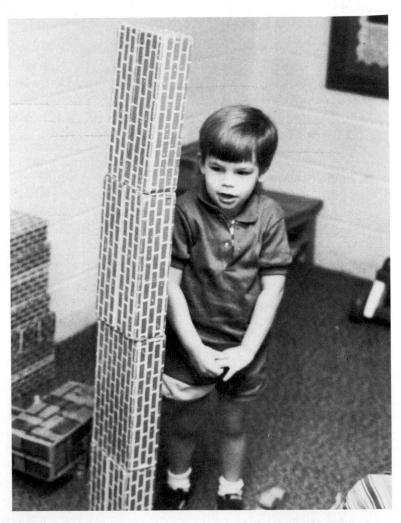

FIGURE 9–4
A 3-year-old compares his height with stacked cardboard bricks by mimicking the counting strategy.

Figure 9–5 shows an area that can be measured directly—the area of a bulletin board that can be measured by counting the sheets of construction paper that cover it. Later, this area can be indirectly determined by computation using the area formula, also shown in Figure 9–5. Likewise, volume can be found directly by counting how many wooden cubes fit into a shoe box. Later, volume can be found indirectly by using the volume formula.

Capacity is measured directly by counting how many calibrated jars of water it takes to fill a bucket. Indirect measurement of capacity occurs through readings, such as the readings of a mechanical water meter. Mass can be directly measured by counting how many pencils it takes to balance a chalkboard eraser on a simple balance. Second graders performing this type of activity are shown in Figure 9–7.

Mass is measured indirectly through the mechanical springs or electric sensors in a calibrated scale. Although temperature is not measured directly by children, it is measured indirectly through the expansion of mercury in a thermometer. One way children can measure time directly is by counting how many birthday candles will burn down sequentially before an ice cube melts. Time can be measured indirectly by using clocks. Later in this chapter, indirect and direct measurement of value (money) is discussed.

Application of Standard Units

In the schooling of children, the application of standard units comes early for some attributes and late for other attributes. Use of standard units depends on the experiences children have had in their home, preschool, and elementary school environments. Children should not be expected to apply standard units before they have had adequate experiences and growth in the stages just discussed. The most commonly used standard units for the customary and metric systems are presented in Table 9–2. Generally, only the linear units are

Direct	Indirect
12 sheets	3 × 4 = 12 sheets

FIGURE 9–5
Area Measure with Nonstandard Units

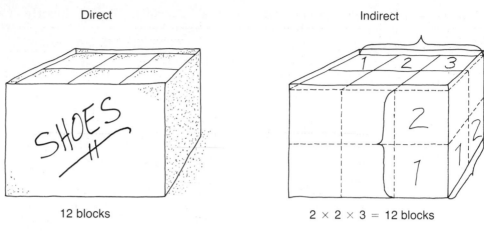

Direct

12 blocks

Indirect

$2 \times 2 \times 3 = 12$ blocks

FIGURE 9–6
Volume Measure with Nonstandard Units

TABLE 9–2
Commonly Used Standard Units and Their Abbreviations

Attribute	*Customary*	*Abbreviation*	*Metric*	*Abbreviation*
			Standard Units	
length	inch	in.	millimeter	mm
	foot	ft	centimeter	cm
	yard	yd	decimeter	dm
	mile	mi	meter	m
			kilometer	km
area	square inch	in.^{2}	square centimeter	cm^2
	square foot	ft^2	square decimeter	dm^2
	square yard	yd^2	square meter	m^2
	square mile	mi^2	square kilometer	km^2
volume	cubic inch	in.^{3}	cubic centimeter	cm^3
	cubic foot	ft^3	cubic decimeter	dm^3
	cubic yard	yd^3	cubic meter	m^3
capacity	ounce	oz	milliliter	mL
	cup	c		
	pint	pt		
	quart	qt	liter	L
	gallon	gal		

TABLE 9–2 (continued)

Attribute	Customary	Abbreviation	Metric	Abbreviation
		Standard Units		
mass	ounce	oz	gram	g
	pound	lb	kilogram	kg
temperature	degree Fahrenheit	°F	degree Celsius	°C
time	second	sec		
	minute	min		
	hour	h		
	day	d		
	week	wk		
	month	mo		
	year	yr		
money	cent	1¢		
	nickel	5¢		
	dime	10¢		
	quarter	25¢		
	half dollar	50¢		
	dollar	$1		
	five dollars	$5		
	ten dollars	$10		
	twenty dollars	$20		
	fifty dollars	$50		
	hundred dollars	$100		

learned in the first grade, but most of the units listed are covered by the third and fourth grades.

The units are not necessarily learned in the same order as they are presented in the table. The teacher should take opportunities as they arise for teaching measurement, although a guide, Table 9–6, for informal and formal learning experiences with measurement is presented in this chapter. This guide is organized according to stage of development, attribute, and the approximate age of the child. For example, feeding the classroom gerbil could become a measurement activity. Students could use measuring cups to determine the amount of food and water for the gerbil. Figure 9–8 shows a kindergarten student setting a manual clock to record what time the gerbil was fed. The value of these types of opportunities is that students "own" the

FIGURE 9–7
**These second graders are counting how many blocks it will take to balance
an object on a simple balance.**

problem of measuring the gerbil's food and water as opposed to solving
textbook and teacher-developed problems all the time.

Making the transition from nonstandard units to standard units involves
certain considerations. For linear measure, the measurement task changes
from lining up discrete units, such as the paper clips mentioned earlier, to
using a measuring stick or tape that has inches or centimeters continuously
marked on it. That is, the standard unit is already iterated along a path
designed for direct comparison. Children generally have their first formal
exposure to standard linear units in first grade. Unfortunately, these lessons
are not always preceded by experiences representative of the four stages that
should come before. To find the area of a bulletin board, instead of multiplying

FIGURE 9–8
By using a manual clock, this kindergarten student is showing what time the classroom gerbil was fed.

the number of discrete units of construction paper down a bulletin board by the number across (described earlier as an example of nonstandard measurement), the measures of length and width are obtained by using a measuring stick or tape and are multiplied. This product determines the square inches or square centimeters that are imagined to be continuously arranged on the bulletin board. Square measures of standard units are learned in third grade. Cubic measures of standard units, needed for volume, are introduced in the fourth grade. See Figure 9–9 for illustrations of the previous discussion.

The attribute of capacity is measured using liters and milliliters. Rather than using additional prefixes with younger children, the custom has been to use fractions of liters, such as a half liter (500 mL) or a quarter liter (250 mL). Instead of a deciliter ($\frac{1}{10}$ L), 100 milliliters is used. Most children know approximately how much a liter is since many popular soft drinks are sold according to liters. Capacity containers should be available for use with water or other pourable materials, such as sand, salt, or rice. Give children ample opportunity to pour a given capacity of a substance into several different-shaped containers to reinforce their understanding of conservation of capacity.

At first, mass should be measured using discrete standard unit weights and a simple balance. Commercial sets of gram and kilogram (1000 g) weights are available. However, these weights can be duplicated by using chips, paper clips, sand, or lead fish weights affixed or grouped together in a container like a paper cup. After ample experiences with these weights using a simple

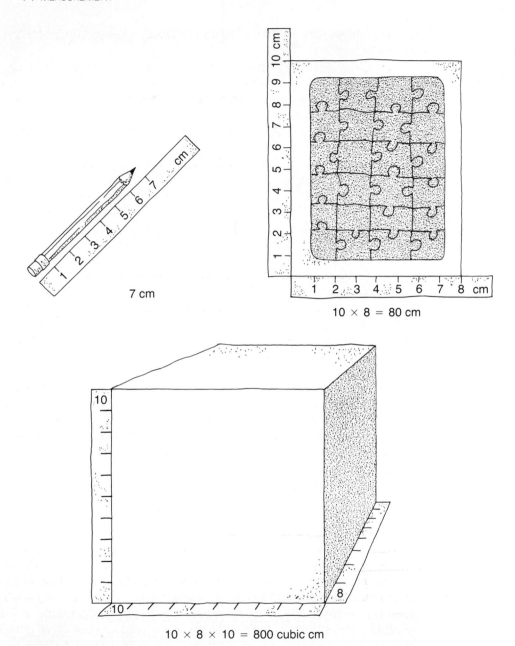

7 cm

$10 \times 8 = 80$ cm

$10 \times 8 \times 10 = 800$ cubic cm

FIGURE 9–9
Measurement of Length, Area, and Volume

balance, have the children compare those results with the results from calibrated scales.

Two-year-olds understand hot and cold, but it isn't until second or third grade that children learn to measure *temperature* by reading a thermometer. A large demonstration thermometer should be available in the classroom. Children should have many opportunities to measure many common temperatures such as body temperature, room temperature, outdoor temperature, the freezing temperature of water, and the boiling temperature of water.

Learning about time includes understanding the duration of time, the sequencing of events, and the mechanics of reading time pieces, such as watches, clocks, and calendars. Initially, duration is best studied as part of the attribute recognition stage, where birthday candles, melting ice cubes, or hand-made sand timers are used to observe change occurring. Sequencing can also be studied from these experiences. Calendar readings and discussions should be a natural part of every school day from kindergarten forward. Kennedy (1984) makes the following recommendations for teaching children how to tell time.

At first, telling time should be taught using an analog rather than a digital clock. Learning to tell time with a digital clock is an easy task after learning with an analog clock, but the reverse order does not work nearly as well. Sometimes children become so dependent on clocks with digital read-out that they avoid learning to read analog clocks altogether.

To teach time with an analog clock, start with a simple clock face that has just the 12 positions labeled. Begin by exploring what the position of the hour hand indicates. After this concept is well-established, add the minute hand to the clock. At this point the partitioning of hours into minutes (5-minute segments that correspond to the marks on the clock face) needs to be thoroughly developed. After the children have learned to read the clock with the hour and minute hand, they can explore the changing positions of the hands. Using synchronous play clocks or real clocks would be very helpful. The children can follow the movement of the hour hand from 4 to 5 as the minute hand moves from 12 to 6 to 12.

Until fraction concepts are fairly well established, it would be wise to omit phraseology such as "a quarter after 3," or "half past 7." Using the terminology "10 minutes until 2 o'clock" should also be delayed until the children have a clear understanding of "50 minutes after 1 o'clock." Teaching both terminologies at the same time can cause children a lot of confusion.

Children in modern society begin to learn about money at an early age—between the ages of 2 and 3. Learning about money includes understanding denominations, equivalences, how to count money, how to read price tags, and how to count change. Of course, money is so pervasive throughout our culture that its applications are not only obvious but also necessary. One of the first concepts that children must understand is the value of coins and paper money. Often, we just tell children that a dime is the same as ten pennies and simply expect them to believe it. Trading games using coins offer a more convincing method of helping children to understand that value is not directly related to size. There are many opportunities in the lunchroom, on field trips, or when playing "store" games in the classroom to introduce money naturally. Use these opportunities to help children understand and acquire the skills they need to deal with money. *STORE*

As children are learning to measure, teachers should introduce the issue of appropriate units of measure. Through many measuring experiences, children can be guided to an awareness that measurements need to be expressed in terms that clearly communicate the quantities in the given situation. Over time they'll learn that saying a hamster ran 7 meters is more meaningful than saying it ran 7000 millimeters; that expressing a book's mass in kilograms is more meaningful than expressing its mass in grams; and that measuring the time it takes for a 100-yard dash in seconds is more meaningful than measuring it in hours. In the conventional system, the units of inch, foot, yard, mile, cup, quart, gallon, ounce, pound, and ton are used. In the metric system, the most frequently used units of length are the millimeter, centimeter, meter, and kilometer, of mass are the gram and kilogram, and of capacity are the milliliter, liter, and kiloliter. The other units are seldom used.

The abbreviations shown in Table 9–2 warrant some additional comments. Notice that *in.* is the only abbreviation shown that has a period. The period distinguishes it from the word *in.* Also, notice that the abbreviation for liter is a capital *L* in order to distinguish it from the number 1. The square and cubic notation is listed in the table for teacher use only. It is not there to suggest that children in the primary grades should use it.

When children are ready for the stage of standard units of measure, they should be given many opportunities to become acquainted with the units that are appropriate for them to use at this age. (See Table 9–6 for a scope and sequence of measurement attributes and stages of development.) As children have more and more experience with the most common standard units for a particular attribute, such as length, they will learn that there are 100 centimeters in a meter or 12 inches in a foot. For children to be successful at measuring with standard units, they need experience and practice, especially using real objects and real measuring tools. Worksheets alone will not facilitate the construction of a good foundation in measurement.

Conversion Within a System

Conversion between the customary and metric systems should not be taught beyond encouraging students to recognize rough equivalences between the two systems. These rough equivalences are indicated in Table 9–2 by horizontal alignments of customary and metric units. For example, the customary unit *yard* is in the process of being replaced by the metric unit *meter*. These units are not equivalent, but there is an understanding that they replace each other as units. That is, when a yard is referred to in the customary system, the meter—not the centimeter—is the comparable metric unit.

Conversions within the customary system or within the metric system will occur during the first or second grades at the earliest. One of the hallmarks of the metric system is its use of prefixes. Table 9–3 shows the values associated with the prefixes that are part of the curriculum as well as part of daily living for a student in the early elementary grades. In addition, Table 9–4 shows the application of these prefixes to the basic standard units. Those prefixes and

TABLE 9–3
Metric System Prefixes

Prefix		Value
kilo	=	1,000
.		.
.		.
.		.
basic standard unit	=	1
deci	=	$\frac{1}{10}$
centi	=	$\frac{1}{100}$
milli	=	$\frac{1}{1,000}$

TABLE 9–4
Conversions Within the Metric System

Linear Conversions			Area Conversions		
kilometer	=	1000 meters	1 square meter	=	1 square meter
.		.	1 square decimeter	=	$\frac{1}{100}$ square meter
.		.	1 square centimeter	=	$\frac{1}{10000}$ square meter
decimeter	=	$\frac{1}{10}$ meter			
centimeter	=	$\frac{1}{100}$ meter			
millimeter	=	$\frac{1}{1000}$ meter			

Volume Conversions			Capacity Conversions		
1 cubic decimeter	=	$\frac{1}{1000}$ cubic meter	1 milliliter	=	$\frac{1}{1000}$ liter
1 cubic centimeter	=	$\frac{1}{1,000,000}$ cubic meter			

Mass Conversions		
1 kilogram	=	1000 grams

their corresponding values that are not used for routine measurements are not included. The position of the basic standard unit is indicated in order to provide a more complete picture of the use of prefixes.

Conversions in temperature, time, and money operate differently than the attributes described previously. Table 9–5 shows the common temperature readings that children should know. No conversions in degrees Celsius are listed. Equivalent time units and equivalent values for money are given in order to provide a visual impression of the complexities children face when learning these units.

It is important to provide experiences for children at each stage of measuring for *each* attribute. When teaching time and money, put effort into helping children recognize the attributes of change and value. The temptation to immediately require children to master clock readings and money denominations is very risky. Children need to have a deeper and broader conceptual understanding of the units involved. Pay special attention to the activities in the Instructional Planner for Measurement to get ideas on how to facilitate this understanding.

TABLE 9–5
Unit Values for Temperature, Time, and Money

Temperature

100° C	Boiling point of water
.	
.	
.	
40° C	Hot day
.	
.	
.	
37° C	Normal body temperature
.	
.	
.	
10° C	Cool day
.	
.	
0° C	Freezing point of water

TABLE 9–5 (continued)

Time Conversions

1 year = 12 months =		52 weeks =	365 days
1 month	=	4+ weeks =	28+ days
1 week		=	7 days
1 day		=	24 hours
1 hour		=	60 minutes
1 minute		=	60 seconds
1 second			

Money Denominations

$100	=	one hundred dollars		
$50	=	fifty dollars		
$20	=	twenty dollars		
$10	=	ten dollars		
$5	=	five dollars		
$1	=	one dollar		
100¢	=	one dollar	=	one hundred cents
50¢	=	half dollar	=	fifty cents
25¢	=	quarter	=	twenty-five cents
10¢	=	dime	=	ten cents
5¢	=	nickel	=	five cents
1¢	=	penny	=	one cent

THE TEACHING OF MEASUREMENT

Although much research has been done on how children learn about measurement, Wilson and Osborne (1988) point out in their review of the foundations of the concepts of measurement that the research completed has not included sufficient detail to know when instruction should occur. They do, however, present a list of principles for teaching measurement. In addition to the stages of learning measurement that were previously presented in this chapter, the following excerpts from the Wilson and Osborne list of principles are offered as a guide for teaching measurement.

Children must measure frequently and often, preferably on real problem tasks rather than textbook exercises.

Children should encounter activity-oriented measurement situations with them doing the experimenting rather than passively observing. The activities should encourage discussion to stimulate the refinement and testing of ideas and concepts through oral interactions.

The emphasis in instructional planning should be on the important foundational ideas of measurement which transfer or work across measurement systems.

Do not rush the teaching of formulas for measurement: rather wait until the children have an adequate understanding to make the generalization—the formula. (p. 109)

USING THE CALCULATOR TO LEARN MEASUREMENT

A hand-held calculator can be a useful tool in the study of measurement. From their own hands-on experiences, children will have a definite understanding that real objects are seldom 4 cm thick or 10 cm long, but instead are more likely to be 4.2 cm thick or 9.8 cm long. The use of a calculator in computations concerning measurements has two advantages. The first is that children can concentrate on the concepts involved and not be distracted by laborious paper and pencil calculations; the second is that the measures can be more realistic numbers that emphasize the practical nature of mathematics.

USING THE COMPUTER TO LEARN MEASUREMENT

Any child who is interacting with a computer to increase hand-eye coordination (i.e., playing a video game) learns a great deal about distance, speed, and angles of rotation. Except for the angles, the measurements involved are nonstandard units, nevertheless, proportional thinking is enhanced. In addition to video games, there are other programs available. The computer language Logo uses simple commands for drawing figures on the screen (as well as performing other tasks) using a turtle or movable triangle. The turtle can be moved forward 50 steps, then turned right 90 degrees, and then moved forward 20 steps to form a design. Although the steps are not standard units, they are proportional and the degrees of turning are accurate. Children can learn a great deal about relative lengths and angle measures by using Logo.

ESTIMATION AND PROBLEM SOLVING

Measurement and estimation go hand-in-hand. Before the actual measurement is done, ask children to guess how long the table is, how much the gerbil weighs, or how many square centimeters the footprint covers. Estimating can provide a natural way to introduce concepts of length, capacity, mass, time, or money for standard and nonstandard units. Even preschoolers are interested in finding out how many marshmallows are needed to fill a cup, how many paper clips are needed to make a chain that will wrap around your ankle, and how long it takes to count to one hundred. The possibilities for estimation are endless. If children are encouraged to guess or estimate first, then, later, they are usually more interested in getting a precise answer to a question. If some children become unwilling to guess (because their estimates are far from the actual measurement), don't give up on them or let them give up on themselves. Take some extra time with them and ask guiding questions that will help them to make better estimates. For example, suppose they are going to measure the mass of an object with which they're familiar, such as a tennis ball or one of their books. Encourage them to test their guess with a simple balance. Then, ask them if they can find a second object that has about the same mass as the object in question. Let them test this object, too. Help them get closer to the actual mass by having them respond to questions whose answers lead to a more reasonable estimate. Good estimation skills are especially important in the area of measurement. The wise teacher will help students to cultivate these skills.

The term *low tolerance for error* refers to children's reluctance to give an answer they know is not exact. In the real world, we live with inaccuracies; children need to learn when exactness is important and when it is not important.

In conclusion, measurement is a vital part of a young child's mathematical education. However, it is frequently overlooked when planning for instruction. The fact that it is overlooked is unfortunate since measurement, both direct and indirect, is one of the most practical applications of mathematics. People doing jobs ranging from engineering to house cleaning need to understand how to measure objects and amounts—from angles of rotation to the amount of floor cleaner that should be used in a bucket of water. Many opportunities are available in the normal classroom setting for developing children's concepts and skills in measuring. A wise teacher will make these opportunities count.

SUMMARY

The focus of this chapter has been the development of measurement concepts in young children. Measurement concepts proceed in stages: attribute recognition, conservation, comparison, application of nonstandard units, application of standard units, and conversions within standard systems. Suggestions for teaching measurement were given, along with ideas of how to use calculators and computers to help with some measurement concepts. This chapter emphasized that estimation and problem solving go hand-in-hand with both learning concepts of measurement and acquiring skills in measurement. Table 9–6 is a summary of the stages of learning measurement and the ages at which children learn the various attributes of measurement. This table was adapted from the work done by Kennedy (1984) and Sohns and Buffington (1977).

TABLE 9–6
Development of Measurement Concepts and Skills: A Guide

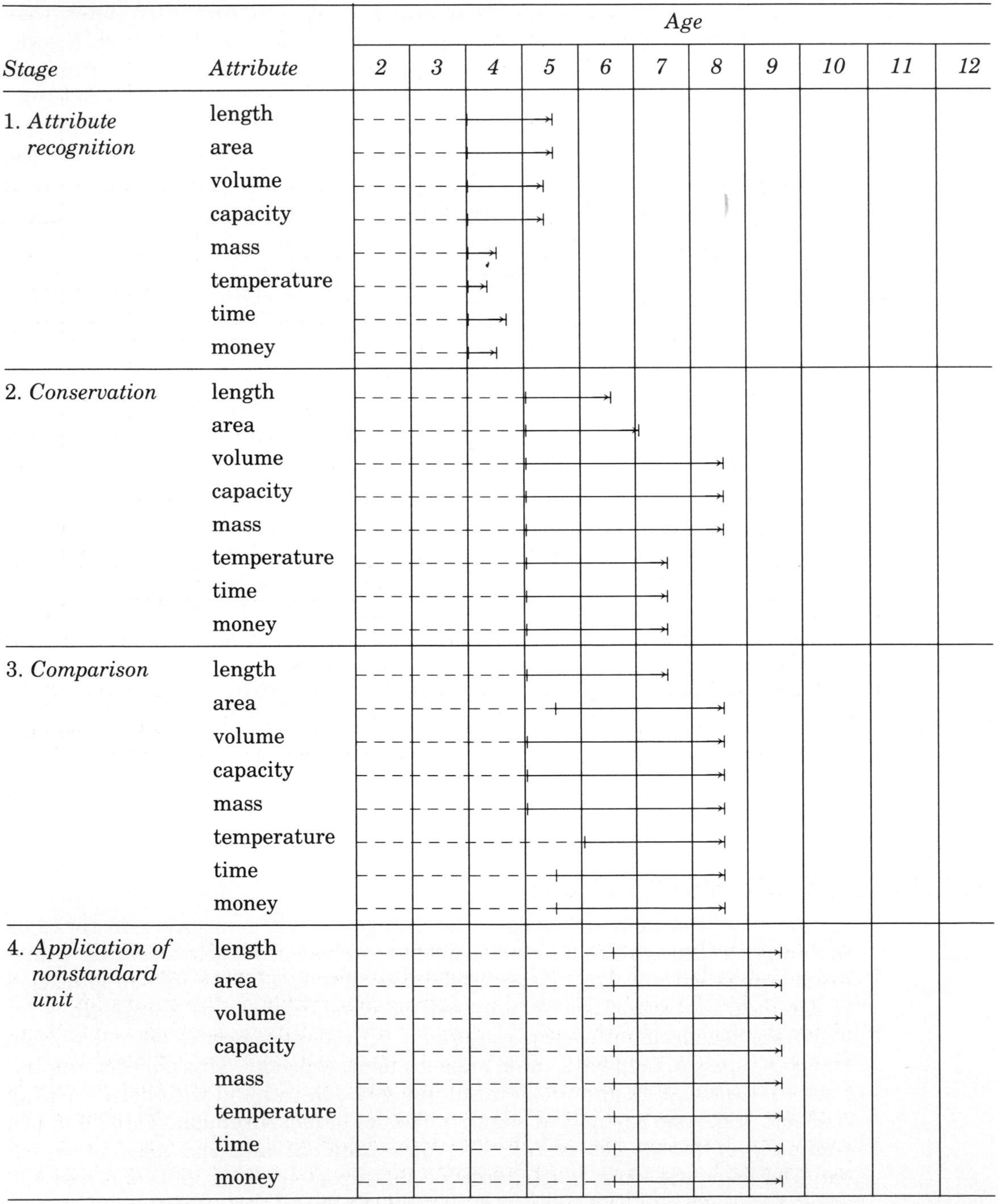
Age
Stage
Attribute
2
3
4
5
6
7
8
9
10
11
12
1. Attribute recognition
length
area
volume
capacity
mass
temperature
time
money
2. Conservation
length
area
volume
capacity
mass
temperature
time
money
3. Comparison
length
area
volume
capacity
mass
temperature
time
money
4. Application of nonstandard unit
length
area
volume
capacity
mass
temperature
time
money

TABLE 9–6 (continued)

Stage	Attribute	2	3	4	5	6	7	8	9	10	11	12
5. *Application of standard unit*	length	–	–	–	–	–	+					→
	area	–	–	–	–	–	+					→
	volume	–	–	–	–	–	+					→
	capacity	–	–	–	–	–	+					→
	mass	–	–	–	–	–	+					→
	temperature	–	–	–	–	–	–	–	–	–	–	→
	time	–	–	–	–	+						→
	money	–	–	–	–	+						→
6. *Conversion within a system*	length	–	–	–	–	–	–	–	+			→
	area	–	–	–	–	–	–	–	–	+		→
	volume	–	–	–	–	–	–	–	–	+		→
	capacity	–	–	–	–	–	–	–	–	+		→
	mass	–	–	–	–	–	–	–	–	+		→
	temperature											
	time	–	–	–	–	+						→
	money	–	–	–	–	+						→

Note: – – – – – informal learning
——————— formal learning

Sources: From GUIDING CHILDREN'S LEARNING OF MATHEMATICS, Fourth Edition, by Leonard M. Kennedy © 1984 by Wadsworth, Inc. Adapted by permission of the publisher; Sohns, Marvin L., *Inservice Guide for Teaching Measurement* K–8, Figure 9, P. 19, "Model for Activity Measurement Programs" by M. L. Sohns and A. V. Buffington, 1977, THE MEASUREMENT BOOK, p. 4. Adapted by permission of Price Stern Sloan, Inc.

PLANNING FOR INSTRUCTION

Although the development of measurement concepts is largely dependent upon the cognitive level of the child, some carefully designed experiences may serve to maximize the conceptual understanding achievable at the child's level. As discussed earlier, children learn measurement best by measuring and talking about what they are doing. There is no prescribed sequence for teaching the various attributes of measurement. The Instructional Planner that follows is organized according to attributes and stages of learning. The activities given in the next section are not intended to be comprehensive but rather are intended to be starting places to stimulate the teacher's thinking about the variety of ways children can have experiences with measurement.

INSTRUCTIONAL PLANNER
Measurement

Attribute	Stages					
	Attribute Recognition	Conservation	Comparison	Application of Nonstandard Unit	Application of Standard Unit	Conversion
length	1	2	3	4	5	(5)
area	6	7	8	9	10	
volume/capacity	11	12	13	14	15	
mass	16	17	18	19	20	
temperature	21	22	23	24	25	NA
time (change)	26	27	28	29	30	
money (value)	31	32	33	34	35	32

ACTIVITY 1

Age: 2–6

Objective: Length, Attribute recognition

Materials: Yarn, straws

Instructions: Have children make a path on the floor or the table with yarn. Then, let them duplicate the path with straws.

ACTIVITY 2

Age: 2–7

Objective: Length, Conservation

Materials: Popsicle sticks

Instructions: Give each of the children five or six popsicle sticks and ask them to make a path. Then, ask them to make another path with the same sticks. Talk with them about what is the same for each path. Ask them if they could make a third path, and let them make it.

ACTIVITY 3

Age: 3–7

Objective: Length, Comparison

Materials: Straws, yarn

Instructions: Give each of the children a length of yarn that is about 30 cm to 40 cm. Ask them to find objects in the room that are shorter than their piece of yarn. After this comparison is done, ask them to make a path of straws that is shorter than their piece of yarn. Next, ask them to make a path of straws that is longer than the yarn.

ACTIVITY 4

Age: 5–9

Objective: Length, Application of nonstandard units

Materials: Straws or popsicle sticks

Instructions: Have the children measure objects in the classroom, such as the blackboard or table, using the straws. Encourage them to discuss their findings. Ask if they found any objects that had an exact length in straws or if they had to approximate the length.

ACTIVITY 5

Age: 5–9

Objective: Length, Application of standard units

Materials: Rulers or meter sticks

Instructions: Have the children measure objects, such as tables, chairs, or chalkboards, in the classroom using centimeters, inches, or feet. Discuss with children that even though the table stays the same size, the length in centimeters will be a larger number than the length in meters. Help them see that more centimeters are needed to describe the length because centimeters are smaller than meters.

ACTIVITY 6

Age: 4–7

Objective: Area, Attribute recognition

Materials: Newspapers or construction paper

Instructions: Have the children cover the floor or a table with newspapers or construction paper. Discuss how this activity is different from measuring the floor or table with string.

ACTIVITY 7

Age: 5–9

Objective: Area, Conservation

Materials: Index cards

Instructions: Give each of the children five or six index cards and ask them to use the cards to make different arrangements. Ask them to find another child who has the same number of cards but whose arrangement is different. Let the children make several different arrangements with their cards. Each time ask them if the cards cover the same amount or different amounts.

ACTIVITY 8

Age: 5–9

Objective: Area, Comparison

Materials: Index cards

Instructions: Have the children cover an object, such as a book, with index cards. Then, have them cover another object, such as a table top, with index cards. Discuss with them which object required more or fewer cards. Ask them why one object requires more cards than the other.

ACTIVITY 9

Age: 4–9

Objective: Area, Application of nonstandard units

Materials: Square pieces of index cards or square pattern blocks

Instructions: Ask the children to find out how many square pieces of cards or pattern blocks are needed to cover the table top. Discuss their findings with them; emphasize how many pieces of cards or blocks were needed.

ACTIVITY 10

Age: 6–9

Objective: Area, Application of standard units

Materials: Centimeter grid paper or inch grid paper

Instructions: Ask the children to measure the sections of the grid paper to find out how big each square on the paper is. Then, ask them to find out how many of these squares are needed to cover some object in the classroom, such as a book or a table top.

ACTIVITY 11

Age: 2–7

Objective: Volume, Attribute recognition

Materials: Popped popcorn and boxes of various sizes

Instructions: Have the children fill several different boxes with popcorn. Encourage discussion about the popcorn inside each box. Let children fill the boxes to different levels but, at this point, they do not need to discuss whether there is more or less popcorn in particular boxes.

ACTIVITY 12

Age: 3–8

Objective: Volume, Conservation

Materials: Water and containers of various shapes

Instructions: Give the children about one cup of water each. Let them pour the water into different containers. Discuss how the shape of the container influences the level of water that is shown. Help them to see that the amount of water has not changed, even though the level of the water in the different containers varies.

ACTIVITY 13

Age: 4–8

Objective: Volume, Comparison

Materials: Many different sizes of cardboard boxes and popped popcorn

Instructions: Ask the children to select two boxes that they think might hold different amounts of popcorn. Then, ask them to fill the larger box with popcorn and empty it into the smaller box. Discuss how much popcorn was left over. Have children do this several times, then reverse this action and have them fill the larger box from the smaller one.

ACTIVITY 14

Age: 5–9

Objective: Volume, Application of nonstandard units

Materials: Children's building blocks and shoe boxes

Instructions: Ask children to find out how many of the blocks are needed to fill each shoe box.

ACTIVITY 15

Age·   5–9

Objective: Volume, Application of standard units

Materials: Centimeter or inch cubes and small boxes with open tops

Instructions: Have the children find out how many cubes are needed to fill each of the boxes. Discuss how the number would vary if the cubes were larger or smaller.

ACTIVITY 16

Age: 3–7

Objective: Mass, Attribute recognition

Materials: Various objects such as cotton balls, building blocks, books, toys

Instructions: Have the children hold different objects in each hand. Ask them how the objects compare in heaviness. Have them pick up and compare other objects.

ACTIVITY 17

Age: 3–7

Objective: Mass, Conservation

Materials: Paper plates, building blocks

Instructions: Have the children arrange five or six building blocks on a paper plate and lift it with two hands. Then, have them stack the blocks on the plate and lift it again with two hands. Discuss whether changing the arrangement of the blocks affects the effort that is needed to lift the plate.

ACTIVITY 18

Age: 4–8

Objective: Mass, Comparison

Materials: Boxes of the same size and shape, sand, and cotton balls

Instructions: Fill two identical boxes, one with sand and the other with cotton. Put them on a table at the front of the room. Ask the children to guess which box is heavier—even though they don't know the contents. Let some of the children try to lift the boxes, one in each hand. Give each of the children a small box filled with sand and ask them to find at least one object in the classroom that is heavier than the box is. Discuss how different materials make an object heavier or lighter.

ACTIVITY 19

Age: 5–9

Objective: Mass, Application of nonstandard units

Materials: A simple balance, bottle caps or similar small objects

Instructions: Ask the children to select a toy or object in the classroom and to find out how many bottle caps it takes to balance that object. Encourage discussion. Have them practice this activity with different objects.

ACTIVITY 20

Age: 5–9

Objective: Mass, Application of standard units

Materials: Envelopes, a postal scale, and small objects such as paper clips, foam packing materials, index cards, etc.

Instructions: Have the children find out how many grams or ounces an empty envelope weighs. Then, have them place different objects in their envelopes and weigh them again. Ask them to try to make the envelope and its contents weigh more than two ounces, less than five grams, or similar weights.

ACTIVITY 21

Age: 3–6

Objective: Temperature, Attribute recognition

Materials: Cup of hot water, ice cubes

Instructions: Have the children touch the ice cubes, the cup of hot water, and then someone's hand. Talk with them about the different temperatures.

ACTIVITY 22

Age:　　3–6

Objective:　Temperature, Conservation

Materials:　Items from the refrigerator

Instructions:　Let the children touch different items from the refrigerator. Talk with them about how these items feel to the touch. Ask them if the items feel the same.

ACTIVITY 23

Age:　　4–7

Objective:　Temperature, Comparison

Materials:　(None needed)

Instructions:　Ask the children to name a food or drink that is usually colder than ketchup. Ask them to name a food or drink that is usually hotter than a soft drink and a food or drink that is usually hotter than oatmeal. Also, discuss the temperatures that children experience in winter or summer (if they don't live in a temperate climate).

ACTIVITY 24

Age:　　5–9

Objective:　Temperature, Application of nonstandard units

Materials:　Cards with the words *very hot, hot, warm, cold, very cold,* and pictures of objects that have different temperatures

Instructions:　Have the children choose labels that describe the temperatures of the objects in the pictures. Discuss how they can decide which label should be used for a particular picture.

ACTIVITY 25

Age:　　5–9

Objective:　Temperature, Application of standard units

Materials:　Objects of different temperatures, thermometers

Instructions: Let the children use thermometers to measure the temperatures of the objects. Discuss the temperature changes with the children. Ask them to estimate the temperatures of some of the objects before using the thermometer.

ACTIVITY 26

Age: 4–7

Objective: Time, Attribute recognition

Materials: A jar for water and another empty jar

Instructions: Punch a small hole in the top of the jar of water. Turn it upside down over the empty jar. Ask the children to find out how long it takes for the top jar to become empty.

ACTIVITY 27

Age: 6–9

Objective: Time, Conservation

Materials: Two small birthday candles, matches

Instructions: Tell children that you want them to march in place while the candle burns. Light one of the candles. (Be very careful using these materials with small children.) Then, ask the children to swing their arms while the second candle burns. Discuss with children how long both these activities took.

ACTIVITY 28

Age: 5–9

Objective: Time, Comparison

Materials: An ice cube and a small birthday candle

Instructions: Ask the children to predict whether it will take longer for the ice cube to melt completely or for the candle to burn down. Light the candle and place the ice cube on a small dish. While the children are watching, discuss with them tasks in their lives that seem to take a long time, and tasks that seem to take a short time.

ACTIVITY 29

Age: 5–9

Objective: Time, Application of nonstandard units

Materials: (None are needed)

Instructions: Have the children use their pulses to count how many heart-beats it takes for some event in the classroom to happen. Some typical events could be counting heartbeats from a certain time until the bell rings, counting heartbeats to determine how long it takes for the teacher to erase the board, or counting heartbeats to find out how long it takes a bug to crawl across the table.

ACTIVITY 30

Age: 5–9

Objective: Time, Application of standard units

Materials: A clock or watch with a second hand

Instructions: Have the children measure in seconds how long they can hold their breath. Have the children measure in minutes how long it takes for the class to walk a mile or around the school building five times. Find other events children can time, such as running, jumping, or climbing stairs.

ACTIVITY 31

Age: 5–7

Objective: Money, Attribute recognition

Materials: Play money made of index cards marked with $1, $2, and $5 and pictures of items with price tags (as appropriate for the children's ages)

Instructions: Give assorted amounts of play money to the children. Have them guess whether they have enough money to purchase the pictured items. Then, let them trade in their money for the pictures of the items.

ACTIVITY 32

Age: 5–6

Objective: Money, Conservation

Materials: Pieces of play money in coins

Instructions: Pass out the pieces of play money and ask children to count the money they have. Ask them to trade money—two nickels for a dime, ten pennies for a dime, and five pennies for a nickel—with other students. Now, ask them how much money they have.

ACTIVITY 33

Age;   4–8

Objective: Money, Comparison

Materials: Play money

Instructions: Distribute play money to the children. Show various amounts of money to them and each time you show them a different amount ask them to stand up if they have less money than the amount you showed. Next time, have those children with more money than the amount you showed stand up.

ACTIVITY 34

Age: 5–8

Objective: Money, Application of nonstandard units

Materials: Play money made from index cards in denominations of $1, $2, and $5 and objects or pictures of objects with price tags that are appropriate to the children's ages

Instructions: Pass out various amounts of play money to the children. Then, show them the objects. Ask them to determine if they have enough money to purchase each of these objects. For older children, you can ask how much more play money they would need to buy a more expensive item or how much change they would get if they bought a particular item.

ACTIVITY 35

Age: 6–9

Objective: Money, Application of standard units

Materials: (None needed)

Instructions: Use occasions where children have an opportunity to purchase items with their money, such as when they're on a field trip or in the lunch room. Ask how they will make decisions about what to spend and how they will know when they have received the correct change. Vending machines also offer similar opportunities to talk about money. Because vending machines don't require sales tax, they are easier for children to understand than many other money situations.

STUDY QUESTIONS AND ACTIVITIES

1. Study the measurement activities in some preschool or early childhood instructional materials (a textbook series is a good source for K–4).
    a. Identify for which attribute and for which stage of development each activity is written. (Some activities will be found to overlap in attributes as well as in stages.)
    b. While identifying attributes and stages, make note of which stages are skipped altogether for each attribute!

2. Remember that it is important to have mathematics grow out of children's personal experiences. When a child's learning occurs from personal goals and motivations, then he or she becomes engaged in the mathematics.
    a. In this chapter, a classroom gerbil was mentioned. List as many measurement activities as you can that could be generated from this classroom pet. Identify each activity according to attribute and stage of development.
    b. List as many measurement activities as you can that could be generated from snack or lunch time. Again, identify each activity according to attribute and stage of development.
    c. Do the same as in items *a* and *b* for a birthday party, a field trip, and an art activity.

3. Observe (and videotape if possible) a child in either a home, a preschool, or an elementary school environment. Make note of all the opportunities for developing the language and conceptual development needed for attribute recognition.

4. Choose one attribute and describe the possible opportunities for collecting and graphing data for that attribute. The following example shows data to compare the number of pets the children in a class have.

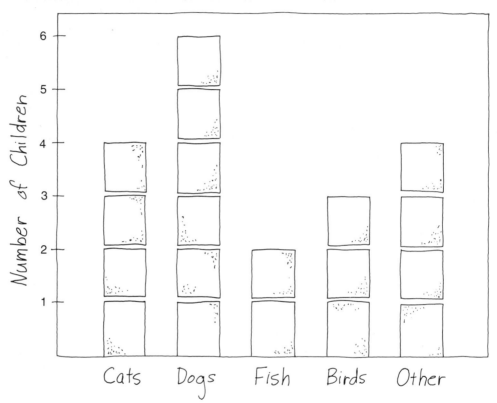

REFERENCES AND RESOURCES

Copeland, R. W. (1984). *How children learn mathematics: Teaching implications of Piaget's research*. New York: Macmillan.

Immerzeel, G., & Thomas, M. (Eds.). (1982). *Ideas from the ARITHMETIC TEACHER: Grades 1–4 Primary*. Reston, VA: NCTM.

Kennedy, L. M. (1984). *Guiding children's learning of mathematics* (4th ed.). Belmont, CA: Wadsworth.

Piaget, J. (1965). *The child's concept of number*. New York: W. W. Norton.

Piaget, J., & Inhelder, B. (1964). *The child's conception of geometry*. New York: Harper & Row.

Price, S. S., & Price, M. E. (1978). *The primary math lab*. Santa Monica, CA: Goodyear.

Reisman, F. K. (1981). *Teaching mathematics: Methods and content* (2nd ed.). Boston: Houghton Mifflin.

Robinson, E., Mahaffey, M., & Nelson, D. (1975). Measurement. In J. N. Payne (Ed.), *Mathematics learning in early childhood* (pp. 227–250). Reston, VA: NCTM.

Sohns, M. L., & Buffington, A. V. (1977). *The measurement book*. Sunnyvale, CA: Enrich, Inc.

Troutman, A. P., & Lichtenberg, B. K. (1987). *Mathematics a good beginning: Strategies for teaching children* (3rd ed.). Monterey, CA: Brooks/Cole.

Wilson, P. S., & Osborne, A. (1988). Foundational ideas in teaching about measure. In T. R. Post (Ed.), *Teaching mathematics in grades K–8* (pp. 78–110). Boston: Allyn and Bacon.

Appendix

Activity Resources Co., Inc.
P.O. Box 4875
Hayward, CA 94540

Creative Publications
5005 West 110th Street
Oak Lawn, IL 60453

Cuisenaire Co. of America, Inc.
12 Church Street, Box D
New Rochelle, NY 10802

Dale Seymour Publications
P.O. Box 10888
Palo Alto, CA 94303

Delta Education
Box M, Math Department
Nashua, NH 03061

DIDAX, Inc.
Educational Resources
5 Fourth Street
Peabody, MA 01960

DLM Teaching Resources
P.O. Box 4000
One DLM Park
Allen, TX 75002

Index